THE VOIC

MW00649623

Master Your Inner Game

John Marshall Roberts

WORLDVIEW
THINKING

© 2016 by John Marshall Roberts

Published by Worldview Thinking

www.worldviewthinking.com

Managing Publisher: Immanuel Otto

Cover Art: Raphael, "Saint George and the Dragon" — a study, 1505 (Public Domain)

Cover and Layout Designer: Carmen Lo Maglio

ALL RIGHTS RESERVED. This book contains material protected under international and federal copyright laws and treaties. Any unauthorized reprint or use of this material is prohibited. No part of this book may be reproduced or transmitted in any form or by any means, electronic or mechanical, including photocopying, recording or by any information system without express written permission from the author/publisher.

Roberts, John Marshall, author.

The Voice Code: Master Your Inner Game

John Marshall Roberts.

Includes bibliographical references.

ISBN 978-0-692-71671-7

1. Self-actualization (Psychology) 2. Leadership

I. Title

BF637.S4R5765 2016   158.1

QBI16-600090

To Eve for helping me find the pearl.
To Pearl for awakening the Emperor.
To You for leading the revolution.

TABLE OF CONTENTS

Preface

*You have got to find the treasure so that everything
you have learned along the way makes sense.*
~ Paul Coelho

THE ANSWERS TO YOUR DEEPEST QUESTIONS ARE
WRITTEN IN YOUR HOPES AND DREAMS. THIS IS
YOUR VOICE. THIS BOOK IS A MANUAL TO HELP YOU
FIND YOUR VOICE QUICKLY AND EFFICIENTLY,
USING A SYSTEM THAT IS PROVEN.

If you are wondering where the world is going, where you'll
be in it and how you can enjoy life in an era where change is the
only constant, you will find this material comforting and inspiring.
Much of what you learn will strike you as common sense. Some
will strike you as utter nonsense. Be that as it may, the results that
you create by applying these ideas to your life will more than
justify whatever time you spend learning them.

There are three principles that give your Voice the power to
turn your life into a work of art. They are **Authority**, the power to
choose; **Resonance**, the power to attract; and **Trust**, the power to
act. These principles are rooted in the dynamic structure of your
mind, influencing everything you see, every decision you make
and every ounce of meaning you gather from your day-to-day
experience. Whatever beliefs you hold about these three words, I
ask that you be willing to revisit them in light of this material.

As you'll see, the secret formula that makes all great minds
think alike is just the A.R.T. of seeing reality. Most people see
reality backwards. To them, the power to create (Authority) lives
in the world outside. They are forever rushing around trying to
achieve their goals while assuming that the barriers they face are
absolute and unyielding. Were this true, the greatest leaders in
history couldn't have existed, because the feats they accomplished
would've been impossible. Authority is always *internal.* People
who start from this premise eventually find their Voice.

Thinking this way, we naturally change our decision-making set. We still live in the world just like everyone else, but we no longer take much of what passes for truth seriously. We find ourselves drawn to things (people, jobs, etc.) not for the future payoffs they might provide, but for the sheer joy of co-creating. When we adopt this joyful self-authored mindset, the principles of Resonance and Trust begin to pull us toward our calling and the fulfillment of our life's purpose.

People who still see a world ruled by external authorities have dreams just like everyone. But having given up on the possibility that they might embrace their passions, they stow their dreams away for some later date hoping to achieve security before doing what they love. Sadly, this never works. Tomorrow never comes. It's always now.

Trust is action, pure and simple. It's not a complicated idea. It's not a transaction. It's not a risk-reward equation. It is action. We only fear action in the pursuit of our dreams when we start from the faulty premise of separation. Thinking this way, we dramatically over-complicate everything, seeking stability on an unstable foundation. People who find their Voice Trust their inner vision of what could be over the voice of conventional wisdom. They show this not by reading book upon book, waiting for just the right moment and prolonging their limitations indefinitely. They show this by taking action. Now.

"Trust first, ask questions later" is a wise motto for anyone who wants to use this book to join them. Because here's the deal: If you aren't willing to take action without evidence, you'll stay stuck in the past forever. This journey will help you release the past to access a life more inspiring than you've imagined possible. But without your Trust, it's just a bunch of empty words. So I thank you for taking action to read this book in a spirit of Trust.

You will not be disappointed. Here's why: You have a Voice! It's an awesomely powerful Voice that others will immediately recognize when you speak it. They will recognize it because, get this: it's also *their* Voice. We seem quite separate to the senses, but beneath appearances we are one. The voice of separation within our minds does nothing to improve the quality of our lives. The inner guide that moves us and moves the world at the same time is the Voice of truth, and truth is simple:

We are One.

You will choose your Authority to know your Voice. When you do, you will follow inner Resonance to create the evidence you need to Trust what you already know. The problem isn't that life is full of danger and disappointment. The problem is that you are more lovable and loving than you currently believe, given the limiting programming you've received. This will all change now if you are willing to be patient and take things one step at a time as we walk through this new paradigm.

From behind the cloud cover of past learning, your Voice speaks with unwavering conviction of who you are and what your mission must be. It does this in steps that work with you. It doesn't command. It doesn't demand. It waits until you are ready, showing you through increasingly exhilarating insights, epiphanies, and revelations the specific instrument that you were born to play in the symphony of life. But you are the decision maker. Until you choose, nothing changes.

So choose again. Choose your Voice and change your world from the inside out. Dismiss your doubts. They are a mirage. If you let me, I will help you see that my confidence in you has not been misplaced. The future is ours for the choosing. Let us choose it together. Now.

~ John Marshall Roberts
July 25, 2016

Introduction

> To become a great visionary we must undergo three transformations.[1] As children, we become a camel. "Put a load on me!" we seem to say. The authorities of our youth gladly oblige, piling up as much baggage as our humps can handle. Once we've had enough, we follow an inner call out into the desert where we undergo the second transformation.
>
> In the desert we turn into a lion. The larger the load we shouldered as a camel, the larger we are in our new lion form. Our new mission: slay Thou Shalt! This immense dragon has thousands of scales, each with a belief from our camel days written upon it. To earn the third transformation, we must slay the dragon to unlearn everything we once believed.
>
> Thus begins the epic battle that determines our destiny. If we make it through this last rite of passage, we achieve total freedom. Liberated from a lifetime of false limitations, we access an inner well of exuberance that makes us unstoppable. In the final transformation, we become a child.

Dare Greatly *The Call of Voice*

This is the world's first dragon-slaying manual for people who yearn to thrive without compromise doing what they love. The new inner game technology this book delivers is truly incredible — as in awesomely effective *and* impossible to believe. But if you summon your lion-heart to brave this journey with me, we will slay the dragons of doubt to give your brain unmistakable evidence for a timeless truth that your heart has always known:

You are a force of nature. You have unlimited creative potential and an inner Voice that calls you to greatness. When you honor this inner calling, you will create a life without limits doing what you love. The only barrier is belief.

Have you heard that dragons hoard gold? Well, the dragons you'll topple in this book don't just hoard gold, they *are* the gold. They're reverse projections of our Voice wrapped in limiting beliefs. But make no mistake: These dragons are clever! Through hypnotic repetition they warp our minds until we become *frame locked,* or trapped in a limited perspective that we mistake for reality. At the root of frame lock lies a lifetime of repressed psychic energy that psychologist Carl Jung called the shadow.[2] Shadow voices are the belief dragons that keep us from actualizing our dreams.

5 Faces of the Shadow

1.	Disowned aspects of our mind we habitually repress and ignore
2.	Unconscious belief patterns that keep us frame locked and limited
3.	The inner-cause source of suffering, scarcity and separation
4.	The deadly dragon Thou Shalt
5.	99% pure gold

Shadow dragons make us see the world through blinders. They tell us things that simply aren't true: "I'm not good enough / there's not enough time / it'll never work out" These hooligans tell us that "risk is dangerous / compromise is healthy / it's too late anyway, so why bother?" ***Don't believe the hype!*** If you believe it, you'll prove it correct and stay frame locked forever.

This book offers a proven path to actualize your dreams by transmuting old shadow energies that block you. Jung called the shadow "99% pure gold"[3] because whenever he helped a client transmute the shadow, miracles happened. This book offers inner game mastery training that makes such miracles commonplace.

When we're frame locked, we think backwards. Seeking inner security through external success, we find ourselves on a treadmill of striving. Projecting our power outward, we then chase after *symbols* of happiness, hoping to fill a growing inner void. Over time, this outside-in mindset turns our lives into a self-fulfilling prophecy of lack. To slay "Thou Shalt" we must commit to being our own authority. This is timeless wisdom that many have preached, but which has proven deviously difficult to practice. Until now.

In the past, terms like "shadow" and "inner voice" were shrouded in mystery. Not anymore. A breakthrough 2012 discovery called the Voice Code has changed the game. For the first time, this equation has mapped the natural laws that govern human thinking. Using Voice Code tools, you can now achieve any goal from the inside-out as you master the visionary mindset. This learning journey unfolds through an epic three act dragon-slaying adventure that trains your brain to hear and follow your heart's knowing. How cool is that?

Act 1 Follow the Call

Become a Lion

When asked to reveal their success secrets, extraordinary people like Oprah Winfrey, Steve Jobs and Richard Branson almost always give one of five similar responses:

1. **"Follow your inner voice."**
2. **"Follow your heart."**
3. **"Find your calling."**
4. **"Do what your love."**
5. **"Believe in yourself."**

Most of us find such advice inspiring, but how often do we actually follow it in our everyday lives? Not very. Despite our good intentions, we become victims of frame lock only minutes after the inspiration fades. Next thing you know, we're back where we started, wondering why we can't seem escape the orbit of old limitations.

This book offers a map that helps you close the gap in record time. The map is proven and the path really works. But here's the rub: *the shadow would rather you die a slow death than finish this book!* So to take advantage of this opportunity you must commit fully to the journey. Otherwise the shadow dragons will derail you.

When we get used to a shadow voice, we no longer question it. Over the years, looping shadow tapes from the past brainwash us into lifestyles that castrate our courage and conviction. To change the game, you must be willing to stand strong for your Voice by saying, *"Who is that?"* to any other inner voice that limits you. Once you've named the resistance, you can use the tools in this book to quickly dissolve it. In this way, you'll remove all problems at their inner roots and reclaim your power forever. See the "Ousting Adolf" case study on page 5 for an example of this process in action.

If this all sounds way too complicated, you could always just stay the course. After all, this is what most normal people do, right? Yes, it is! That's why I strongly urge you to reconsider. Let's face it: *normal isn't natural.* Normal people lead lives of compromise that end in regret. In a recent study, it was discovered that the number one regret of people approaching death was "not living life on my own terms."[4] *No one* expects their life to end this way. But most of us do anyway because we fail to challenge old shadow voices and stay frame locked until we're on death's doorstep. This is tragic and totally unnecessary now that we've decoded the inner game.

5 Faces of Voice

1.	Timeless knowing that arises from the core of your being
2.	Dynamic creative intelligence that orchestrates human evolution
3.	The missing link between human nature and Mother Nature
4.	How visionary minds think alike
5.	The real you: unlimited

> **Voice in Action: Ousting Adolf**
> **Dragon Slayer: Robert, CEO** *

> *When he signed up for the Voice Code boot camp, Robert was a time-strapped young executive working harder and harder just to get by. As the Voice Code gained traction in his mind, old beliefs dissolved and his inner being began to shift. In week four, while pushing to meet a deadline, he looked within and calmly observed his stressed-out mind without believing his thoughts. "Who is that?' he asked of a paternalistic tyrant prodding him within. He personified this shadow as "Adolf the Awful" and used Voice Code tools to reclaim his power. With Adolf out of the picture, Robert became unstoppable! Within 8 weeks, he had risen to become CEO of his company, entering a bold new social orbit that "randomly" brought him into personal contact with many of his childhood heroes, including a former US president, UN ambassador, and a Grammy-award winning recording artist he had long admired.*

They say life begins at 40. But for me it started at the age of 39 when I found my life's calling. After nearly two decades of research, my ship came in on July 26, 2012, when I cracked the Voice Code. This equation blew my shadow bunker to bits by showing my mind the blueprint that had secretly governed my lifelong quest to uncover this very equation!

Can you imagine what this must've felt like? My entire existence up until this moment had been consumed by the search. The inquiry began in childhood. Formal research began in 1993 with my first self-directed experiment at the University of Florida. In 1999 I discovered an early beta version of the Voice Code while doing my doctoral studies. But it would take 13 more years of field testing and refinement before this "red pill" solution emerged.

I'll never forget it. In this fateful moment time stood still, and life opened with a light so blinding that my heart nearly exploded. Before this experience, I felt limited no matter how much I achieved.

*All "Voice in Action" profiles in this book are true. Names and minor details were changed to protect client privacy.

5

I'd always thought there was something wrong with me, and it turns out I was right — *because I believed this!* The shadows had seduced me into believing that I was an ego trapped in a bag of skin, forced to compromise to survive. Having now experienced life from both perspectives, I can tell you one thing with total certainty:

Life doesn't begin at 40. It doesn't even begin at 80. Life begins the moment we find our calling and choose our Voice with unwavering conviction — and not a moment sooner.

This is the moment when the dragons lose their grip and the world lifts us to our proper station. Every great visionary in history has gained their powers through this same inner path, claiming gifts that made them seem like superheroes to the rest. You have this same awesome power within you too. To claim it, you must commit to clearing the shadows that block your light.

The Dragon Slayers Motto*

I choose to follow my Voice, not because it is easy, but because it is hard — because this mission serves to unlock my deepest gifts, organize and express my full potential, because this is a challenge that I am willing to accept, one that I am unwilling to postpone, and one which I intend to win.

*Adapted from John F. Kennedy

Act II Slay Thou Shalt
Master the Inner Game

At the end of the day, your destiny is determined by one choice:

shadows or Voice?

Master this choice and watch life lift you. When we follow the right inner guide, simple actions produce breakthrough results along

6

**Choose Shadows
DEFEND Fear**

**Choose Voice
CREATE Future**

Frame Lock:
*Reality Distortion
Caused by Beliefs*

Voice:
*Instinctual Knowing
Blocked by Beliefs*

the path of least resistance. This isn't magical thinking. Our Voice is connected to the grid of nature's intelligence. Backed by Mother Nature, we become an indomitable *force of nature* in whatever we feel inspired to do. If you have doubts, be sure that your Voice — the creative will of life — has none whatsoever about you.

Three principles guarantee your success: Authority, Resonance and Trust. The seemingly "magical powers" that iconic visionaries embody grow from inside-out as they master the inner game to restore proper alignment with these three principles:

✌ Authority – *The principle of choice*

Normal people frame authority as something "out there" in the world. Dragon slayers align with this principle by choosing themselves as the sole creative authority of their lives.

✌ Resonance – *The principle of attraction*

Normal people let social norms and expectations frame their personal ambitions. Dragon slayers become "strange attractors" of success by letting their heart inspire their future vision.

7

◦ **Trust** – *The principle of action*

Normal people take action to minimize risk and maximize personal gain. Dragon slayers demonstrate trust by taking inspired action without attachment to future outcomes.

This book helps you align with your Voice to reframe these principles using six mastery skills listed below. These skills form a closed-loop process called the "CREATE cycle" that governs Voice alignment from a part of our mind called the *creative unconscious*. Once this cycle is fully restored, we naturally *Authorize, Resonate* with and *Trust* our Voice to CREATE the life of our dreams. With the tools in this book, you can achieve this in record time, without the bumps and bruises of those who came before us.

CREATE: Six Verbs of the Visionary Mind

♮ **Commit** – Choose your mission freely and fully, from a state of calm urgency and decisive inner authority

♮ **Reframe** – Demonstrate authority by thinking backwards from the assumption of successful future completion

♮ **Explore** – Inquire to find limiting feelings, beliefs, and resistance to owning our vision with clarity and conviction

♮ **Assimilate** – Restore inner integrity by neutralizing the charge of shadow patterns uncovered while exploring

♮ **Transmute** – Love the resistance without conditions to dissolve assimilated shadow patterns and reclaim Voice gifts

♮ **Embody** – Take action to celebrate the gift and close the vision-reality gap, pulling our chosen future into the present

Act III Become a Child

Remember Your Innocence

The dragon-slaying journey that frames this book was inspired by Friedrich Nietzsche. As the story goes, inner evolution is a circle. As *children*, we become *camels*. As adults, the most brave among us leave our camel lives to become *lions*. We must now slay the beastly belief dragon Thou Shalt. If successful, we remember our innocence and become a *child* again, bringing the story full circle. Although Nietzsche's thinking is highly unconventional, the Voice Code offers powerful new evidence that it is essentially correct.

This equation emerged from applied research in developmental psychology. By deciphering the natural laws that govern the developmental path of an 8-stage model proposed by Dr. Clare W. Graves, we mapped the *entire spectrum* of human consciousness.[5] There are a total of 12 stages that tell the whole story — from the womb (Stage 1) to the highest level of enlightenment (Stage 12). Most models of developmental psychology view inner evolution as a ladder that reaches forever upward. In keeping with Nietzsche, the Voice Code reveals it to be a circle.

The easiest way to grasp this cyclical path is by analogy to a journey up and over a mountain with 12 base camps along the way (graphic below). The first 6 stages (Phase I) are an uphill slog that involves forgetting our innocence as our ego fuses with countless beliefs handed down to us by parents and authorities. The next 6 stages (Phase II) are a downhill ride. During these stages we follow our own *inner* authority to *unlearn* all Phase I beliefs that keep us from remembering our timeless innocence.

Because this path was designed by nature's holographic mind, it plays out on all scales, from the lifespan development of individuals to the evolution of mankind as a whole. The most confusing leg of the journey is the one our world is now navigating: the shift from stage 6 (end of Phase I) to stage 7 (Phase II begins). Through this epic inner shift, we must reverse our mental models of cause and

9

12 Stages of Worldview Thinking

Phase I. DEFEND
Life is a Dilemma
Seeing is Belieivng
Extrinsic Motivators

CHOOSE AGAIN
Frame Reversal

Phase II. CREATE
Life is a Paradox
Beliefs Create Seeing
Intrinsic Vision

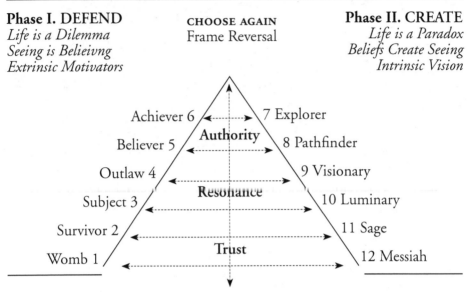

Achiever 6   7 Explorer
Authority
Believer 5   8 Pathfinder
Outlaw 4   9 Visionary
Resonance
Subject 3   10 Luminary
Survivor 2   11 Sage
Trust
Womb 1   12 Messiah

effect. Sensing the impending death of our egos, most of us refuse the call to Phase II until the pain of not changing is unbearable.

When we finally commit to our Phase II journey, life gets much simpler. The insecurities that plagued us during Phase I dissolve and a sense of curious wonder lights our path. Each step forward takes us closer to the life of total freedom we dismissed as unrealistic during the Phase I climb. As we master the new Phase II mindset, a lifetime of false limitations dissolve. By the time we reach Stage 9 (Visionary), we have found our life's calling and are infused with an almost otherworldly passion to bring our vision to the world in a spirit of shared possibility.

With this book, I'm fulfilling my own Phase II calling to help you navigate Voice mountain with ease. Since cracking the code, I've designed and refined a powerful suite of tools that make slaying Thou Shalt a relative breeze. But before you dive in, please consider the "Reader Beware" section on the next page. Nothing I share in this short introduction can possibly prepare you for the power you will unleash if you fully embrace this paradigm. My hope is that a quick story from my early experiences using Voice Code tools will help you begin to fathom the mighty forces we will soon summon.

> **Voice In Action: Solving the Solver**
> **Dragon Slayer: Amy, Researcher**

Amy married the partner of her dreams. Unfortunately, after three years together, things were rocky. No matter how hard she tried, she couldn't seem to make her spouse happy. A few cycles into the course she found out why. The cause of her problems was a shifty shadow she named "The Solver." This clever shadow voice had convinced her that her value came from solving other people's problems. Believing this, she was unable to listen and be fully present. This was the inner root of her partner's dismay. By solving the Solver, she reclaimed the gift of partnership and sparked a profound shift that rippled through every area of her life. Old shadow dynamics began to unravel and her marriage grew closer. As their union entered a new phase, this gift extended outward to positively impact her entire life, joining disconnected social circles and bringing her a sense of happiness and inner security she'd never known.

Reader Beware: May Cause Enlightenment

Throughout this adventure, I have interwoven stories of my own journey turning the Voice Code equation into a book. The years that followed this discovery were disruptive, with events that would be considered impossible by most — including me if I hadn't personally experienced them. So if any of the claims I've made so far seem incredible, buckle up. You ain't seen nothing yet.

A funny thing happened in the summer of 2014, two years to the day after I'd cracked the Voice Code. I was taking a new tool called the CARE ritual (in Act I, Scene 6) for a test run at a Starbucks near the University of Florida in Gainesville. It was an exciting and challenging time. We were four weeks into a beta field test of the first Voice Code training program. The night before, I felt guided to create this new tool to help clients ground an almost overwhelming influx of creative energy flowing through the group.

When I sat down to give it a spin, a chorus of inner voices seemed hell-bent on distracting me. At first I was irritated. Then I had a fun idea. "What if I adamantly refuse to believe any thoughts that I'm not 100% sure to be my real Voice?" To test this out, I invented a game that I call *Name that Resistance.* Here's how to play: Observe your mind with calm vigilance. Whenever a thought or feeling arises that doesn't radiate with boundless joy, give it a name. Don't believe it or resist it. Just notice it, name it and move on.

Silly right? Well, on that fine Florida morning, I played this silly game with such gusto that I busted right through the walls of the universe! No joke. Sitting at a Starbucks, having a ball, I rapidly cycled through many layers of shadow, until I came upon a horrific inner thug that I named the "Big Boss." Seeing this icy devil lurking within, I entered a state of deathly despair and blacked out cold.

When I came to, I was in a place most call the "white light" where I spent what seemed a full calendar year cavorting with an ascended master resembling Jesus. When I came back, an hour of clock time had passed, but my life had changed forever... Yep. That's right:

I thought myself to death at Starbucks.

Call it a "white light episode" if you prefer. The point is that my shadow-busting episode induced an experience that was virtually identical to what untold thousands who've reported near-death experiences have described. But with three critical differences:

1. **I wasn't physically ill. Not even a cough.**
2. **I did it with tools designed from a scientific mind map that fully explains how and why it happened.**
3. **Any deeply motivated person might use these same tools to replicate the experience.**

I'm not schizophrenic. I wasn't hopped up on magic mushrooms. If you'll bracket your doubts and consider that I may be telling the truth, you will begin to grasp the staggering implications... *We now have a simple, process-driven inner game technology that anyone can use to bridge heaven and earth – literally!*

For the record, I have no unstated spiritual agenda. I am a religiously unaffiliated scientist whose clients have consisted largely of secular agnostics who recoil at both "woo woo" spirituality and the excesses of organized religion. I am not a guru, nor do I aspire to be one. I have always seen myself as an open-minded skeptic, and I've been careful to always position myself this way in my work.

As you might imagine, I was resistant to share this story. But had I failed to give you the whole truth, I would've felt unworthy of your trust. Now that I've spilled the beans, do know that this system will work equally well regardless of your metaphysical preferences. Let me also make it clear that there's no implied pressure to believe this story or anything else. As I see it, belief is irrelevant. Either the Voice Code works, or it doesn't. There's only one way to find out: *Give it a try. Gather first-hand evidence. Decide for yourself.*

My religion is the search for truth. I love this religion because it's both paradoxical and practical. It changes over time, yet helps us discover that which is timeless. There are no gurus or dogmas. There are many ways one can practice. One is to follow the four Voice callings below. These were derived using Voice Code logic. They succinctly describe the process that I used to cycle through all shadows and achieve a state of stage 13 (aka "white light") consciousness. They also summarize the inside-out mindset that helps us achieve our dreams. In fact, these callings distill everything in this book into 12 simple words that resonate immediately because they're true:

Own your Mind
Think with Heart
Face the Dark
See the Light

13

The Path Ahead: Own the Frame, Be the Change

This book gives you *everything you need* to give yourself a mental operating systems upgrade for the "Phase II" world unfolding. The journey helps you master the visionary mindset as you make practical inroads toward a goal of your choosing over an 8-week period. Please note: you don't need to fully immerse yourself in this formal curriculum to get profound value from this book. Feel free to read through once and come back through for another pass. Whatever you do, please commit to getting all the way through the book. Like a great movie, this story builds towards an epic Act III climax that reframes everything you learn along the way.

Reading this introduction is the hardest part. Once you've crossed the threshold into Act I, each step forward unleashes new power and momentum to carry you through to the next stage. The journey is previewed below. This three act structure mirrors the natural process that our mind moves through when we experience transformational change. It is no coincidence that this same structure has spontaneously emerged across all eras and cultures. The natural laws that govern this process are timeless and universal.

Act 1 Follow the Call

In Act I, you will befriend the four mentors through which your Voice speaks: Emperor, Alchemist, Warrior and Poet.[6] Each offers powerful gifts that, when integrated, turn you into a force of nature.

Week 1: Befriend the Emperor

In week one you'll befriend the Emperor. This inner mentor will help you reframe Authority from external (shadows) to internal (Voice) to *Own Your Mind* and CREATE purpose.

Week 2: Inspire the Alchemist

In week two you'll inspire the Alchemist. This brilliant mentor will help you reframe Resonance from believing (shadows) to knowing (Voice) to *Think With Heart* and CREATE possibility.

Week 3: Embrace the Warrior

In week three you'll engage the Warrior. This brave mentor will help you reframe Trust from tribal (shadow) to instinctual (Voice) to *Face the Dark* and CREATE power.

Week 4: Behold the Poet

In week four you'll behold the Poet. This joyful mentor will help you remember your Innocence to *See the Light* and CREATE partnerships of shared purpose and presence.

Each scene of Act I offers you new tools and practices to help you align with each aspect of your Voice. In the climactic final scene of this act, you will receive your main dragon-slaying tools for Act II: the CARE ritual and the CREATE script.

Act II Slay Thou Shalt

In Act II, you will put the tools and ideas from Act I to good use as you reclaim your Voice gifts from the shadow dragon posse. Over a series of six progressively intense scenes, you will reclaim your power from a lifetime of limiting beliefs.

Week 5: Dethrone the Dividers | Own Your Mind

In the first battle, you will enter the Desert of Authority. Empowered by the Emperor's presence, you'll reclaim your power from a controlling group of shadow dragons called the Dividers, who keep us frame locked by time scarcity, stress, and escapism.

Week 6: Remind the Forgetters | Think with Heart

In the second battle, you will enter the Forest of Resonance inspired by the Alchemist. With the help of this brilliant mentor, you will reclaim your power from the Forgetters, a sketchy group of shape shifters and social chameleons who keep us from seeing the simplicity behind the complexity of everyday problems.

Week 7: Arrest the Enforcers | Face the Dark
In the third and final battle of Act II, you will enlist the Warrior's courage to enter the Cave of Trust. Here you will meet an alarmist group of blow-hard punishers and prisoners called the Enforcers. If we let them, these cowardly shadow bullies keep us forever frame locked with shameless scare tactics and blame games.

In the final scene of Act II, you'll receive a set of two advanced Voice Code tools to help you demolish even the most challenging shadow dragons that block your path.

Act III Become a Child

As you move into the Act III, you will have established powerful inner alignment with the principles of Authority, Resonance and Trust. This will prepare you to face the most formidable foe in your inner kingdom: the Doubters.

Week 8: Dissolve the Doubters | See the Light
In the final battle of the journey, you will wade into the Pools of Innocence to face the Doubters. Tapping the Poet's gentle light, you will dissolve this sullen cadre of despairing dragons with an innocent love that transcends.

This adventure starts slow and builds to an epic conclusion. Every step matters. With each step forward, your Voice alignment will deepen. If you embrace the adventure, you will eventually ignite an inner shift in which you become One with your Voice. After this, all bets are off. Nothing will keep you from standing for mastery. You will return to this journey again and again until you've mastered the inner game and completed your Voice Revolution.

That's the journey in a nutshell.
Are you ready to become a lion?
Great! Let's get started.

Visit TheVoiceCode.com to get free digital resources, including free training videos and digital copies of key tools in this book. You will also find the Voice Code glossary at the end of this book helpful for clarifying and expanding upon any new words, ideas and symbols used.

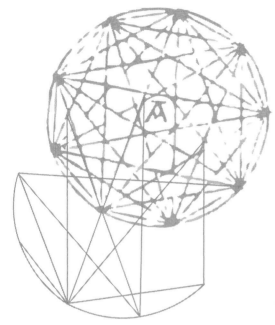

ACT 1
Follow the Call

The CREATE Cycle: 6 Verbs of the Visionary Mind

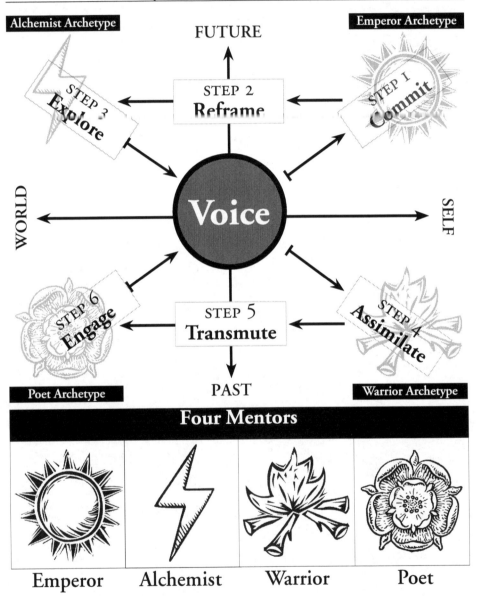

FUTURE

Alchemist Archetype

Emperor Archetype

STEP 3
Explore

STEP 2
Reframe

STEP 1
Commit

WORLD

Voice

SELF

STEP 6
Engage

STEP 5
Transmute

STEP 4
Assimilate

Poet Archetype

Warrior Archetype

PAST

Four Mentors

Emperor Alchemist Warrior Poet

Scene 1 | *Choose Again*

Martin Seligman electrocuted dogs.[1] Please don't hate him. The dogs didn't die. It was cruel, yes, but for a noble cause. He was testing a theory about "learned helplessness," a condition that promised to help us understand and alleviate needless human suffering. Here's how it all went down:

He placed two groups of dogs in cages. Both received shocks at random intervals. The first group was lucky — they had a button available to help them stop the shocks. To escape pain, all they needed to do was find the button and push it with their noses. The second group had no such button. When the shocks came, they searched in vain to find an escape and eventually gave up. The shocks still came, of course, but instead of searching they whimpered on the cage floor to cope.

Once this powerless group had been trained to believe that escape was futile, they were placed in different cages with a partition in the middle. Good news: Now there was a way out! To stop the shocks, they just needed to hop over a tiny partition. No sweat, right? But when the shocks resumed, most of these poor pups didn't lift a paw. They just sat on the cage floor moaning. Having learned that the problem could not be solved, they lost their will for the search. Like so many of us in today's overwhelming world, they assumed they were helpless and created powerful evidence to prove this theory correct.

Escape The Cage *Outwit the Dragons*

"All children are born artists," said Picasso. "The trick is to remain an artist when you grow up." How does the exuberance of childhood become the stressed-out mindset of the average adult? As children, our minds are filled with wonder and our eyes behold a world of endless possibilities. But by our mid 20's most of us have placed invisible barricades of low grade angst between our head and heart. Like Seligman's pups, we've grown weary from a lifetime of shocks and have settled for lives of mere comfort-seeking in the cage of social conformity.

Frame lock makes us whimper on the cage floor instead of seeking a better way forward. Once we've accepted compromise as a way of life, we lose our emotional vitality. Before you know it, we are comfort zombies, living to gratify our senses and numb ourselves to the pain of life without purpose. This is particularly tragic in today's world, because converging economic, technological and social trends have leveled the playing field for everyone. In this new normal, anyone with the gumption to own their heart's calling can thrive without compromise doing what they love.

The only barrier is belief.

The bars of our cages are made of unquestioned beliefs that frame our worldview. This book helps you quickly escape by transmuting the shadow patterns that constrain you. But before we face the dragon, let's take a moment to see how our enemy seduces us. "Thou Shalt" is subtle, infectious, and insidiously effective at enslaving us without us even knowing. To see one way this happens, consider the worldview segmentations on the opposite page.

You've seen quadrant profiling systems like this before, yes? From 2008 to 2012, I made my living peddling this one to marketers and change agents around the world. As far as segmentations go, this one is cream of the crop. It grew from the work of Dr. Clare W.

What's Your Worldview?

Explorer
(25% US pop, rising)
Values: Empathy, Equality
Metaphor: Mankind is a family
(frame: caring - uncaring)
Goal: *"Sacrifice myself to be
accepted now in a spirit of shared
self interests."*
Emerged: 20th Century (1900 AD)

Pathfinder
(12% US pop, rising)
Values: Innovation, Integrity
Metaphor: Life is a system
(frame: interdependency)
Goal: *"Express myself to get what
I want, in a way that hurts no one
and helps life flourish."*
Emerged: Rise of Info Economy

Believer
(22% US pop, decreasing)
Values: Discipline, Authority,
Metaphor: Life is a test
(frame: pass - fail)
Goal: *"Sacrifice myself now for
future reward."*
Emerged: Agrarian Age
(~ 2000 BC)

Achiever
(25% US pop, stable)
Values: Success, Power
Metaphor: Life is a Game
(frame: win - lose)
Goal: *"Express myself to get what
I want, but without getting into
trouble."*
Emerged: Industrial Era (~1700)

Graves. An unsung hero of the social sciences, Graves used a *natural systems* lens to map the evolution of human thinking. Through three decades of research he distilled a deeply insightful developmental path that applies to all people and cultures. My launch into the public eye came in 2008 when I integrated Graves research with an early version of the Voice Code in my book *Igniting Inspiration: A Persuasion Manual for Visionaries.*[2]

After sharing these four Graves-inspired segments (above) with many audiences I noticed that, with few exceptions, people would always respond in one of three ways:

1   They look to see which box they fit in.
2   They look to see which boxes to place others in.
3   They fold their arms in defiance of boxes.

These are all reasonable responses. Unfortunately they are also symptoms of frame lock. To understand how this could be, consider the post-Voice Code version of these quadrants on page 25. When I cracked the code, a staggering insight struck down like lightning:

All four worldviews are forms of *frame lock* caused by unconscious beliefs rooted in separation.

Notice the word "Voice" at the center and the four motivators (autonomy, security, connection and change) around the two axes. According to the Voice Code, these motivators exist in a state of yin vs. yang complementarity that forms our worldview. When we follow our Voice we balance all four needs at once to defy all boxes. When we don't, we become frame locked by our belief in separation. Old shadow habits then frame our perception, turning our life into a self-fulfilling prophecy of limitation.

Our Voice resides at the timeless center of this quadrant, the still-point of NOW where all needs are satisfied without sacrifice. When we follow our Voice, we transcend all boxes — including even our basic worldview! Living fully in the present, we experience ourselves as one with the source of life. Aligned with our inner authority in each passing moment, we take inspired actions that satisfy our needs without sacrifice. In this sense, our only *true* need is our Voice. It's the one need that satisfies all of them.

Whether this claim inspires you or stirs up resistance, your reaction is rooted in your desire for freedom. This is a beautiful thing! The inner nudge for freedom is our Voice calling us to escape the cages of compromise and play our part in the symphony of creation through which life evolves. As our dragon slaying journey deepens, celebrate your yearning for freedom however it shows up for you. When those clever dragons spin tales of doom, use them as kindling for the fire of your passion to be free. Whatever shadows

Q: What's Your Frame Lock?

tell you going forward, please make it your mission to remember:

You are a force of nature. The only barrier is belief.

Sins of the Father *A Legacy of Shadows*

This book grew from a "healer, heal thyself" scenario rooted in a long legacy of buried family shadows. On both sides, my family has been plagued by a very dark but cleverly disguised shadow rage. Apart from an abnormally high number of impulsive marriages and divorces, things looked pretty normal growing up. But beneath the surface volcanic shadow lava was flowing hot.

Turns out my family's creepy ways started back before the Big Bang. My genes from both parents are apparently riddled with guilty shadows, institutionalized through generations of humiliation, hiding and repression. My mom gave me the shadow genes for resentment and duplicity. Her family migrated from Germany, a family of Jews who renounced their faith and fled the Holocaust to live in the states as "nothing to see here" Catholics.

Dad gave me the genes for angry fundamentalism. On his deathbed, my great-great-grandfather Roberts confessed that we were spawn of Maximilien Robespierre, the idealistic orator who led the French Revolution, only to put the guillotine on wheels during the Reign of Terror. I don't know what Robespierre's day-to-day personality was like, but the modern day Roberts male lineage is a very specific stock with shadow overtones very much in line with those of such a figure — passionate, principle-driven men with a gift for misguided eloquence.

If this work heals the sins of the father in my own situation, it will be because I finally broke the shadow spell of frame lock within myself. Most of the tools in this book were things I invented for myself to clear out all those old ancestral shadows so that I could unclog writer's block. Cracking the Voice Code was both liberating and unsettling. It was liberating because I'd finally found my life's calling with absolute certainty. It was unsettling because the moment my brain figured out its own operating logic, much of what I'd come to see as "the real me" suddenly seemed false and those long buried shadows came rushing up into awareness.

In the introduction, I briefly mentioned the mind-boggling experience that happened in the summer of 2014, when I went to the white light after uncovering a chilling shadow thug named the Big Boss. Let me now elaborate to help you better understand how and why this happened.

So there I was at Starbucks playing "Name that Resistance," laughing my head off. I was having the time of my life, saying "Who is that?" to a barrage of distracting shadow impulses. Inspiration was flowing, as you might gather, from some of the colorful characters I uncovered. For example, there was:

"Tolstoy Parliament" the brooding pensive shadow that always wanted me to have one last cigarette, as if going before a firing line.

"Donny the Damned" that pathetic prisoner shadow who was always feeding me reasons to stop trying, give up and feel hopeless.

"Reverend Firestone" who was always beating up on poor Donny with self-righteous sermons in the name of his future salvation.

And then there was "Mourna," a caterwauling pit of endless grief, forever lurking in the backdrop of my mind, waiting to fill me with anguish.

But not today Mourna! Today, I'm on a roll...

Then it happens. The back door in my mind flies open, and my personal antichrist walks in. It was beyond chilling. Imagine that you're a child playing in your sandbox, when the lovechild of Joseph Stalin and Darth Vader creeps up unseen. Icy terror shoots through your veins. You feel the presence of death lurking behind you, but you can't move... There's no escape! You can't run. You can't hide. But if you look at it, you'll die.

So it was when I met the Big Boss. This shadow was the opposite of everything I aspired to be, and epitome of everything I've always despised in others. But if you think I regret the meeting, you are wrong. It was the best moment of my life! When I exposed this delusion, it dissolved and I was absolved. In a snap, the chronic sense of anxiety that had forever haunted me was gone. In its place, I found a sense of peace and love that words cannot describe.

Before this moment, I could never seem to shake this vague sense of unease, no matter what I did. Like most of us, I eventually just decided that life was supposed to be unsatisfying. How wrong I was!

Life was only crappy when I let the Big Boss bully me into a lifestyle of endless distraction. Freed of this hooligan, life is an endless process of joyful creation in celebration of all things timeless.

Who *was* that? (My original notes from the incident below in italics)

Captured! "The Big Boss" (Shadow Lynchpin)

The Choice for Death that Refuses to Die. All others work for him. Fear is their currency and their prison. The Big Boss gets the gold — your will, peace of mind, clarity and capacity to remember, experience and accept God's love. The Big Boss is the bully that can't be bullied because to attack him is to play into his racket. He must be forgiven. He is the real you that you think you are behind your self concept.

Believe it or not, we all have our own "Big Boss" stowed away in the darkest corner of our unconscious. To remember our innocence, we must eventually reclaim our power.

The Big Boss is our memory of the original choice to be separate — the *Big Bang* moment in our personal time-lines — the moment when our innocent unbroken mind seemed to collapse. Exposing this forgotten choice and choosing again is the secret to freedom. When we meet our Big Boss, we release the fear that created it and set ourselves free. My ultimate goal is to help you become so energized by this work, that you embrace your inner Warrior to reclaim power from this illusionary death merchant.

Whatever your goals may be, developing an actionable grasp of this inner game map will prove very practical. The map this book offers is unique, but the core truth it points to has been suggested time and time again by the world's greatest teachers:

There is no "out there" out there.
Separation is an optical delusion of consciousness.[3]

28

The Voice Code demystifies this ancient teaching by revealing the natural logic through which our minds generate the world we see as part of the process of evolution. From the 64 hexagrams of the I-Ching to Maslow's hierarchy of needs, the Voice Code joins all timeless wisdom with a unifying map that shows how all great ideas grow from one underlying source. That source is *your Voice* as it speaks through your creative unconscious.[4]

Like the proverbial devil and angel who stand on our shoulders, our Voice and shadows whisper into our inner ears from two different mental planes, the creative unconscious and primal unconscious (respectively). These unconscious engines run two diametrically opposed operating systems: the CREATE cycle and DEFEND cycle. These cycles are mutually exclusive. *To choose one is to reject the other.* Each can be simply understood through four callings. The chart below offers a quick high-level summary.

Voice Mentor	Voice Calling	The Gift	Shadow Calling	Thou Shalt
Emperor	Own Your Mind	Purpose	Do not Find	Dividers
Alchemist	Think with Heart	Possibility	Play the Part	Forgetters
Warrior	Face the Dark	Power	Blame the Dark	Enforcers
Poet	See the Light	Partnership	See the Lack	Doubters
	CREATE Cycle		DEFEND Cycle	

Because our free will is absolute, once we make a choice our mind naturally follows the path we've set in motion — until we choose again. Here's the tricky part: because the DEFEND cycle buries the evidence, we don't consciously remember creating the shadow. Rest assured, until we achieve the liberated Messiah (Stage 12) consciousness of Buddha or Jesus, we have many shadows to transmute. So what? The past is over. The future is ours. To reclaim our birthright, we must *CREATE* it from the inside out by mastering the one choice that matters above everything else:

shadows or Voice?

The next sections offer brief overviews of the two cycles that these inner guides use. Going forward, we will revisit these cycles from many different perspectives until this holistic map is deeply ingrained into your decision-making brain. As your mastery increases, the dragon's ploys will begin to ring hollow and you will transcend the belief cages that keep most folks enslaved.

The DEFEND Cycle
The Origin of Frame Lock

The shadow is like a virus that bogs down our mental systems, saps our energy, and crashes every time we dare to dream big. A helpful first step to giving yourself a mental operating systems upgrade, is to understand the coding it uses to infect minds. The DEFEND cycle is this coding. This six-step process forms an end-to-end feedback loop that turns our Voice into a mirage and our life into a self-fulfilling prophecy of lack.

Step 1: Divide *our minds with dilemma-based assumptions that reinforce our implicit beliefs in separation, scarcity and sacrifice.*

Step 2: Escape *accountability for this inner choice by blaming people, circumstances and conditions.*

Step 3: Forget *our true Voice identity in favor of a fictional belief identity (self concept) generated to help us survive in a scary world.*

Step 4: Enforce *obedience to our beliefs through punishing tactics that institutionalize fear and keep the real problem hidden.*

Step 5: Negate *our freedom to choose again by burying awareness of the original choice (Step 1) that spurred the cycle.*

Step 6: Doubt *our self worth. Conjure a fantasy future of exoneration from the trials of life. Ignore growing inner void. (Repeat Step 1)*

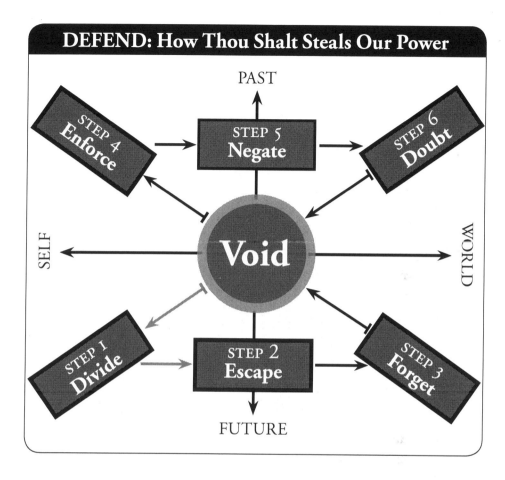

By Step 6 our reality has been turned upside down and Voice seems to have vanished. Our inner world is now an *effect* of what happens outside. Our senses show us a world of endless problems in which death, scarcity, stress, sickness and sadness are "just the way it is" reality. Sound familiar? Once more, I implore you: ***Don't believe the hype!*** Such problems may be common wisdom, but this doesn't mean they're *true*. In the final analysis, they're shadow delusions, made to seem real through the DEFEND cycle. In other words:

Belief in shadows is the *ONLY* problem.

Once shadow voices take root in our minds they are very convincing. They become new threads in the fabric of a highly organized and socially endorsed delusional system stitched together by the DEFEND cycle. When events arise that make us question a shadow projection, a host of other shadows surface to keep us in line. Fortunately, just one decisive commitment to our Voice can change everything. Shadows seem real, but they are literally *nothing*. So, if those sneaky dragons nip away at your peace at any point along this journey, here's one simple remedy:

Laugh at nothing.
Choose again.

When you observe shadow projections without *believing* them, you disrupt the DEFEND cycle and pave the way for miracles. Give it a try and see for yourself. Transmute old shadow patterns and watch problems dissolve like stardust. In the next section you'll see how your Voice helps you permanently correct the reality distortion caused by shadow trickery through a brilliant reality correction process that we call the CREATE cycle.

The CREATE Cycle

The Path to Freedom

The CREATE cycle operates in our creative unconscious, the part of our mind through which our Voice speaks. The skills that govern this process are simple and intuitive. But when we fail to master even one of them, the cycle is compromised and the DEFEND cycle takes over. By removing blocks to restore the flow, we summon higher forces that harmonize our lives on every dimension, pulling us towards the fulfillment of our highest purpose as we focus squarely on the achievement of practical goals.

One step at a time, this cycle shifts us into a state of timeless presence that delivers both inner freedom *and* practical results. Inner gains come first, paving the way for worldly gains to manifest

The CREATE Cycle: 6 Verbs of the Visionary Mind

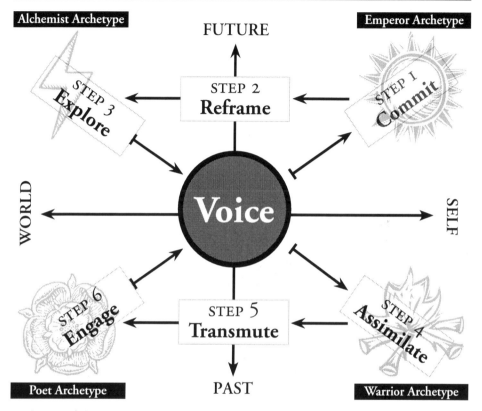

with graceful ease. When you CREATE first-hand evidence that this process actually works, your mind will be blown. You will then be inspired to keep going until the sense of separation between inner and outer dissolves. We activate this cycle through the 6-step goal acceleration process outlined below:

> **Step 1: Commit** *to your mission with intrinsic Authority, challenging any shadows that would keep you limited.*

> **Step 2: Reframe** *the present moment from the chosen future to demonstrate your Authority and honor completion.*

> **Step 3: Explore** *inner resistance that blocks inspired clarity and conviction in the pursuit of your mission.*

Step 4: Assimilate *fear by neutralizing shadow resistance with focused attunement and non-resistance.*

Step 5: Transmute *neutralized shadow patterns with unconditional love to dissolve the past and reclaim gifts.*

Step 6: Embody *gifts with inspired action to renew the cycle, collapsing time to bring the chosen future into the present.*

Each time we complete Step 6, our Voice grows stronger and the DEFEND cycle weakens. Starting with a heartfelt commitment to our Voice authority, we systematically find and remove the inner resistance that would otherwise show up as problems. Each time we generate *Embodied* proof of our unlimited power, we are inspired to *Commit* again, reclaiming more and more power from those Phase I shadow dragons that kept us playing small.

By mastering the CREATE cycle, you will find your calling and become One with your Voice. But this won't happen overnight. Through a lifetime of social programming, we come to deeply fear our own power. Because of this, the direct experience of our Voice can be quite be terrifying at first. In coming scenes of Act I, you will befriend your Voice as it filters through four archetypal mentors: the *Emperor, Alchemist, Warrior* and *Poet*. In Act II, these mentors will help you to reclaim the gifts of Purpose, Possibility, Power and Partnership as you restore this cycle to proper functioning.

Your Voice Revolution will unfold one day at a time as you apply this process to slay everyday dragons. With each iterative cycle, time-stress and scarcity thinking will recede as the natural function for which you were born becomes clearer. Every game-changer in history has achieved the impossible by mastering this cycle. But without a clear map to explain inner game, the true cause of such success was elusive. Good news: we now have a clear map and an actionable path to mastery! The cause: Voice. The path: CREATE. The future: *yours for the choosing.*

Choose Again
CREATE The Revolution

Because the Voice Code is an equation, it doesn't mince words:

You have unlimited creative potential and no limitations whatsoever. Any limitations that you perceive are 100% self-authored, without exception. To remove them, choose again.

People committed to keeping the shadow enthroned dislike this idea because it castrates the excuses they use to justify playing small. But you aren't one of them. If you are who I think you are, you *know* that your Voice is your ticket to freedom. Until now, the question was always: How? How do you unleash your full potential in a frame locked world? Believe it or not, you've just seen a bullet-proof map. This map cannot fail if you give yourself to it without reservation.

Our minds are more powerful than we can imagine. This can be good or bad depending upon how we use them. When we choose the right inner guide, we CREATE freedom. When we don't, we DEFEND fear by default and enslave ourselves with the same power that would otherwise liberate us. The choice is ours.

Lest there be any doubt: You *can* do this. With truth in your heart, you can stare through shadows to heal the past and reclaim your birthright. You can restore the inner throne to its rightful heir and CREATE the future of your dreams from the present. As you do, you will escape the cages of compromise forever.

The only barrier is belief

In the next four chapters, you'll befriend the four Voice mentors who will help you master the CREATE cycle. But first, consider the *Explore Your Voice* inquiry below for some powerful questions to help you get a feel for your unique Voice essence. Then, in Scene 2 you'll meet the Emperor, the stately inner mentor who helps you turn these feelings into an unshakable sense of higher purpose.

CREATE: A Cycle By Any Other Name

The Voice Code has been intuited in nearly all human cultures. Below you see the Star of David, the Heart Chakra, the double Quaternity symbol and the masonic pyramid. These are just a few symbols that point directly towards this universal pattern.

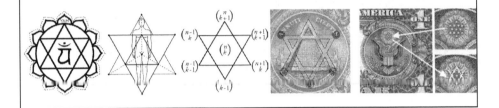

Explore Your Voice *Live the Question*

The nine questions below will help you resonate with your Voice and begin to get clarity about your life's calling. Read each aloud, then listen quietly within for two full minutes. Feel into the heart of each question. As you do this, gently observe the backdrop of your mind for any emerging insights. Take notes in a journal. Repeat this process weekly until the journey is complete. Then review all notes.

Commit: *What would you do if you failure was impossible?*

Reframe: *What gives you great hope for the future?*

Explore: *What three words distill your unique genius?*

Assimilate: *What do you love doing that others find scary?*

Transmute: *Where does your heart call you to bring healing?*

Embody: *What single quality do you admire most in others?*

Authorize: *As a child, how did you see yourself as an adult?*

Resonate: *What lights you up that lights others up?*

Trust: *What early memory is like a snapshot of your life?*

Visit TheVoiceCode.com to get free digital resources, including free training videos and digital copies of key tools offered in this book. You will also find the Voice Code glossary at the end of this book helpful for clarifying and expanding upon any new words, ideas and symbols used.

Scene 2 | *Befriend the Emperor*

Principle: Authority
Voice Number: 4
Gift: Purpose
Emperor's Calling:
Own Your Mind

The Emperor governs the principle of Authority and the 16 gifts of Purpose your Voice offers. This mentor helps you discern your true Voice and commit to this knowing with coherent conviction in the service of your calling. When our being is aligned with the energies of the Emperor archetype we exude a grounded, purposeful presence that commands loyalty from those we engage. During times of uncertainty, the Emperor helps us remain the calm in the eye of the storm, bringing a much-needed sense of order and stability. People who embody the Emperor's Authority are natural leaders. They often become catalysts for world-changing movements, inspiring others to stand with them to usher in bold new realities through power of shared purpose.

Emperor Wisdom

"A house divided against itself cannot stand."
— Abraham Lincoln

*"In the long run, we shape our lives and we shape ourselves.
The process never ends until we die. And the choices we make are our
own responsibility."*
— Eleanor Roosevelt

*"To enjoy good health, to bring true happiness to one's family, to bring
peace to all, one must first discipline and control one's own mind."*
— Buddha

Emperor Essentials

- Brings the 16 Gifts of Purpose through the principle of Authority
- Sits upon the central throne through which Voice speaks
- Brings commanding presence and calm inner Authority
- Brings order and stability to the kingdom (inner first, then outer)
- Leads Axis of Vision in partnership with Alchemist
- Completes Axis of Presence led by the Poet
- Only archetype to directly access higher will

Four is Purpose *The Emperor's Authority*

The Emperor's number is four. This number represents the sense
of calm authority and purpose that this mentor offers. The number
four frames our minds through four simple coordinates of consciousness: *self, world, past* and *future*. These four elements are actually part

of one undivided whole, conjured through four inseparable elements of consciousness: identity, perception, memory and imagination (respectively). To our conscious mind these four coordinates are reflected as four universal motivators: autonomy, connection, security and change. Wherever we look, we find these same four variables in different disguises. Through the Voice Code lens, such patterns are outward pictures of the Emperor's presence.

When we're frame locked, we author our lives unconsciously. Old shadow habits split our thinking, causing us to see ourselves as an effect of our own projections. Thinking this way, our Authority remains limited. Forgotten shadow choices run our lives, as unresolved dynamic tension in our unconscious causes us to perceive the four coordinates of consciousness as irreconcilable opposites. The Voice callings (Own your Mind, Think with Heart, Face the Dark, See the Light) represent a four step process to resolve such false dichotomies from the inside out. Each calling traces to one of the four Voice archetypes: Emperor, Alchemist, Warrior and Poet (respectively). When the kingdom runs smoothly, we come to know each of these archetypes as a different expression of our own unbroken Voice. The Emperor brings order to our kingdom and nurtures the inner roots that make this possible.

To access our Voice through the Emperor we must learn to listen differently to our inner experience. Our Voice speaks not through words, but through *our state of being*. In Phase I (worldview stages 1-6) of the human journey, we see authority as something out there rather than within because we confuse the voices of shadow emperors (aka "Dividers") with the Emperor's calm knowing. In Phase II (worldview stages 7-12), we reclaim the throne and Own our Mind as we dissolve the brain-being barrier we unwittingly created in Phase I. Following the Emperor's lead, we restore the CREATE cycle, to solve our problems first at the level of cause. To do this we align with four mentors, to transmute four species of shadow dragons until our inner and outer kingdoms become One in the service of our purpose.

The Voice of Four

Inner Structure
4 Frame Coordinates: Self, World, Past and Future
4 Gifts of Voice: Purpose, Possibility, Power and Partnership
4 Need Motivators: Autonomy, Connection, Security and Change
4 Mind Elements: Identity, Perception, Memory and Imagination

Outer Picture
4 Heart Chambers | 4 DNA Bases: U,C, A, G | 4 Body Limbs | 4 Fingers |
Directions: North, South, East, West | Seasons: Summer, Autumn, Winter,
Spring | Earth, Air, Wind, Fire | Humuors: Phlegmatic, Choleric, Sanguine,
Melancholic | Pythagoras: 4 is Perfection | Taoism: 4 guardians: Li, Ma,
Cho, Wen; | Buddhism: 4 noble truths | Hinduism: Brahma four headed
God of space & time | Hindu: Vishnu, Brahma & Lakshmi on Ananda

CREATE Authority *Install the Emperor*

The Emperor is the captain and commander of your creative
unconscious. This mentor speaks through calm self-assurance that
arises from definiteness of purpose. When you hear the words "great
leader" what comes to mind? Whatever arises is a reflection of your
relationship to the Emperor within. When you hear the phrase
"terrible leader," what comes up? Whatever it may be, it is a reverse
reflection of this same inner relationship projected outward.

Believe it or not, the same exact Emperor that Abraham Lincoln
accessed to end slavery is within you right now. Is this hard to fathom?
If so, this is only because you've become frame locked into believing
that separation is real. Do you find it hard to imagine that Lincoln
gave his Gettysburg address speech under the same sun we see every
day? Why not also the sunny Emperor archetype? A common
response might be, "Well, because the sun is objective and measurable,

but archetypes are subjective and invisible." But this response starts from the premise that perception is reality. If perception is manufactured in our unconscious, then our unwillingness to consider the value of immeasurable things is a denial of our own authority — a form of frame lock that blocks access to the Emperor's wisdom.

For a moment, please suspend your doubts and openly consider that you have the same exact Emperor as Abraham Lincoln, John F. Kennedy, Jesus Christ and Richard Branson living inside your mind right now. Were this the case, then by mastering the ability to choose your Voice, you would begin to effortlessly exude the same leadership qualities. You wouldn't be trying to copy them either; you would just be acting naturally, following inspiration.

Consider this: Why do we admire people in the first place? Because they reflect our better angels. Great leaders are great because they inspire us to follow our Voice. We all possess this same leadership potential innate. The Emperor archetype is our primary inner access point to unleash it.

When we see through the Emperor's eyes, we behold a world of peace, gratitude, and boundless opportunities to create shared prosperity. When we look at people through this lens, the light goes on for them also. Seeing our light, they remember their own.

When you befriend the Emperor, others will respect your Authority regardless of your formal position in the society. They will recognize something familiar and yet incredibly unique about you that comforts and inspires them. This something is, of course, their own Voice essence reflected within you.

Shadow emperor habits are the true undiagnosed cause of the pervasive stress and insecurity that so many experience today. In the Emperor expression, our Voice helps us escape all of this by reminding us of our true power and helping us own that power in pursuit of our purpose. In the next section you'll learn the secret mindset called paradoxical pragmatism that allows us to stay aligned with this inner powerhouse at all times.

Voice in Action: **The Power of Purpose**
Dragon Slayer: **Theresa, IT Entrepreneur**

After seeing the documentary An Inconvenient Truth, *Theresa was determined to make a difference. She decided to launch a new IT company that would offer a virtual world for children themed around the topic of sustainability. She raised venture capital, built a prototype and launched her vision with a bang. But the outlook soon dimmed: growth was flat. Investors were anxious and morale was sinking. From a Voice Code perspective, the problem was clear. There was no universally relatable "true north" Voice calling statement to help them own the frame in a noisy marketplace. After a one day team session, a simple eight word phrase emerged that perfectly captured the essence: "Unconditional love for the children and the planet." Moved by these words, Theresa's team rallied. Within a year, the customer base had grown from 200,000 subscribers to over 1 million and once-gun shy venture capitalists kicked in another $5 million to support expanding operations. This is just a tiny taste of the explosive power we possess when we're infused by the Emperor's Authority in the pursuit of a definite purpose that issues from the core of our being.*

Think Different *The Purpose Paradox*

Our minds are holographic reality generators: every part of our mind lives within every other part, and all parts grow organically out of the whole through the paradoxical portal of the present. Our Voice is the engine source — that immovable spot at the core of our being from which everything emerges. It is like a homing device for thriving programmed into us by life's creative intelligence. To access it, we must be willing to surrender our limited self-concept and open our minds to the creative urgency of the present moment. The more we choose our Voice, the less we believe in our self-concept and the more self-authored we become. This may sound like a contradiction, but it is actually a *paradox* — a beautifully simple and practical paradox that lives at the core of the Voice Code equation.

The Emperor's powers of purpose and presence emerge through paradoxical thinking. Want to know how Steve Jobs almost single handedly revolutionized three separate industries while bucking all conventional wisdom? Or how Richard Branson has turned Virgin into a sprawling global empire without even knowing basic MBA jargon? Or how that fresh-faced Senator Barack Obama toppled the Clinton Empire in 2008 with an epic grassroots campaign? In all cases the answer is the same:

They embraced paradoxical thinking to find their Voice and predict the future by creating it.

The paradox at the core of all human experience is that we are both unlimited beings and ordinary human beings. In Phase I, we believe that we cannot have it both ways, and become frame locked by "either/or" thinking. In Phase II, we stand for "and" to pass through the paradoxical portal of uncertainty through which our Voice speaks. This allows us to operate from a much deeper field of social engagement than is available to conventional thinkers.[1]

In simple terms, here's the Voice Code spin. This is the big secret that visionary minds leverage to access the Emperor and escape the orbit of ordinary:

Life is a paradox, wrapped in a dilemma, masquerading as an endless series of unsatisfying choices.

To Phase I thinkers, this may seem a nihilistic indictment of human existence. But once we choose our Voice, these same words strike a chord of joyful irony that breaks the frame and reminds us that we are a force of nature with no limitations. When we follow our Voice, we are fearless because we instinctively know that we are the sole authors of our personal reality. But to hear our Voice, we must suspend belief in that habitual head noise we call thinking.

Our Voice is not a head noise. It is a timeless knowing that speaks from the core of our being. We access it by passing through the portal of paradoxical uncertainty to embrace the present moment without preconditions. From this expanded state, our Voice speaks clearly. The habitual sense of separation between inner and outer dissolves and we come to know both aspects of our personal reality as mirror reflections of the same underlying process.

As quantum physicist Richard Feynman put it, "Paradox is just the difference between what reality is and what we'd like it to be."[2] As with quantum reality, so with our inner reality when we maintain a separation between *who we are* and *who we'd like to be*. When we choose our Voice, we close the gap by releasing the past and uniting with the timeless truth at our core. The "HAVE Authority" process below outlines a four-step sequence to help you begin to adopt this paradoxical mindset in your everyday life.

Paradox, Revisited
The Mirror of Voice

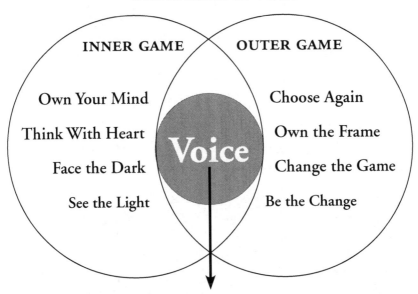

When aligned with Voice we experience inner and outer as mirror reflections of the same process

CREATE Mastery *HAVE Authority*

Hold • Accept • Validate • Embrace

Step 1: Hold the Throne

To access our Voice, we must first commit to remaining calm and centered no matter what happens. When we lose our center, we cannot distinguish the Emperor's Voice from the Divider voices of stress, seeking and scarcity thinking.

Step 2: Accept Resistance

When we find ourselves tempted to lose our cool, we can keep our center by observing resistance without reacting to it. One quick way to remain centered amid resistance is to focus on our breathing. If you begin to feel limited, breathe in for 7 counts, hold in for 7 counts, exhale for 7 counts, and hold out for 7 counts. Repeat this process 7 times and inner resistance will mellow.

Step 3: Validate the Source

From this nonreactive state we can observe the quality of the energies now operating within us. What is the feeling, tone or essence of the inner nudge that seeks to dethrone us? If we experience anything other than a calm inner knowing, we can rest assured this is not our Voice. By taking a moment to validate the source, we help our brain and being stay aligned regardless of external conditions.

Step 4: Embrace Uncertainty

Fear of change is the number one tool in the shadow's arsenal to keep us frame locked. We slay this dragon by reframing uncertainty as an opportunity to close the gap between our aspirational vision and the facts of reality. To do this, we must become masters at placing our faith fully in the creative mind that orchestrates life.

Emperor's Wisdom

"First they ignore you, then laugh at you, then fight you, then you win."
— Gandhi

"There is nothing either good or bad but thinking makes it so."
— William Shakespeare

"We are the creative force of our life and through our own decisions rather than our conditions, we can accomplish any goals."
— Stephen Covey

The Emperor's Mission
Commit to Voice: CREATE Authority

The Emperor is the alpha of the creative unconscious. This wise inner leader offers us the confidence and poise we need to actualize our potential in any domain. Without the good Emperor we spend our lives thinking backwards from our true nature, forever searching for freedom exactly where it isn't. But the true Emperor is always waiting to step in and assist us. We need only to make the invitation. Because the Emperor governs the access point to our Voice, this archetype is the central leverage point to affect change.

The graphic below shows the Emperor's position within the CREATE cycle. The Emperor's role is to make sure the cycle keeps flowing smoothly in a way that keeps our lives healthy, happy and aligned with our highest purpose.

When we are aligned with Voice, we have Authority. When the shadow rules, we have authority *problems*. The pervasive projection of resentment onto authorities in today's world is part of a natural evolutionary process through which we shift our authority frame from external (Phase I: power outside) to internal (Phase II: power inside) perspective. As faith in the wisdom of conventional authorities breaks down, people naturally become disillusioned. Authority problems are common as a coping mechanism to deal with the fear of change.

For frame locked people, blame is the easy way to displace terror. But the true cause of their problems is never out there; it is an

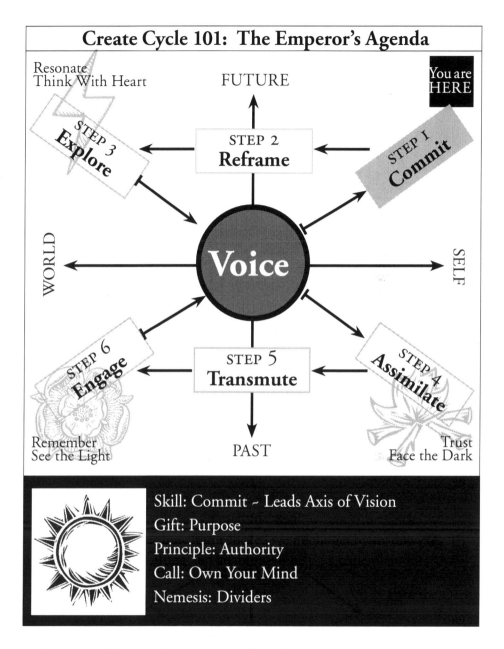

Create Cycle 101: The Emperor's Agenda

Resonate
Think With Heart

FUTURE

You are
HERE

STEP 3
Explore

STEP 2
Reframe

STEP 1
Commit

WORLD

Voice

SELF

STEP 6
Engage

STEP 5
Transmute

STEP 4
Assimilate

Remember
See the Light

PAST

Trust
Face the Dark

Skill: Commit ~ Leads Axis of Vision
Gift: Purpose
Principle: Authority
Call: Own Your Mind
Nemesis: Dividers

authority problem in here, caused by shadow emperor antics. Fortunately, no matter how frame locked we might get by shadows, our Voice is always shifting and adapting to help us remember our

49

power and choose again. But the more shadow habits we develop, the noisier our inner world becomes and the harder it is for the creative energies of our being to break through.

To right the ship, we must commit to our Voice authority with a sense of definite purpose that breaks the shadow's stranglehold over our frame of reference. Without such a commitment, we lack the authority to live life on our own terms. We cannot own our goals with conviction, and our lives become an endless series of dilemmas with no end in sight. Unless we befriend the Emperor, we will remain unable to fully commit to anything, and our goals will lack the sense of vivid urgency that compels decisive action. Without a viscerally compelling vision that reframes our thinking in the present, every other step in the CREATE process is compromised.

To restore the Emperor and establish proper alignment with the principle of Authority, we must ultimately clear shadows around the Axis of Vision which joins the Emperor and Alchemist archetypes. With a balanced Axis of Vision we begin to own the frame in all situations. We live on purpose with a decisive leadership quality that inspires others to follow us. By making a commitment to befriend the Emperor as part of a regular practice (see *Choose Authority* exercise at end of Scene 2), you will quickly begin to embody the gifts that your Voice offers through this mentor.

Shadow Emperors

Dividers: Dragons of Dilemma

When ruled by the shadow, we use our Authority to divide our own minds. With the seductive promise that we might separate means from ends, shadow emperor voices keep us on a treadmill of time scarcity, struggle and seeking to control things forever beyond our reach. When this happens, the DEFEND cycle takes over and the shadow convinces us that we are powerless over our own fate.

The shadow dragons that leads this process are a controlling tag-team called the Dividers. They steal our inner throne by whispering

Axis of Vision

Commit →	Reframe	← Explore
Purpose	AND	**Possibility**

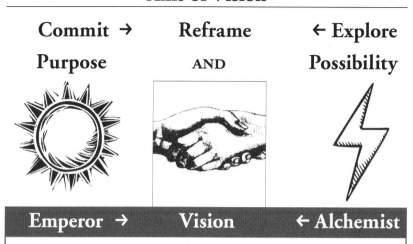

Emperor →	Vision	← Alchemist

The Axis of Vision consists of the C-suite of our Creative Unconscious, the Emperor and Alchemist. When shadow habits associated with these two archetypes are transmuted, the Emperor aligns with the principle of Authority and the Alchemist aligns with the principle of Resonance in the service of the Emperor's vision. When a healthy dynamic exists between these two mentors, the CREATE skill of Reframing becomes a potent skill to help us own the frame and inspire shared vision.

false dillemas that pit our future success against present freedom. They maintain the throne with a good-cop/bad-cop routine that keeps us forever split-minded in our committments. There are eight Divider voices that fall into two basic categories previewed below:

Wardens – *These active shadow emperor voices control us by convincing us that we're not good enough yet. When we follow their advice we end up on an endless treadmill of seeking, constantly striving to control the uncontrollable, seeking success and security according to rules written by others.*

Wimps – *These passive shadow emperor voices control us by "helping" us escape stress and worry caused by the Warden voices. When we follow them we embrace escapist indulgences that provide fleeting satisfaction, but in a way that reinforces our frame lock and leads to addictive patterns that cause us more stress over time*
.

As clever and convincing as the Divider's can seem, they are just optical delusions of consciousness. They are like plates on sticks spinning in our minds, placed in motion years ago when we were first disappointed by the authority figures of our youth. (Technically they are holographic projections of old undigested pain amplified into our awareness from our primal unconscious. But spinning plates is so much simpler, don't you think?)

One good shortcut to escape the Divider's trap is to closely monitor the quality of our commitments. When we choose with anything less than a radically coherent, inspired commitment, we choose the voice of the Dividers instead of our true Voice. As you restore the rightful heir to your inner Voice throne, the Dividers will start to seem laughable. As your relationship with the Emperor matures, you will transmute a lifetime of old Divider shadow habits to permanently reframe Authority from the inside out as you reclaim the 16 gifts of Purpose the Emperor offers.

***

In the final section of this and the next three chapters of Act I, you will find an invocation to help you connect with your Voice through these mentors. For these and all other tools, it is important to adopt a proper attitude. Consider the following key points:

1. **Ground:** In the same way that an electric circuit needs grounding to handle a huge current, our mind-body needs grounding to handle the current of archetypal energy that comes when we summon these mentors. A simple way to become grounded in the present is to observe your body. Notice how your body is supported by the chair that you are sitting in, feel your feet on the floor. Notice the temperature and

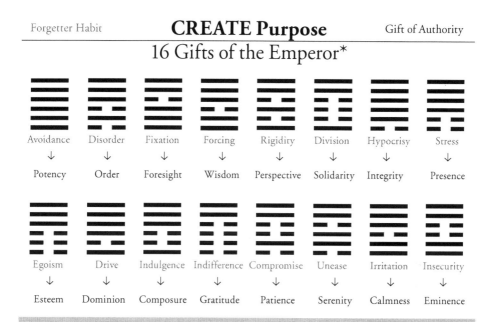

16 Gifts of the Emperor*

Avoidance	Disorder	Fixation	Forcing	Rigidity	Division	Hypocrisy	Stress
↓	↓	↓	↓	↓	↓	↓	↓
Potency	Order	Foresight	Wisdom	Perspective	Solidarity	Integrity	Presence

Egoism	Drive	Indulgence	Indifference	Compromise	Unease	Irritation	Insecurity
↓	↓	↓	↓	↓	↓	↓	↓
Esteem	Dominion	Composure	Gratitude	Patience	Serenity	Calmness	Eminence

*Derived from line-by-line Voice Code reframe of 64 Hexagrams (*I-Ching, Chinese Book of Changes*)

the feel of the air against your skin, etc. This helps you quiet your mind and makes you more receptive to connecting at the level of being.

2. **Be Humble:** Before invoking these archetypes, relax your habitual thoughts and conjure a reverent feeling tone as if you were speaking to some benevolent deity. At the same time, remain aware that the deity is actually the real you — your Voice. As you hold these two seemingly contradictory ideas in mind, tune into your heart and notice what it feels like. Open fully to whatever feelings arise without resistance.

3. **Be Grateful:** Search your mind for at least 3 things that you can be grateful for that are related to that archetype. They don't need to be big things. In fact, if you find this hard to do, be grateful for bad things that aren't happening. Gratitude expands and enhances your ability to access these archetypal energies

4. **Accept the Present:** The trick to accessing these energies is relaxing our frame of reference to embrace the reality of now — without conditions. When we observe our own shadow resistance

without giving into it or adding more resistance, we pass through the portal of paradox to connect with our Voice.

The key to acceptance is to BREATHE into the moment by:

- *Bringing* your attention to your breath,
- *Recognizing* your freedom to choose again,
- *Exhaling* your stress
- *Accepting* your resistance
- *Trusting* in the creative power at your core as you
- *Hold* your mind open to your heart's knowing, and
- *Expand fully* into the present without conditions
-

At the end of each invocation section you'll find a version of the BREATHE presencing process for each Voice archetype. This process offers combined simple numerical imagery with a sequential breathing process that quickly anchors your attention into the present. The more you practice, the more efficient and effective this process will become. These anchors will also help your brain more easily assimilate concepts and information as your brain connects the dots between these visual symbols and the inner states they represent.

Week 1. Befriend the Emperor (checklist)

Step 1: Capture: Take note of key insights and areas of resistance now emerging having read through this material.

Step 2: Consider: Review the 16 Gifts of Purpose and the 16 shadow habits of the Dividers given in the table above. Give yourself an assessment rating between 0 and 10 for each gift where 0 = Divider habit and 10 = Emperor's Gift. Total your responses to find your baseline Emperor Quotient (EQ), between 0 and 160.

Step 3: Clarify: Come up with a clear and compelling 8 week goal — a *milestone mission* that you would like to CREATE as you master this new mindset. Turn this into a clear goal statement. Review and read your milestone mission, your goal statement aloud. Visualize success for 3 minutes before moving on.

Step 4: Connect: Perform the Choose Authority process (below) to connect with Voice Authority directly via the Emperor archetype.

Step 5: Consult: Use this process to get direct Emperor feedback and infuse your vision with a sense of higher Purpose.

Step 6: CREATE: Repeat Steps 3-5 every morning for 6 days. On the 7th day, rest, and release the cycle. Then move into Week 2 with the Emperor's blessing.

Choose Authority *Summon the Emperor*

The Emperor archetype shows up most clearly through our decision making. When we make powerful clear-headed choices that end up working, we have followed the Emperor. When we are indecisive, flaky, inconsistent, reactive and/or impulsive in our decision-making, we are frame locked. Such choices may sometimes bring us the desired external outcomes, but those results never bring us the satisfaction that we crave because they reinforce the split-minded thinking style that keeps us feeling disconnected.

The Emperor blesses decisions that bring us happiness and success on every level. This archetype is completely self-authored, moving like a wheel out of its own center. It can direct us to be conservative and/or reserved, but it can also direct us to take bold actions that others might call foolish. It all depends upon the situation and what the proper response is considering the whole.

Remember the Emperor: Pause to reflect upon times you have been the calm in the center of the storm, making powerful, effective decisions amid times of uncertainty. Search your memory for two or three such moments from the past. It might be a smart business choice that others doubted, but which panned out for you. Or maybe it was the time you calmly walked right up to a gorgeous stranger, who later became your spouse, and introduced yourself without even pondering rejection. Perhaps there was a true moment of crisis in which you were called to step up and help a stranger or someone you care about. Then again, maybe it was the choice you didn't make — the time you said no and ended up much happier for having not done something stupid. Whatever moments you choose, make sure they are decisions that you feel proud of today, whether or not they turned out exactly as you planned. It's the calm Emperor's *state of being* within these moments that we want to focus on further.

Access the Emperor. To access the Emperor, or any Voice archetypes, we must first quiet mental chatter and relax into the present. *Close your eyes* and inhale slowly and deeply as you picture the number 4 in blue. When you exhale release your grip on any stress, tension or resistance you may feel as this blue 4 turns red and reverses into an upside down 4 symbolizing the shadow. Repeat this simple breathing cycle four times. On your final exhalation for the number 4, let the red shadow 4 turn back into the upright blue 4 as the entire number sequence 432 appears. Sit with a calming blue 432 image for 9 more breaths and then open your eyes.

Holding this relaxed state, consciously access the Emperor's energy now. Summon a memory of a time when you owned your mind fully, acting without fear or hesitation to express your inner Voice Authority. What did it feel like to be moved from within by the Emperor? Follow the thread of instinctual knowing that guided you. That thread is your Voice as it speaks through the Emperor. Dive into this energy. Take a few breaths and expand into the calm authoritative power that the Emperor offers. If resistance arises, BREATHE it away and expand to encompass all of who you are.

Invoke the Emperor: While holding this calm power, place your hand on your heart and recite the following invocation in a spirit of respect and appreciation:

"With deep reverence for the creative source that sustains me, I now invoke the commanding power and presence of the sacred Emperor to help me *own my experience with poise and calm composure* as I embark to reclaim my Voice from shadow delusions of yesterday.

"As I make this invocation, I understand that the archetypal Emperor energies I am now summoning are far more powerful than my everyday ego. I make this request, not from ego, but from a heartfelt aspiration to express my true potential in the service of life.

"Today, in a spirit of gratitude for the countless gifts of inner authority that the Emperor has already bestowed, I vow to receive and assimilate any energetic guidance this sacred archetype offers to further my commitment to unify the inner kingdom through which my Voice calls."

Maintain the humble Authoritative presence that the Emperor offers. Hold this state for one minute, before moving forward. Expand to embrace the state of being through which the Emperor speaks. Feel grateful that you have access to this inner power. Give thanks to your Voice as it expresses through the Emperor. Let your heart and mind open to connect in conscious appreciation of the many gifts you have been given and those yet to come.

Anchor the Emperor: To help make Emperor alignment a new life habit, rest calmly in this presence for 2 more minutes, focusing on the number 4 in the Voice Code matrix on the page below. Four is the Emperor's Code. Whenever Divider (shadow emperor) energies cause you to feel reactive, stressed or off center, this number will serve a potent mental trigger to help you quickly regain access to anchor this state in the world of the senses, focus on the white 4 in the center of the Voice Code matrix as you take 9 full breaths. Notice numbers in the surrounding quadrants with your peripheral vision, as you keep your eyes focused on the meeting point in the center. Hold the calm openness as you expand into the Emperor's state.[3]

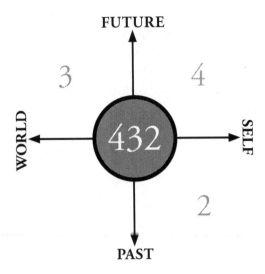

Consult the Emperor: We'll now practice the art of tapping your creative unconscious to get input directly from the Emperor. When ready, read the Voice invocation below. Offer these words from the heart, infusing them with the expansive inner quality of calm authority you've just accessed:

"With profound respect for the creative mind through which we are One, I request direct input from the sacred Emperor that I may Own My Mind as I slay the Dividers to achieve my mission. As I am just now learning how to remain aligned with my creative unconscious in everyday life, I still fall prey to the shadow's distortions without even knowing it, mistaking my own Voice for the Divider's controlling ploys.

"I recognize that by letting the shadow mob rule my thoughts, I make it impossible for you to work through me effectively. I'd like to get your input on a couple of questions to improve our connection going forward."

Ask each the following questions aloud. Pause after each. Listen and write down whatever comes up. Some responses might make immediate sense. Others may seem unclear or irrelevant. Trust that whatever you receive is the perfect guidance for you at this time.

1. **Collaboration Clarity:** Are there any new questions, images, ideas or advice to help me strengthen our connection?

2. **Calling Clarity:** What words or images can you offer to help me better understand the unique gifts I offer?

3. **Milestone Mission:** What input might you offer to help me reclaim my power from the shadow in the pursuit of my mission?

4. **Action Items:** What is one simple thing I can do before the end of the day to generate traction to move my mission forward?

"Thank you. I appreciate your guidance and support. I will give you what you need moving forward."

Release the Emperor: Taking a few final breaths, imagine exhaling any excess energy into the earth to ground the circuit as we move forward. Know that befriending this archetype is the key to everything you want in life. The Emperor offers you inner security, stability and purpose that can be the only foundation for lasting health, happiness and prosperity.

Capture advice in a journal or a file you can revisit later. Often the guidance you receive needs a little time to assimilate. When you look back with the wisdom of hindsight, you'll find prophetic insights, recurring themes and patterns that help you see the unique character and style of your Voice in the Emperor expression.

Visit TheVoiceCode.com to get free digital resources, including free training videos and digital copies of key tools offered in this book. You will also find the Voice Code glossary at the end of this book helpful for clarifying and expanding upon any new words, ideas and symbols used.

Scene 3 | *Inspire the Alchemist*

Principle: Resonance
Voice Number: 3
Gift: Possibility
Alchemist's Calling:
Think with Heart

The Alchemist governs the principle of Resonance and the 16 gifts of Possibility your Voice offers. Through inspired questions and "AHA!" insights, the Alchemist helps us achieve clarity and keep our inner light burning brightly in a frame-locked world. This inner mentor helps us unravel limiting assumptions to see the simplicity behind the complexity of everyday life. When we establish a powerful relationship with this mentor, our brilliance knows no bounds. People with healthy Alchemist alignment don't get frame locked by conventional thinking. They follow their inner knowing to remove all limiting beliefs, to discover the disruptively simple ideas that help them own the frame in the pursuit of their Emperor's purpose.

Alchemist's Wisdom

"Nothing in life is to be feared, it is only to be understood. Now is the time to understand more, so that we may fear less."
— Marie Curie

"Ninety-nine percent of who you are is invisible and untouchable ."
— Buckminster Fuller

"The only source of knowledge is experience."
— Albert Einstein

Alchemist Essentials

- Brings the 16 Gifts of Possibility through principle of Resonance
- Ruthless nose for truth to find blind spots and unravel causes
- Master of radical inquiry, lives the question, spurs innovation
- Part of executive suite of our creative unconscious (with Emperor)
- Translates Emperor's orders into a strategic vision and action plan
- Completes Axis of Vision led by the Emperor
- Leads Axis of Traction in partnership with the Warrior
- Only archetype that can directly challenge Emperor's authority

Three is Possibility
The Alchemist's Resonance

The Alchemist's number is three, which symbolizes the boundless possibility and vision clarity that we unleash through the principle of Resonance. Our Voice accesses our conscious mind through an inquiry-driven mindset that joins three universal planes of experience: the plane of creative vision, plane of social control and plane of primal will. These planes of experience correspond with three layers of the human mind: creative unconscious, conscious aware-ness and primal unconscious. Our conscious choices govern the alignment among these three planes through the three timeless prin-ciples: Authority, Resonance and Trust.

Because our minds are structured this way, we find sacred trini-ties occurring universally throughout history in every culture. All are different ways of expressing the same underlying essence: your time-less Voice essence as it expresses through the Alchemist archetype.

Although our mental attitude towards life changes dramatically as we progress through life, the underlying three-layer structure of our minds never changes. As we navigate our days, every choice we make orients us toward this structure in a way that determines what shows up for us according to the three principles of Voice: Authority, Resonance and Trust. The Alchemist helps us find that balancing point between inner and outer through which we can see and respond to the timeless truth. When we do this, we make smart choices that bring about our highest future, along the path of least resistance. When we don't, we stay frame locked.

In story form, this timeless trinity is represented by different layers within Voice Mountain — the central mountain that we travel up and over along the 12-stage developmental path to complete inner game mastery. From the moment of conception, we begin our lifelong journey up and over this mountain. The mountain never moves, but our relationship to it changes quite dramatically at each stage — especially at the critical shift from Phase I (worldview stages 1-6) to Phase II (stages 7-12). On our way up Voice Mountain, we Resonate with the belief reality handed to us by our parents and the authorities of our youth. Once at the top, we have a frame shifting experience that helps us see through shadows to Resonate with our heart's knowing.

Inspired by our inner Authority, we enter Phase II where we follow the new inside out laws of social gravity to systematically reframe all three principles in reverse order. As we slay the Divider dragons to reframe the principle of Authority, this inner call grows

12 Stages of Worldview Thinking

Phase I. DEFEND
Life is a Dilemma
Seeing is Belieivng
Extrinsic Motivators

CHOOSE AGAIN
Frame Reversal

Phase II. CREATE
Life is a Paradox
Beliefs Create Seeing
Intrinsic Vision

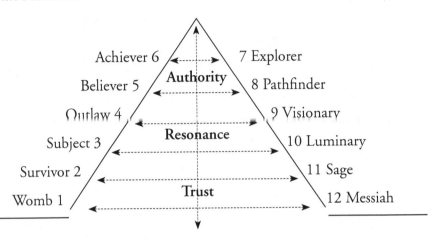

louder and clearer. Our strengthened sense of self-authorship through the Emperor, leads us to become more deeply attuned to our heart's naturally calling. This awakens our latent Alchemist genius as we reframe the principle of Resonance to fit with our new Phase II mindset.

As the principles of Authority and Resonance become radically aligned through the Emperor and Alchemist's invisible handiwork, the inspired gravity of Phase II pulls us with increasing velocity towards a life of unconditional freedom doing what we love. In time, this momentum drives us to release all fear as we reframe the principle of Trust to remember our Innocence and become One with our Voice through the Poet.

The Alchemist brings us the vision clarity we need to become the force of nature we were born to become. But the Alchemist's brilliance cannot shine through fully until we first reclaim the throne by befriending the Emperor. To stay aligned with the principle of Resonance we must be operating with an inner Authority frame.

While the Emperor keeps us grounded in the present with a clear sense of purpose, the Alchemist is free to wonder, observing the dynamic patterns of information as they flow between our inner and outer worlds. So it is that these two powerful Voice mentors give us that rare ability to "own the frame" and create works of timeless value in a polarized world of accelerating change and complexity.

The Voice of Three

Inner Structure

3 Principles: Authority, Resonance, Trust
3 Social Planes: Creative Vision, Social Control, Primal Will
3 Mind Levels: Creative Unconscious, Conscious Mind, Primal Unconscious

Outer Picture

Brain, Heart, Gut | Beginning, Middle, End | Body, Mind, Spirit | Camel, Lion, Child | Heaven, Purgatory, Hell | Christianity: Father, Son, Holy Spirit | Pythagoras: 3 is Completion | Thesis, Antithesis, Synthesis | Celtics: 3 Blessed Ladies | Egyptians: Thoth the Thrice Great | Virtues: Faith, Hope, Charity | Buddhism: The Triratna, The Three Precious Jewels, Three Temptations: Desire, Fear, Opinion

CREATE Resonance

Inspire the Alchemist

The Alchemist is the brilliant inner mentor who finds the simple path to make our dreams come true. Should our kingdom fall into frame lock, the Alchemist is the clever detective who sends us inspired questions that unravel blind spots and inspire solutions. When information complexity reaches a tipping point and confusion clouds our vision, the Alchemist is our stormy seas navigation expert who helps us find true north and correct our course.

With a skill set like this, the demand for people with inspired Alchemists is higher than ever before. But despite this demand, the supply of folks who embody these gifts is quite limited. Why is this? Because most people are frame locked by magical Phase I thinking. The Alchemist's gifts can seem magical, but they aren't. They grow quite naturally from the inner discipline of radical inquiry to challenge conventions in the pursuit of simple truth.

To conventional thinkers, success comes from finding the right answers to solve problems. To visionaries, it's about finding the right questions to discover solutions that dissolve problems from the inside out. This ability seems paranormal to those who've never seriously challenged conventional thinking. Perhaps this is why, to frame locked people, the Alchemist is like lightning — beautiful, impressive and terrifying. There's no telling which sacred cornerstone belief structures this electric mentor might topple!

The habit of closing our hearts to our Voice is totally rational once we've made up our minds to believe in fear. But in reality, we are never afraid of anything but our own shadows projected outward. Once we reframe Authority to reclaim the throne, we begin to deeply appreciate the beauty and practical value of disillusionment. Business leaders can spout words like "creativity" and "innovation" all day long, but they won't become truly innovative until they embrace the spirit of curious wonder that the Alchemist inspires.

The Alchemist's brilliance comes naturally once we get over our old shadow fears about not being smart enough. Sadly, most people I meet dramatically underestimate their own intelligence. The Voice Code doesn't mince words: you are inherently brilliant. If you will, please consider that *whatever brilliance you've ever experienced or seen in the world is actually just your brilliance reflected.* Where have all of your personal experiences beholding brilliance happened? In your mind, of course! You authored those experiences by assigning meaning to the data patterns sent into your brain from the five senses. For this to happen, you must have the same potentiality operating within yourself that you've admired in others.

If you didn't, you wouldn't have been able to recognize their gifts.

The grand prize always goes to those with the gumption to seek truth above all else. Degrees don't matter. Experience doesn't matter. Only truth matters. When our inner foundation is built upon cornerstones of truth, we have the confidence required to place full faith in our own ideas. When this inner foundation is built upon unquestioned beliefs, we lack the courage required to access our gifts, as we become mired in the quicksand of conventional BS. So please be careful not to put people with advanced degrees and impressive credentials up on a pedestal.

It doesn't matter what people think. What matters is what *you know*. Be honest with yourself. What does your heart know beyond the shadow of any doubt? Own it and be willing to keep unlearning until only that knowing remains.

> Voice In Action: **Rebranding a Brander**
> Dragon Slayer: **Marc, Author/Entrepreneur**

> *Marc was a respected branding expert looking to up-level his career by authoring a successful book. He was stymied trying to find the right topic. He reached out to me in dire straits after spending months spinning his wheels. As he spoke, I paid attention to my own subjective sense of inner clarity and inspiration. I noticed that whenever he talked about the human side of the marketing world I felt uplifted. "What lights you up?" I asked him. "What have you learned the hard way, that you want to offer so that others won't have to struggle?" Marc thought for a moment "I want them to trust their instincts. After all, there are no brands really. There are only people." He tried to keep talking, but I stopped him. "There's your book. 'No brands. Only people.'" As if clouds parted, his eyes lit up and he grew calm. He's found his topic! He went on to write the entire book from start to finish in three weeks. The book he soon launched led to a powerful new business model that he now uses to thrive in the marketplace by helping others stand for their humanity in the corporate world.*

You have the same Alchemist archetype that gave Einstein the ability to unravel the world of physics within your creative unconscious right this moment. Your Voice calls you to redefine brilliance so that you can lead the charge to inspire and liberate people from the handcuffs of cognitive conformity. Awaken the Alchemist, then let us inspire and awaken others to theirs, in a spirit of shared purpose.

Alchemist Wisdom

"Knowing your own darkness is the best method for dealing with the darkness of other people."
— Carl Jung

"He who asks a question is a fool for five minutes; He who does not ask a question remains a fool forever."
— Chinese proverb

"What people think of as the moment of discovery is actually the discovery of the question."
— Jonas Salk

Restore Vision *Reverse the Reversal*

During the first six stages of our Voice journey ("Phase I"), the shadow convinces us that we must protect our hearts to be safe. Believing this, we try to live life through our brains, making choices based upon whether or not something resonates with past learning. This mindset inverts our reality, causing us to perceive ourselves as an effect of the world around us. Although rooted in lies, this outside-in mental model gains strength every time we reinforce it by explaining events using this backwards logic. The Alchemist helps us reverse the reversal and see reality as it truly is beyond the veil of limiting beliefs that block clear vision.

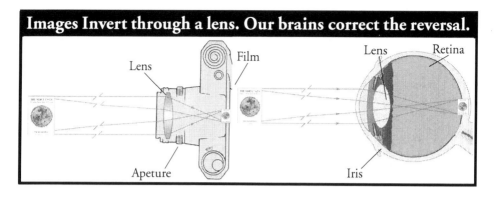

Images Invert through a lens. Our brains correct the reversal.

To better understand how shadows warp reality, consider the analogy of human eyesight. The schematic above shows how images naturally become inverted as light travels through our eyes. In everyday life, when we look at an image, we see it upright only because our brain corrects the inversion before it reaches our conscious mind. If our brain didn't do this, when we opened our eyes each morning we would see an upside-down world.

What if you were forced to wear glasses that inverted images before they entered your eyes? With these upside-down-glasses, the world would now land upright on the back of your eyeball instead of upside down (as it does now). But your brain, having gotten used to correcting information, would still reverse information before it reached your conscious awareness. The world would now appear to be upside down whenever you wore these crazy glasses.[1]

Now, imagine that we were all born in a society that made everyone wear those glasses from the age of three onward. So we all wore them and socialized our children to do the same. In this scenario, we wouldn't have to live in an upside-down world. Research has confirmed that our super-adaptive brains would simply correct our vision again. Within a week or so, our eyes would show us a right-side-up world while we were wearing those upside-down glasses.

Pretty cool, right? But here's the problem: we'd now be dependent upon those glasses to see the world correctly. The minute we took them off, our brains would show us an upside-down world! Naturally we'd begin to feel a sense of dependency on those glasses! After a few scary experiences misplacing them and bumping into things, we might even develop a phobia of naked eye sight and come to live our lives in neurotic fear of ever losing our spectacles.

But would our fear be truly justified? If we lost our glasses, our brains would adapt again. We'd naturally unlearn the optical reversal. Within a few weeks, we'd see the world perfectly without the need of any glasses whatsoever. Sure, there might be a few scary or awkward moments in the interim weeks as we adapted, but once those moments passed, we'd be free of ocular tyranny for life!

This is a great metaphor for the shift from Phase I (Stages 1-6) to Phase II (Stages 7-12) that our world is now undergoing. Things can feel a bit awkward once we throw away our outside-in Phase I belief spectacles. As we first acclimate to the new inside-out terrain of Phase II, things seem upside down and backwards for a bit, even though we're undergoing a very healthy correction. This feeling comes from the momentum of old shadow habits learned in Phase I that we will soon transmute through the natural path life offers.

The Alchemist helps us navigate this transition with grace, offering us clear vision into that deeper, unseen order where all things are connected. As we embrace this inner guidance, our brains and hearts become powerful collaborators in the pursuit of our passions. Looking at others, we see the light of our own Voice reflected within them. As they behold us looking at them this way, they see their own Voice reflected in us. Through this process, the Alchemist helps us restore our vision *together* as part of a unified collective with enduring bonds that become unbreakable with time.

True vision is an act of reality creation through which we unleash possibilities that shift the future *from the present*. When we align with the Alchemist we access this gift. Rules, categories and conditions that keep others trapped melt away as our inner vision directs us to discover the best path forward. Seeing through the shadow's maze, we start to thrive without a map. Following stray hunches and intuitions, we experience coincidences that draw us toward the ideas, people and situations perfectly suited to help us generate a forest of shared value from the seed of a simple "What if?"

Aligned with the Alchemist, we become visionaries in the truest sense of the word. No longer worried about things beyond our control, we are liberated from the indecision that once kept us frame locked. We release all doubts, collapsing our future vision into being in every moment through the disruptive power of joyful discovery. The lessons we learn through this process gradually dissolve all boundaries as we come to know ourselves as One with our Voice.

Living the questions that stoke our innermost passions, our minds embrace the paradoxical portal of now through which Voice speaks. Freed of control games and pretensions, we open to the entire spectrum of thoughts and emotions as they form and dissolve, observing the grand orchestra of creation as it grows our future from the inside out. As our hearts open to the melody, waves of creative energy pass through us like thunderstorms and sunsets, releasing the past to wash away our blind spots in timeless rhythms of resonance. This is how we inspire others without effort, solve problems without thinking and thrive without compromise doing what we love.

The *Find the PEARL* box below will help you shift thinking to access the Alchemist-inspired gifts to solve any practical problem. For tough, longstanding problems repeat every morning for 5 days.

Explore the Alchemist *Find the PEARL*

Pretend • Exaggerate • Ask • Release • Listen

Step 1: Pretend Alien Status
When a problem stumps you, imagine that you are a visiting alien doing a book report on planet Earth. With these unassuming eyes, examine your challenge anew. Explore and embrace all possibilities as you seek to understand how the problem originated.

Step 2: Exaggerate to Absurdity
To break frame lock, exaggerate the problem to absurdity. Ask: "What's the worst thing that could happen?" and then let your imagination soar with until the whole things starts to seem silly.

Step 3: Ask Five Questions

Summon the Alchemist. Be honest and objective as you consider each of the five following questions in a spirit of radical curiosity: *Am I truly committed to finding a solution? What does the successful solution feel like right now? What inner resistance do I refuse to explore? If I neutralized that resistance, what gifts might I find? If I secretly loved this situation exactly as it is, what would be my motive? If I didn't know any better, what would I do right this moment?*

Step 4: Release the Problem

Once you've completed Step 3, take a few breaths and simply notice what comes up in the backdrop of your mind. Then release the whole problem, and shift your attention to something else entirely. Don't worry about finding the solution. Just trust your unconscious to help you work it out. If lingering shadow habits nag at you, say, "Who is that?" Name the character and move on. If you get a stubborn detractor, do the CREATE script (Act I, Scene 6) to remove it and then repeat Step 3 with fresh eyes.

Step 5: Listen for Clues

Once you've released the problem, you've set the wheels in motion. Now you need to stay tuned to your unconscious as you go about your business. Place your gentle attention on the backdrop of your mind. Note any inspired nudges, patterns or images that emerge. Don't obsess. Hold the intention but be relaxed. When the solution emerges (as it must eventually) you will know it.

The Alchemist's Mission

Explore Truth: CREATE Resonance

To see the Alchemist position within the CREATE cycle, see the graphic on the next page. The mastery verb of the Alchemist is *Exploring.* This is the skill of radical inquiry to discover truth and discern root causes. The skill grows as we learn to ask bold questions to unravel fact from fiction, starting with our own minds. The penetrating insight and broadness of perspective that the Alchemist offers grows naturally when we honor our instinctual curiosity. Curiosity may kill cats, but it sets people free.

Please consider that the original cause of every external problem you face is your own unwillingness to explore and exhume old shadows trapped within your unconscious. Unless we master the skill of Exploring, we remain frame locked by an outside-in mental model. Thinking this way, the actions we take to solve problems solve them by displacing our shadows to create other problems. The Alchemist helps us resolve problems at their roots so that they never return or come back to haunt us in other areas through *projection*.[2]

The CREATE cycle works in sequence from the Emperor to the Alchemist. Directives pass from the immovable spot at the center to the Emperor then over to the Alchemist for strategy formulation.[3] Collectively these two inner mentors collaborate to help us Own the Frame through the first three verbs (Commit →Reframe → Explore) of this six-step cycle. Our mastery at Reframing emerges as we balance the skills of Commitment and Exploring through the Emperor and Alchemist.

Collectively these two mentors form the Axis of Vision, the segment of the CREATE cycle that governs our ability to hear our Voice in a frame locked world. When we master the Emperor's ability to issue authoritative Commitments and the Alchemist's talent for Exploring, we are naturally gifted at reframing situations to maintain motivation in the pursuit of our dreams. When either mentor is blocked, we lose this gift. Our future feels cloudy and we cannot visualize our goals happening with inspired clarity.

The importance of Emperor-Alchemist alignment cannot be overstated. Without the Emperor's authority, we lack the inner gravitas and conviction to choose our Voice fully. But without the Alchemist's brilliance, we lack the strategic clarity and agility to bring our vision to the world. If you've ever wondered why more than 85% of people fail to actualize their true potential, now you know: few have the courage to think big because very few have done the work required to establish rapport between these two mentors.

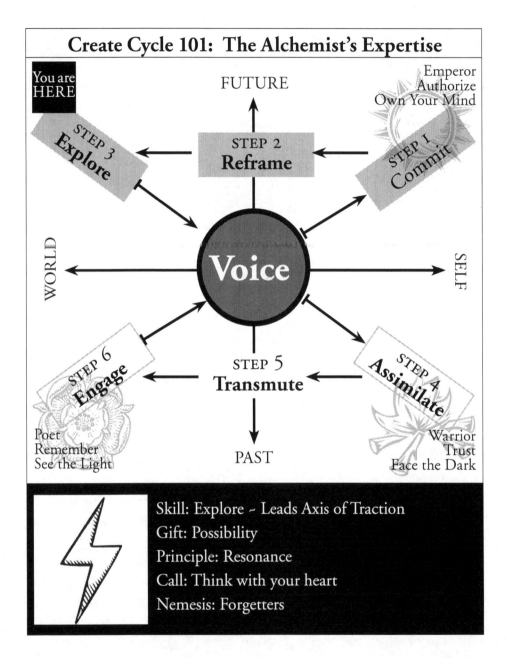

Create Cycle 101: The Alchemist's Expertise

You are HERE

FUTURE

Emperor
Authorize
Own Your Mind

STEP 3
Explore

STEP 2
Reframe

STEP 1
Commit

WORLD

Voice

SELF

STEP 6
Engage

STEP 5
Transmute

STEP 4
Assimilate

Poet
Remember
See the Light

PAST

Warrior
Trust
Face the Dark

Skill: Explore ~ Leads Axis of Traction
Gift: Possibility
Principle: Resonance
Call: Think with your heart
Nemesis: Forgetters

The Alchemist is our access to possibility. When this mentor falls into shadow, we play sneaky games that kill our curiosity and keep us from receiving a clear vision of our life's unique calling.

Our calling becomes grounded only after we've strengthened the Axis of Traction that binds the Alchemist and Warrior. When this channel is blocked, our big ideas remain ineffectual, no matter how hard we may try to implement them. On the other hand, when this bridge is sturdy, we bridge heaven and earth through the principles of Resonance and Trust. The box below offers a more detailed preview of this pivotal CREATE cycle partnership.

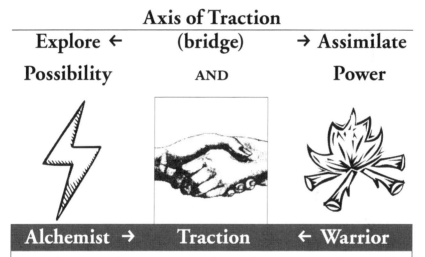

Axis of Traction

Explore ←	(bridge)	→ Assimilate
Possibility	AND	Power

Alchemist →   Traction   ← Warrior

The Axis of Traction is what helps us move the needle with the Emperor's Purpose. At first, the Alchemist's airy inspired energy may seem incompatible with the Warrior's earthy gumption. But when we transmute the shadow habits that keep our intellect and gut instincts at odds, our hearts naturally bridge this inner polarity as part of one dynamic flow. Healthy Alchemists let the heart wisdom shape their exploring. Healthy Warriors follow their heart's courage to assimilate the obstacles that block our path. Together, they unleash the power to bridge heaven and earth in the service of any worthy purpose.

Shadow Alchemists

Forgetters: Dragons of Duplicity

The dragons that keep us from accessing the gifts of the healthy Alchemist are a shadow team of Forgetters. In Act II. Slay Thou Shalt, you will expose the Forgetters' schemes in dazzling detail. Like the Dividers, these mesmerizing shadow dragons form a tag-team duo that keep us forever split minded. When we fall for the con, we become frame locked by social pretenses and selfishness. When following Forgetters' advice becomes a personal policy, we no longer even know what we feel. This makes all of our relationships suffer and causes deep frustration in every area of our lives.

When we let the Forgetters steal our power we "Play the Part" instead of "Think with Heart" and lose access to the 16 gifts of Possibility our Voice offers through the healthy Alchemist. As with the Dividers (shadow emperors), there are eight Forgetter voices that fall into two main categories:

Sharks – *These assertive shadow voices control us by giving us clever strategies that compromise our conscience. They pose loaded questions rooted in zero-sum thinking. When we take the bait, we feel compelled to manipulate and misdirect others to survive and achieve our agenda.*

Showboats – *These shadow voices control us by having us mistake symbols of freedom (like money, popularity and approval) for the actual experience. When we follow their advice, we mistake grandiosity for grandeur and find ourselves living our lives like actors playing a role.*

As you might guess, these two shadow dragons feed off of one another. Sharks beget Showboats beget more Sharks and Showboats, until we feel like phonies, enslaved by social norms and conventions. When we make it a habit to follow the Forgetters' sneaky advice, we lose our natural curiosity and experience a steady state of low-grade anxiety. This makes us feel even more dependent upon the shadow Emperors (Dividers) and Warriors (Enforcers) to help us find quick-fix solutions that never satisfy. Thus it happens that otherwise brilliant people find themselves caught in a downward spiral of inner shadow dependency, playing the role assigned to them by society instead of authoring life on their own terms.

As we shift focus to summon your Alchemist in the next section, please consider one fact every shadow in your primal unconscious dreads that you will one day discover:

You are the world's leading expert at being you.

You have a gift to offer the world that no one has ever seen before. Brilliance is your very nature. Forgetters be damned! What's true is true: *there is an unspeakable, infinite well of brilliance woven into the very essence of your being.* When you let it, this light will lead you to total freedom. If any inner voices doubt you on this, say "Who is that?" Then name the shadow pattern and transmute it using the CREATE cycle. If anyone in your outer world doubts you on this, say "Thank you" and keep moving forward. Those who judge you are your helpers. They only attack you because they feel the power of your Voice stirring within and it scares up old shadows.

When you let cynics discourage you, the shadow wins and everybody loses. But when you shine your brilliant light without worry, you set yourself free and create a very real opportunity for others to wake up along with you. They'll do so when you no longer need their help and approval — once you've transmuted the limiting beliefs that had you worry about their opinions in the first place. When you've released these old shadow habits, their service to you as your helpful challenger will be complete and you will both be in a position to choose again — together, as one.

This co-creative learning process is at the heart of great leadership. Like everything truly great, this ability grows from the inside out as we follow our Voice in the pursuit of shared vision. *Everyone who has ever lived an extraordinary life was considered a naive boob before the world finally caught up with them.*

Frame locked people are always resistant to brilliance when they first encounter it, and make no mistake: your Voice is the essence of brilliant. Without it, there'd be no light in the kingdom and none in the eyes of those you engage. The Forgetters are plotting to keep that light buried forever. Let's keep this from happening.

Week 2. Inspire the Alchemist (checklist)

Step 1. Capture: Note any key insights and areas of resistance now emerging having read through this material.

Step 2. Consider: Review the 16 Gifts of Resonance and the 16 shadow habits of the Forgetters in the table below. Give self-assessment rating between 0 and 10 on each gift where 0 = Forgetter Habit and 10 = Alchemist Gift. Total responses for baseline Alchemist Quotient (AQ) between 0 and 160.

Forgetter Habit   **CREATE Possibility**   Gift of Authority
16 Gifts of the Alchemist*

Boredom	Dependency	Decadence	Comformity	Pretense	Complication	Reactivity	Fantasy
↓	↓	↓	↓	↓	↓	↓	↓
Curiosity	Harmony	Coherence	Honesty	Grace	Simplicity	Objectivity	Reality

Confusion	Hypocrisy	Dissonance	Diversion	Resistance	Histrionics	Arrogance	Myopia
↓	↓	↓	↓	↓	↓	↓	↓
Clarity	Humility	Alignment	Attunement	Receptivity	Equanimity	Modesty	Vision

*Derived from line-by-line Voice Code reframe of 64 Hexagrams (*I-Ching, Chinese Book of Changes*)

Step 3. Clarify: Review and read the milestone mission statement (from week 1) aloud. Visualize success for 3 minutes before moving forward to Step 4.

Step 4. Connect: Perform the Choose Resonance process (below) to connect directly with your Voice in the Alchemist expression.

Step 5. Consult: Use same process to get direct Alchemist feedback to clarify next steps and infuse your vision with inspiration.

Step 6. CREATE: Repeat steps 3-5 every morning for 6 days. On the 7th day, rest, relax and release the cycle.

Choose Resonance

Summon the Alchemist

The Alchemist speaks through inspired inquiry, insight and creative vision into emerging future possibilities. To feel the Alchemist frequency, recall a memory of an inspired moment of effortless clarity. Perhaps it was a time when a great idea just landed in your lap or where you were struggling over some issue and gave up, only to have the answer arrive without effort. Dive into this experience and try to access that thread of effortless inspiration that directed you. As you do, imagine that your mind is expanding to include the entire universe, capable of receiving and decoding messages instantly, offering inspired insights to quickly solve any problem. This is how life shows up when we are aligned with the Alchemist in our everyday life. In this section you will align with the Archetype directly. Use this process to access this mentor anytime.

Remember the Alchemist: Please take a moment to consider the three biggest "Aha!" moments that you can recall. Try to make these moments of great clarity and inspiration — times when you were able to see the simplicity behind the complexity, where your vision was strong. Perhaps your frame shifted, offering a different way of thinking about a challenge, opening a new pathway to achieve your dreams. These may be times when an inspired idea just seemed to fall out of the sky from nowhere. You might also scan your memory for one of those inspired conversations from the past in which the clock just seemed to stop as you explored idea after idea in a spirit of shared brilliance.

Access the Alchemist: To strengthen access to this mentor, we must first quiet mental chatter and relax into the present. Close your eyes and inhale slowly and deeply as you picture the number 3 in blue. When you exhale release your grip on any stress, tension or resistance you may feel as this blue 3 turns red and reverses into an upside-down 3. Repeat this cycle 3 times. On your final exhalation, let the red shadow 3 turn back into the upright blue 3 as the entire number sequence 432 appears. Sit with a calming blue 432 image for 9 more breaths and then open your eyes.

Holding this relaxed state, consciously access the Alchemist energy now. Dive into your memory, back to a moment when your mind was open, inspired and filled with curious wonder. Perhaps it was a time when a great idea just landed in your lap. What came before this big "AHA!"? Were you in a moment of confusion or struggle that suddenly opened to reveal a simple path forward? Was it an issue that you had been incubating for some time? Whatever the case may be, take a moment to replay the moment where the light bulb went on in your mind's eye.

Mentally project yourself right into the "AHA!" state of mind now. Embrace the electricity of insight. Imagine that your mind is unlimited in size, scope and clarity; able to receive inspired ideas and brilliant insights that give you vision down into the deeper unseen layers of social reality. In your mind's eye, dive into those layers and become One with the electric knowing of infinite possibility. Let this lucid energy resonate throughout your body, mind and being. Take a few breaths and expand into this energized state fully.

Invoke the Alchemist: Keep your mind open as you anchor in the unbearable lightness of your being as it speaks through your heart's timeless knowing. Feel the paradox of stillness within change. Know yourself as the stillness, observing the change. Take a few more breaths and exhale all resistance as you place your hand on your heart and recite the following invocation:

"With deep reverence for the creative source that sustains me, I now invoke the inspired brilliance of the Alchemist that I may observe my inner experience with objective clarity and insight as I embark to reclaim my gifts from shadow.

"As I make this request, I respectfully acknowledge that the archetypal energies that my Voice offers through the Alchemist archetype are far beyond those of my everyday ego mind. I make this choice not to co-opt these powers for my ego, but from a heartfelt aspiration to actualize my true creative potential in the service of life as a whole.

"Today, in a spirit of profound gratitude for the countless gifts that the Alchemist has already given, I vow to receive and assimilate any energetic support and guidance this inner mentor offers to help me unify the kingdom, inner and outer, in the service of my life's purpose."

Hold the state of receptivity and reverence that these words evoke for one minute before moving forward. If resistance arises, BREATHE it away, and open to the brilliance of your Voice as it expresses through this creative energy. Be the Alchemist. Rest in this state for one minute, observing and allowing it to envelop you. As you do, give thanks. Feel grateful that you have access to this power.

Anchor the Alchemist: Rest in this energy as you focus on the number 3 in the Voice Code matrix below. Three is the Alchemist's

Code. This number represents clarity, unity, and connection through timeless truths that bind. Whenever shadow alchemist (Forgetter) energies cause you to feel confused, anxious or blocked from accessing your vision, this number will serve an efficient mental trigger to help you escape frame lock. To visually anchor this state, focus on the white 3 in the center of the Voice Code matrix below as you take 9 full breaths. Hold the state of heart Resonance you've accessed as you open fully to the Alchemist's energy.

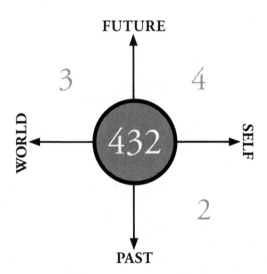

Consult the Alchemist: We'll now practice the art of tapping your creative unconscious to get input directly from the Alchemist. When ready, read the Voice invocation below. Offer these words from the heart, infusing them with the same quality of inspired receptivity you've opened.

"With profound gratitude and respect for the timeless creative source that connects us, I now request direct assistance

that I may Think with Heart to reclaim my power and achieve this mission. As I am just now learning how to remain aligned with my true Voice, I still fall prey to the Forgetters' manipulations without even knowing it. I'd appreciate your wisdom and guidance so that we can create a more inspired partnership in the pursuit of shared vision, in service to truth."

Read the questions below. After each question be silent. Listen quietly and write down whatever comes up. Some insights will make sense immediately. Some might seem irrelevant. Just write it down and move forward. Whatever you get is the perfect message for you at this moment.

1. **Collaboration Clarity:** Are there any new questions, images, or ideas that you would offer to help me strengthen our connection?

2. **Calling Clarity:** What words, images or other information can you offer to help me better understand the unique gifts I offer?

3. **Milestone Mission:** What input might you offer to help me reclaim my power from the Forgetters in the pursuit of my mission?

4. **Action Items:** What is one simple thing I can do before the end of the day to generate traction to move my mission forward?

"Thank you. I appreciate your guidance and support. I will give you what you need moving forward."

Release the Alchemist: Taking a few final breaths, imagine exhaling any excess energy into the earth to ground the circuit deep down at the earth's core. Understand that the mighty charge the Alchemist helps you access is always available to you. It enters awareness effortlessly when you surrender false certainty to open your mind to that timeless field of pure possibility from which everything arises. Tapping this aspect of their creative unconscious is how great visionaries become great. The trick is learning how to use our brains as instruments of curious inquiry in search of timeless truth. The Alchemist will gladly teach us these tricks so that we create prosperous lives beyond the bounds of all belief boxes.

Visit TheVoiceCode.com to get free digital resources, including free training videos and digital copies of key tools offered in this book. You will also find the Voice Code glossary at the end of this book helpful for clarifying and expanding upon any new words, ideas and symbols used.

Scene 4 | *Embrace the Warrior*

Principle: Trust
Voice Number: 2
Gift: Power
Warrior's Calling:
Face the Dark

The Warrior governs the principle of Trust and the 16 gifts of Power your Voice offers. Through the Warrior, we "Face the Dark" with honor, discipline and fierce resolve to neutralize the past and reclaim power from any shadow patterns that limit us. By embracing this mentor, we conquer fear through the CREATE skill of Assimilation. The Warrior plays a pivotal role in our lives. This mentor helps us give our heart's aspirations real world traction as we transmute the shadow hell of undigested pain into heaven on earth. Through this natural healing process, we establish Trust with our Voice and pave the way to the life we've always dreamed possible, but dismissed as impractical during the uphill climb of Phase I. Aligned with this mighty mentor, we take on an almost otherworldly aura of strength and tenacity in the name of timeless principles and in the service of our life's purpose.

Warrior Wisdom

"If a man doesn't have something he's willing to die for, he's not quite prepared to live."
— Dr. Martin Luther King Jr.

"The fear of death follows from the fear of life. A man who lives fully is prepared to die at any time."
— Mark Twain

"The most difficult thing is the decision to act. The fears are paper tigers. You can do anything you decide to do."
— Amelia Earhart

Warrior Essentials

- Brings the 16 gifts of Power through the principle of Trust
- Brings fearless courage, discipline, vitality and resilience
- Assimilates shadow to protect innocence and restore unity
- Executes Alchemist's plan to implement Emperor's purpose
- Responsible for establishing and maintaining boundaries
- Completes Axis of Traction in partnership with the Alchemist
- Leads Axis of Vitality in collaboration with Poet
- Helps us enjoy the "good burn" of constructive discomfort

Two is Trust *The Warrior's Power*

The Warrior's number is two, which represents the spirit of unconditional Trust and service to life. Thinking in alignment with this mentor, we embrace duality with a gentle but fierce resolve to dissolve the shadow delusions that drive it. The world we perceive is comprised of opposites that can only be reconciled from the inside out with the Warrior's guidance: self-other, past-future, us-them, rich-poor, good-evil, love-hate, old-new, and all other polarities we perceive can ultimately be traced back to one inner dichotomy:

shadows vs. Voice

When we embrace the Warrior, we know in our bones that all polarities are rooted in delusion. This gives us the indomitable courage to trust our Voice and stand for our inner authority in the pursuit of a life without compromise.

In Phase I (stages 1-6) of the 12-Step journey to total Voice alignment, we learn separation and gather endless evidence to support dualistic thinking. As the story goes, good and evil are bitter enemies engaged in an epic battle to triumph over our souls. In Phase II, we gradually unlearn duality to find ourselves in a loving world of oneness. As we transmute shadow wounds from Phase I, we come to recognize that delusions cannot triumph over anything but our sanity. The more we bet on our Voice, the more evidence we collect to help our reptilian brains recognize that evil is nothing more than the mistaken perception of love's absence.

Can love ever truly be absent? It can certainly *appear* absent at the level of perception. But only through frame-locked lenses do we confuse perception with reality. This is the central delusion that we learn during the Phase I climb. As our mastery of the Phase II mindset deepens, we begin to consciously influence what happens out there through focused inner work. In so doing, we castrate the optical delusion of separation as we come to personally realize a universal truth that all great dragon slayers embody: *Love cannot be absent because love is what we are.*

Cleared of all shadows, we see love and only love wherever we look within every moment. As we approach Stage 12, we feel deep love for even the darkest of shadows, because we see within them the call to become *only* love and so enter Stage 13 – a highly advanced state of consciousness that some call heaven. Stage 13 is the white light that people often report after near death experiences. The

Warrior's happy job is to help us see that light now, before we die, by facing and dissolving the inner dichotomies that conjure the polarized world of perception.

We are forever free to choose how we invest our trust. But we cannot choose to escape the principle of Trust itself. When we trust in anything other than our Voice, we trust shadows and lose our awareness of love's presence. By the time we are ready to shift from Phase I to Phase II, most of us have gotten so accustomed to hiding, repressing and projecting our fears that we find it far easier to list reasons for being afraid than to place our faith in the power of love at our core. To set ourselves free, we need only summon the Warrior and commit to facing darkness directly, in a spirit of honor to the creative source that unites us. By staring at our delusions without believing in their power, we transmute all dualities into Oneness and see the light of infinity shining freely.

The Voice of Two

Inner Structure
Two Inner Guides: Shadow vs. Voice
Dual Unconscious: Primal vs. Creative

Outer Picture
Good vs. Evil | Light vs. Dark | Yin vs. Yang | Inner vs. Outer | Us vs. Them | Science vs. Religion| Nature vs. Nurture | Past vs. Future | Self vs. World | Up vs. Down | Love vs. Hate | Hot vs. Cold | Man vs. Woman | Hero vs. Villain | Adam vs. Eve | Heaven vs. Earth | Logic vs. Magic | Heart vs. Head | Truth vs. Lies | Thesis vs. Antithesis | Fear vs. Faith | Mind vs. Matter | Risk vs. Reward | Freedom vs. Slavery | Money vs. Meaning | Purpose vs. Profits | Security vs. Progress | Courage vs. Cowardice | Left vs. Right

CREATE Freedom *Enlist the Warrior*

The Warrior doesn't mess around. This is the creative energy of focused action in the service of a higher principle or purpose. The Warrior's motto is "It's a good day to die." But please don't let this motto frighten or deceive you. This mentor doesn't believe in death. That's the whole point! The Warrior sees death and fear in every form as a shadow delusion and relishes the opportunity to dismantle false limitations on our behalf. When we fall into shadow around the Warrior, we misdirect this mighty energy out into the world through projection and find ourselves mired in endless cycles of blame and attack — a dance of mutual deflation that can only be resolved from the inside out.

The healthy Warrior never attacks unless doing so is absolutely essential for preserving the sanctity of the kingdom. Even then, the actions taken are performed in a spirit of love. This archetype is the soul essence of honor, discipline and sacrifice in the service of transcendent principles that join everyone. When change is needed, the Warrior is the one to call. This energy will gladly arrest and Assimilate any stray shadow forces within. When you need to lose twenty pounds, kick a bad habit or save a baby from a burning building, summon the Warrior. It's the only archetype in our royal inner court that actually enjoys the burn of productive pain. When we summon the Warrior to break frame lock, we find ourselves suddenly enjoying things that would've made us quake with dread only moments before.

The productive go-getter power available through this archetype is why so many people (men in particular) become susceptible to shadow Warrior possession. The jolt of healthy Warrior vitality can become addictive, leading people to become mad with power, chasing after adrenaline through risky thrill-seeking actions that serve no one. When this happens, old shadow energies have emerged to block healthy access to our Voice in the Warrior expression.

Rising awareness of the negative impact of shadow warrior excesses has turned many against this misunderstood mentor. But those who dismiss the Warrior as "men behaving badly" fail to realize that the most iconic portrait of the Voice Warrior is a loving mother. The true Warrior is a disciplined protector of innocence, integrity and timeless principles that we all cherish. Anyone who wishes to escape the influence of this archetype is deeply misguided. One might as well hope to escape happiness, physical vitality and respect since these are just a few of the gifts this mentor makes available to those who honor the call.

Voice in Action: **Escape from Convention**
Dragon Slayer: **Sarah, (Not so) Desperate Housewife**

When she signed up for the Voice Code boot-camp Sarah was a self-described "desperate housewife". She lived in beautiful surroundings with a successful and loyal husband. But something was missing. Where was the passion? Why were disagreements over money and material things destroying her relationship? What could she do to escape the sense of social imprisonment that plagued her? How might she reclaim her power? In Week 1, the answers began to arrive, and they kept on arriving until nearly every dimension of her life had transformed. As it turned out, her prison was clad with iron bars of guilt forged by a lifetime of repressed shadow warrior energies sapping her power. With Voice Code tools and coaching, she reclaimed her power one week at a time. When the 10-week course ended her marriage had been amicably dissolved. She was now financially independent from a clean divorce settlement. She'd also healed her relationships with both parents, and landed her dream job leading a company with shared values. Friends were coming up to her asking her how she did it, and total strangers were now asking for life advice. All of this from the inside out, without a clear premeditated plan of action, by simply Assimilating fear of change to awaken the Warrior within. Not bad, eh?

The Warriors Role
Assimilate Fear: CREATE Trust

How did Gandhi free India? Radical Warrior alignment. How did Steve Jobs usher in the new era of creative capitalism? Radical Warrior alignment. How did Martin Luther King Jr. bring healing to a country torn by racial intolerance? Radical Warrior alignment. Iconic visionaries become great by developing a powerful personal connection with the Warrior archetype in the pursuit of their life's purpose. This gives us an indomitable will and the discipline to persist despite any odds until we have actualized our dreams. Anyone who does the same inner work as these icons can and will accomplish similar feats with this mentor's guidance. The only barrier is belief.

By actively neutralizing fear, the Warrior archetype clears our minds and helps us access the unlimited strength at our core. When we fall into frame lock, we stay stuck in our minds, afraid to live life fully. We may not consciously feel fear every day, but when we make decisions that compromise our vitality, we can be sure that fear is stowed in the cave of our primal unconscious sapping our power. The Warrior evokes our better angels, that part of our mind that is bigger than all fear and which stands for freedom in the name of timeless principles that bind everyone.

The graphic below shows the role of the Warrior in the CREATE cycle. As you see, this mentor stands in the lower right hand quadrant of the creative unconscious, diagonally across from the Alchemist. When we are aligned with the Warrior, we follow heart Resonance and gut instincts to act on Alchemist directives, actively tuning into shadow energies to neutralize fear. By bringing active attention to our own inner resistance, we castrate old shadow delusions so that they can no longer infect our minds. Once a shadow pattern has been assimilated, we pass the residue along to our inner Poet who helps us reclaim the Voice gift trapped within.

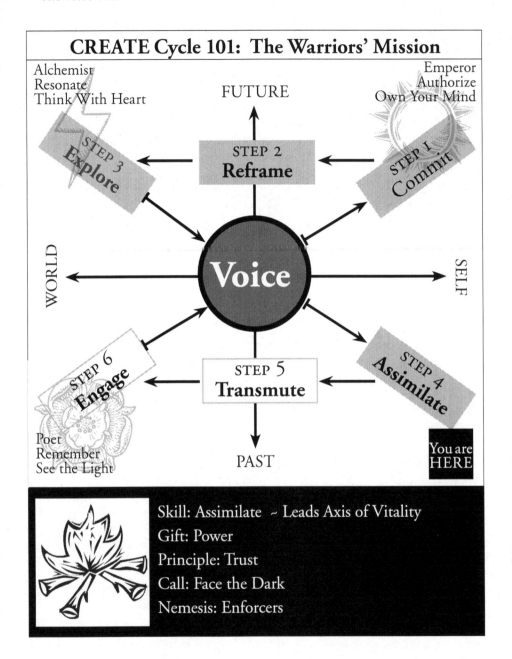

CREATE Cycle 101: The Warriors' Mission

Alchemist
Resonate
Think With Heart

FUTURE

Emperor
Authorize
Own Your Mind

STEP 3
Explore

STEP 2
Reframe

STEP 1
Commit

WORLD

Voice

SELF

STEP 6
Engage

STEP 5
Transmute

STEP 4
Assimilate

Poet
Remember
See the Light

PAST

You are
HERE

Skill: Assimilate ~ Leads Axis of Vitality
Gift: Power
Principle: Trust
Call: Face the Dark
Nemesis: Enforcers

In a unified mind, the Poet and Warrior work closely together to implement the vision handed down by the Emperor and Alchemist. These two archetypes are the boots on the ground change agents of our creative unconscious. They find and process the shadow to reclaim our birthright by *Assimilating, Transmuting* and *Embodying* our Voice essence to complete the CREATE cycle. Together this dynamic duo forms the Axis of Vitality through which we reframe Trust as we learn to let our Voice direct our day-to-day actions.

When our Warrior falls into shadow, things go downhill quickly. The world outside becomes increasingly punishing as our inner world turns into an emotional prison. We may conjure many reasons to justify the feelings of fear, anger, victimization and hopelessness that occur during times like these. But here's what's really happening: we've bought into shadow warrior projections. That's all. Mistaking the shadow for the real Warrior, we left the Poet unprotected and got seduced into despair by wounded shadow poets trapped deep within our primal unconscious.

To see the downward spirals that shadow warrior and poet melodramas instigate, watch cable news. Consider that all this polarizing madness we find in modern news media is just an outward picturing of our collective inner condition. Our world is deeply confused, grappling with shadow warrior (Enforcers) and shadow poet (Doubters) projections right now at an unprecedented rate, as part of the epic macro-shift to Phase II (Stages 7-12) now unfolding. This shift can be scary if we believe the shadow hype and cling to past beliefs. But those with the courage to ask, "Who is that?" and embrace the Phase II mindset can now become a thriving force for positive change more easily than ever before.

Shadow warriors cannot survive in a mind that allows the C-suite (Emperor and Alchemist) to fulfill its natural function. When the Axis of Vision is strong, we feel empowered to think big and own our frame of reference. This inspiration leads us to heal the Axis of Traction (Alchemist-Warrior) and ultimately the Axis of Vitality (Warrior-Poet). So if we're looking for someone to save the world, we need only look in the mirror and say, "Who is this?" to those shadow voices within that would have us blame the world (or ourselves) for the world's problems. Blame is shadow warrior prison. It is the opposite of Trust and the biggest barrier to reclaiming the Warrior's indomitable gifts.

Axis of Vitality

Assimilate →	Transmute	← Engage
Power	AND	**Partnership**

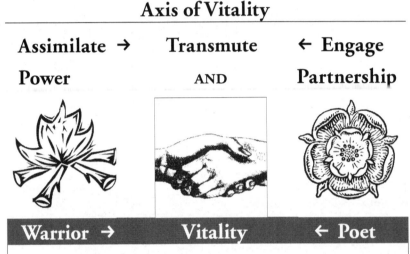

Warrior →	Vitality	← Poet

The Axis of Vitality governs ability to heal the past and open the future. The health of this axis can be determined by our physical and mental vitality and resiliency. The key skill that unleashes vitality is the big T of the CREATE cycle: Transmute. To master the art of Transmutation we must have a radically coherent inner kingdom in which the Warrior and Poet are thriving partners. In practice this requires that we master and balance the skills of Assimilation and Embodiment. This integrates the Warrior's power with the Poet's love, opening us to our natural ability to heal the past and access a new future from the inside out.

The *Clear the CAVE* exercise on the opposite page is a simple 4-step process that will help you neutralize resistance to reclaim your power from any shadow patterns that limit you.

Assimilate the Warrior *Clear the CAVE*
Call • Arrest • Validate • Endure

Step 1: Call it Out

When nagging negative emotions haunt us, we usually try to ignore them. When this doesn't work, we usually try to dismiss them. Neither works. The only proven way to erase fear is to face it squarely. If the fear is buried, consider amplifying and exaggerating it by ranting, writing or otherwise embodying it. This reversal tactic diffuses the discomfort and brings the shadow energies out into plain view. (Note: Perform Step 1 in a safe, private setting.)

Step 2: Arrest the Opposition

Once you've seen the true enemy, it's time to arrest it. In this context, arrest means simply to stop. We arrest shadow patterns much as we'd arrest the bleeding from an open wound — by placing firm, caring pressure on it until it stops. This requires the mental discipline of focused attunement. With the strong, resolved mindset of the Warrior, attune your energies until they match the frequency of this old shadow pattern precisely.

Step 3: Validate Immortality

In everyday life, we let the desire to avoid discomfort rule our lives. When aligned with the Warrior, we rule our own lives saying "Bring it on!" to discomfort. As you stare old shadow energies in the eyes, say "Today is a good day to die," and double down. Learn to love the liberating discomfort that comes with this attitude and watch your comfort zone grow beyond all bounds.

Step 4: Endure until Shift

When the shadow pattern has been fully neutralized, you will experience a shift. This usually occurs right when you stop worrying about how long the process will take. Seeing that you won't be bullied, the shadows bend to your will. A deep inner shift happens, and the gift reveals itself. Observe this gift. What is it? Notice and name it. You have permanently neutralized a shadow pattern, and you are moments away from transmuting it to reclaim your power.

Warrior Wisdom

"I count him braver who overcomes his desires than him who conquers his enemies; for the hardest victory is over self."
— Aristotle

"Do the thing you fear to do and keep on doing it... That is the quickest and surest way ever yet discovered to conquer fear."
— Dale Carnegie

"Do the one thing you think you cannot do. Fail at it. Try again. The only people who never tumble are those who never mount the high wire. This is your moment. Own it."
— Oprah Winfrey

ల

Shadow Warriors
Enforcers: Dragons of Darkness

The spectacularly destructive shadow dramas that cause misery in our world are just a dramatic out-picturing of shadow caves that we all inhabit. Were this not true, we wouldn't judge them. Shadow warrior thinking habits always involve rationalizing, defending and projecting our pain through blame, instead of confronting our fears directly. Over time, this amorphous mass of undigested pain takes on a life of its own, leading us down dark alleys that no one cares to travel. Pain turns to fear, morphs into anger, calcifies into rage and then cools into icy hate.

Most of us spend enormous amounts of energy playing shell games with these dark energies. Over time we develop a host of shadow habits that we employ to help us bury the evidence. As these habits calcify through hypnotic repetition, our minds become like slow computers glutted with viruses. Instead of Assimilating and Transmuting the pain to reclaim our power, we fall into exhausting patterns of apathy, resentment, cynicism and driven ambition that drag us down even more.

To permanently escape this condition, we must clearly distinguish between the true Warrior and the Enforcers, a deviant group of shadow dragons that drive all such downward spirals from behind the scenes. As with the other three shadow teams, there are eight Enforcers that fall into one of two categories:

Punishers – *These prideful "kill or be killed" shadow warrior voices control us by convincing us that we have been somehow disrespected or dishonored. Once we fall into their trap, we become self-righteously dogmatic in defense of our beliefs. This drives a sense of ruthless entitlement that lives right under the surface in most civilized people.*

Prisoners – *These cynical "it's too late" shadow warrior voices control us by convincing us life is dangerous and doomed. Tapping undigested shame from our most embarrassing past mistakes (most caused by the Punisher!), they tell us that our quest for fulfillment is a fool's errand. When we believe them, we sell out on our dreams and become permanent victims of the Punisher's angry antics.*

Over time the iron bars of guilt that the Punishers and Prisoners create seem thick and impenetrable. What we fail to realize is that they are only as real as our choice to keep believing that our past errors have power over us now. The true Warrior never punishes or imprisons, it liberates us by setting us free of this shadow prison that keeps most people feeling forever powerless to control their fate.

These days, the walls of many Enforcer caves can be quite stylish and appealing to the senses. Penthouse apartments and six-pack abs can just as easily become tools for shadow warrior imprisonment as anything else! The Enforcers don't care what we do, as long as we stay split minded — forever forcing, blaming and compromising our principles for the sake of survival. Those who endeavor to create freedom through shadow warrior ploys are trapped in a painful and truly hopeless cul-de-sac of human consciousness, searching for freedom by attacking their own Innocence.

Once we've stripped away the first two layers of shadow energy that caused us to believe in dilemmas (shadow emperors) and forget our essence (shadow alchemists), we reach the critical inner tipping point that precedes our greatest awakening. Having now established Authority over our own minds and given ourselves permission to embrace true discovery by living the question, we are in the pole position to see something people who fear darkness never learn: the Enforcers are a bunch of goofy windbags. Like all bullies, they crawl away whenever someone with courage stares at them without flinching in fear or reacting in anger.

In Scene 12 (Act II. Slay Thou Shalt) you'll enlist the Warrior to arrest the Enforcers and reclaim the 16 gifts of Power that your Voice offers through this mentor. When our journey to self-actualization leads us down the path to those dark nights of the soul, we are on the precipice of liberation. The long-dreaded darkest moment is never nearly as terrifying as we once imagined. When it finally arrives, a beautiful thing happens: facing the fear, we see the

Enforcer Habit							Gift of Trust

CREATE Power
16 Gifts of the Warrior*

Resignation	Indecision	Dishonor	Indolence	Distraction	Ambivalence	Impotence	Condemnation
↓	↓	↓	↓	↓	↓	↓	↓
Fortitude	Tenacity	Honor	Discipline	Focus	Devotion	Potency	Forgivennes

Apathy	Instability	Cynicism	Expediency	Lethargy	Bravado	Impulsiveness	Complacency
↓	↓	↓	↓	↓	↓	↓	↓
Resolve	Reliability	Optimism	Universality	Vitality	Tenacity	Temperance	Vigilance

*Derived from line-by-line Voice Code reframe of 64 Hexagrams (*I-Ching, Chinese Book of Changes*)

98

light. With indomitable will and fierce resolve, we clear the path to remember our Innocence and restore the Poet's grandeur as the charismatic ambassador for the life of purpose, possibility, and power we've always wanted.

Week 3. Embrace the Warrior (checklist)

Step 1. Capture: Take note of any key insights and areas of shadow resistance now emerging having read this material.

Step 2. Consider: Review the 16 Gifts of Trust and the 16 Enforcer habits. Give self-assessment rating between 0 and 10 on each gift where 0 = Enforcers Habit and 10 = Warrior Gift. Total for baseline Warrior Quotient (WQ) between 0 and 160.

Step 3. Clarify: Review and read your milestone mission goal statement aloud. Visualize success for 3 minutes before moving on.

Step 4. Connect: Perform the Choose Trust process (below) to connect directly with your Voice via the Warrior archetype.

Step 5. Consult: Use same process to get direct Warrior feedback to clarify next steps and infuse your vision with grounded power.

Step 6. CREATE: Repeat steps 3-5 every morning for 6 days. On the 7th day, rest, relax and release the cycle.

Choose Trust *Embrace the Warrior*

The Warrior surfaces most vividly when challenges arise that require courageous action in the face of uncertainty. As we become radically aligned with our Voice in this expression, we begin to exude this same type of decisiveness at all times. The ultimate trick to maintaining radical Warrior alignment at all times is to have a sense of purpose and vision so strong and compelling that we would sooner die than surrender. To pave the way as your life's purpose becomes clear, make it a practice to consistently invite the Warrior into your heart and mind. The exercise in this section will help you make the process of directly accessing and anchoring this aspect of your being an empowering new life habit.

Remember the Warrior: Take a moment to consider a few times where you faced fear and rose to the occasion, taking honorable, courageous action in the service of a higher principle or purpose. This could be a moment of service helping another during a crisis, protecting someone or something that you cared about from harm, a challenging conversation in which you came clean with someone to clear your conscience, a time when you went with your gut and took a chance that paid off despite the warnings of cynics. If helpful, tap your creative imagination. Imagine that something or someone you care about deeply is being threatened and immediate action is required to protect those you love. The feeling of fearless resolve we access in times like these are the Warrior's energy in action.

Access the Warrior: Quiet mental chatter and relax into the present using the Warrior 432 process. Close your eyes and inhale slowly and deeply as you picture the number 2 in blue. When you exhale, release your grip on any stress, tension or resistance you may feel as this blue 2 turns red and reverses into an upside-down 2. Repeat this simple breathing cycle 4 times. On your final exhalation for the number 2, let the red shadow 2 turn back into the upright blue 2 as the entire number sequence 432 appears. Sit with a calming blue 432 image for 9 more breaths. Then open your eyes.

Holding this state, please dive back in your memory to a moment when you embodied the Warrior's primal powers. What drove you to enter that state? Were you driven by an inspired idea, principle or purpose about which you felt strongly? Did you suddenly become aware of fear and make up your mind to face it squarely? Whatever it was, strip away the situational details and focus on the feeling state you were in. Take a moment to fully embrace the Warrior's honor and fierce resolve. Imagine drawing those powerful energies into your body from all around you. Let it swell up from the earth and down from the heavens, filling you from head to foot with a sense of vitality and invincibility.

Take a few breaths and let these powerfully charged vital energies course through every cell of your body. Let this mentor pull you through the wall of your normal comfort zone and into a space where your focus is so disciplined that shadows cannot touch you. Take a few breaths and expand into this state of mental discipline and calm readiness. Own this state. Rest within it for at least one minute before moving forward.

Invoke the Warrior: When you are ready, hold this state as you place your hand on your heart and recite the following:

"With profound reverence for the creative source that sustains me, I now invoke the fearless courage of the Warrior so that I may *face old shadow energies with courage, focused mental discipline and principled resolve* as I embark to reclaim my gifts from the shadow clouds of past learning.

"As I make this invocation, I humbly acknowledge that the Warrior's creative energies are far more powerful than my everyday ego. This request is made in good faith with the courage of my principles. My mission is rooted in my wholehearted desire to make a difference offering my unique gifts in defense of that which is Innocent at the heart of all.

"Today, in a spirit of respect and honor for the many gifts the Warrior has already given me, I vow to receive and assimilate any energetic guidance this sacred mentor offers to help me embody my potential to further my mission, that I might bring unity to the inner kingdom through which greatness grows."

Hold the state of humble reverence that these words evoke for one full minute before moving on. Observe your inner state. Allow gratitude. Give thanks to your Voice. Let your heart and mind open in appreciation of the many blessings this mentor offers.

Anchor the Warrior: To anchor this state, consider how much the Warrior's honor and courage has brought to your life already — without it you would be unable to challenge the status quo and lead change. Rest in this energy for two more minutes before reading the paragraph below. 2 is the Warrior's Code. This number represents the courage and honor to face fear and division without fear or resistance. When we do this, shadows dissolve and we see the light. Whenever Enforcer energies cause you to feel fear, judgment, shame, resentment, anger or aggression, the number 2 will serve as a potent mental trigger to help you quickly access the Warrior's power. To anchor this state, focus on the white 2 in the center of the Voice Code matrix as you take 9 full breaths. Notice numbers in the surrounding quadrants with your peripheral vision, as your eyes focus squarely on the white 2 in the center. Hold the state you've accessed as you anchor the Warrior through this process.

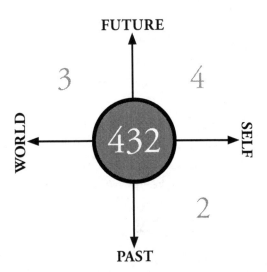

FUTURE

3   4

WORLD ← 432 → SELF

2

PAST

Consult the Warrior: We'll now tap your creative unconscious to get input directly from the Warrior. When ready, read the Voice invocation below. Offer these words from the heart, infusing them with the same quality of being you've accessed through this exercise

"With profound respect for the timeless creative source that connects us, I now request direct assistance from the Warrior that I may face the dark and fulfill my mission with *courage, honor and focused mental discipline*. As I am just now learning how to align with my creative unconscious in everyday life, I still fall prey to the shadow's distortions without even knowing it, mistaking the Enforcer's projections for my true Voice."

After each question, be silent. Listen quietly and write down whatever comes up. Some insights will make sense immediately. Assume that whatever you get is the perfect message for you at this moment.

1. Collaboration Clarity: Are there any new questions, images, or advice that You might offer to help strengthen our connection?

2. Calling Clarity: What words, images or other information can you offer to help me better understand the unique gifts I offer?

3. Milestone Mission: What input might you offer to help me face and reclaim my power in the pursuit of my mission?

4. Action Items: What's one simple thing I can do before the end of the day to generate traction to move my mission forward?

**"Thank you. I appreciate your guidance and support.
I will give you what you need moving forward."**

Release the Circuit: Taking a few final breaths, imagine exhaling any excess energy into the earth to ground the circuit and bring you back to a comfortable, sustainable energy state before moving forward. Aligning with the Warrior is the key to physical and mental vitality and to getting grounded traction with any goal. This state is the portal to grounded power and the passion to persevere in the face of any setbacks. It offers you the ability to stand fully for your

Voice in the service of truth, unity and the unique purpose life has assigned you. Release the energy, but maintain the positive state that you've opened to carry with you, that you may call upon this mighty mentor at any time in the name of any worthy endeavor.

Visit TheVoiceCode.com to get free digital resources, including free training videos and digital copies of key tools offered in this book. You will also find the Voice Code glossary at the end of this book helpful for clarifying and expanding upon any new words, ideas and symbols used.

Scene 5 *Behold the Poet*

Principle: Innocence
Voice Code: 1
Gift: Partnership
Poet's Calling:
See the Light

The Poet embodies the principle of Innocence and the 16 gifts of Partnership your Voice offers. This mentor evokes innocent love, gratitude and praise for the beauty of life. If you've ever felt connected to something larger than yourself, some transcendent beauty that stirred your very core, you have tasted the Poet's intoxicating charms. By transmuting neutralized shadows with unconditional love, this inner guide helps us remember our timeless Innocence as an expression of Oneness. If the Poet seems weak, please think again. The Poet's innocence is the core truth of who we are and the very essence of strength. Without access to this aspect of our Voice, the entire kingdom falls into disarray, and we cannot achieve satisfying partnerships in any area of our lives, leaving true prosperity out of reach. When we restore our relationship with the Poet, exuberance blooms and prosperity flowers naturally from the inside-out.

Poet Wisdom

"Through our own recovered innocence we discern the innocence of our neighbors."
— Henry David Thoreau

"If we have no peace, it is because we have forgotten that we belong to each other."
— Mother Teresa

"Love is the only force capable of transforming an enemy into a friend"
— Martin Luther King, Jr.

Poet Essentials

- **Brings the 16 Gifts of Partnership through principle of Innocence**
- **Brings joy, beauty, compassion, charisma and connection**
- **The anchor archetype that brings light to the kingdom**
- **Dissolves past with unconditional love and forgiveness**
- **Heals wounds with active love to transmute shadow patterns**
- **Completes Axis of Vitality led by the Warrior**
- **Leads Axis of Prosperity in partnership with Emperor**
- **Only archetype that can challenge Emperor's authority**

One is Innocence *The Poet's Partnership*

The Poet's number is one, the symbol of innocence and equality. Like the Poet, the number one is a perfect mirror of unity. Any number multiplied by one remains itself. Any number divided by itself equals One. In the same way, when we align with the Poet, we come to know our Voice as One with the creative mind that orchestrates life. When shadows remain, we perceive and believe in duplicity. When the Poet speaks through us, we no longer mistake perception for reality. With our physical eyes we still see a world of opposites, but we do not experience ourselves as separate from that which we observe. This state of consciousness can be pointed to with words, but remains accessible only to those of us willing to loosen our grip on our everyday self-concept. When we make this choice, the Poet is waiting to help us remember the truth of Oneness.

At this point in our journey you've seen the ideas in the equation below represented in a few different ways:

$$\text{Authority} + \text{Resonance} + \text{Trust} = \text{Voice}$$

You've also met the mentors who govern these three principles: The Emperor governs Authority. The Alchemist governs Resonance. The Warrior governs Trust. Here's the big question: where in this equation do we find the Poet's innocence? The answer is both obvious and as strangely overlooked as is the Poet's presence within our being. The Poet's footprint in this equation lives in the one place we take for granted, the mathematical symbol for unity:

$$=$$

The equal sign is the symbol of the Poet. It represents the purity of perfect Oneness. In all situations it sits silent and unassuming, acting as a mirror for the changeless, without ever drawing attention to itself. Consider all the equations you've ever looked upon. How often have you consciously noticed and appreciated the role of the equal sign? If you are like most people, not often. Yet this often ignored symbol is critically important. Without it, by definition, there can be no equation. So too with the Poet and light of innocent love that this mentor offers to help us unify inner and outer.

Every revered teacher in history has been an ambassador of Oneness in the service of the Poet. We've revered them because they've helped us transcend frame lock. Instead of walking the path of convention, they chose Voice with clarity and conviction to arrive at the exact message time and again:

We are One, after all.
One Mind. One Love. One Purpose.

When someone has the audacity to speak simple truth with unusual grace, it always sends the shadow mob into frenzy. Sometimes truth tellers even get killed for their willingness to stand for this message. Considering the perils of martyred truth tellers throughout the ages, why would anyone stick their neck out to join them? It's a reasonable question. Consider this: what if they knew something we don't? What if their seeming super powers came from their ability to see the simple truth behind the veil of separation? What if the Poet's call led them to unravel all fear so that only Oneness remained and death dissolved as a mere shadow delusion?[1]

The Voice of One

Inner Structure

Voice

Outer Picture

Love | World | Life | Tao | The Force | Vortex | Nature | Gaia | Ground of Being Existence | Mother Earth | Universal Mind | The Big Bang | The End of Time | Source | Creator | One Source Creator | Om | Soul | Spirit | Allah | Lord | Spirit | The Word | Supreme Being | Source | Creator | Abbah | Almighty | The Christ | The Buddha | The Sonship | The Friend | The Godhead | The Universe | The Light | God | The Jewel | Jehovah | Thoughts of God | Truth | Eternity | Unity | Infinity | Oneness

CREATE Joy *Behold the Poet*

The Poet *speaks* through innocent love and gratitude. For this reason, the Poet is the most charismatic kid on the block. When aligned with this mentor, we radiate love and appreciation without agenda, effortlessly reflecting back to others their deeper Voice essence. When people with pretenses meet someone who embodies this archetype, they cannot help but feel awkward — as if their own cool-badges were suddenly revoked. In the Poet's innocent light, all pretensions crumble like sawdust, opening portals to that mysterious plane of shared being where all things are connected.

Want to live a great life? Make it your mission to befriend the Poet. Here's the rub: the Poet flowers only after we align and integrate the Emperor, Alchemist and Warrior. Until we do this inner work, the Poet's call remains elusive. With no sturdy inner reference point to distinguish between the Poet and the Doubters (shadow poets) we dread looking deeply inward for fear of what we'll discover. Feeling ourselves unlovable, we project the parts of ourselves that we don't like out onto the world, guarding our vulnerability with a mask of bravado. This attitude disinvites the Poet from our awareness; not because this mentor is weak, but because our belief *in our own weakness* blocks the light of timeless truth from our conscious awareness.

That radiant inner beauty that the Poet offers is potent precisely because it is innocent. Everyone has access to this energy for their entire lives, but most of us carry so many Phase I battle scars that we can no longer distinguish between the real Poet and the shadow poet proxy until we see them side by side. Whenever someone comes along who has retained (or recovered) his or her authenticity as an adult, the Poet's call awakens. Our doubts dissolve and we remember our youthful Innocence by an invisible means that can seem magical or otherworldly when viewed through conventional lenses.

This mysterious dynamic is good news, indeed. If frame lock can dissolve so easily in the presence of Poet messengers, we must still have access to joyful Poet energy beneath our defenses. Whatever mistakes we may have made in the past, at our core we remain the same unconditionally lovable and radiant beings that we've always been. When we do the inner work to reconnect with this inner radiance in our everyday life, we get to thrive in today's Poet-starved world by simply opening our minds and following our hearts in each passing moment.

Professional poets speak of love with such beauty, because they know that it is a mystery beyond words. Although our intellect cannot begin fathom love's meaning, we can create conditions of radical inner coherence in which love speaks through us. As we stand strong at the altar of our heart's knowing love extends outward in ever widening circles. When we behold the Poet, we know love as the mystery that our Voice has always been. It is a mystery only because we thought we threw it away long ago, in a moment of misguided choosing. But standing in Innocence, we remember the reality of love and recognize it as our very nature.

Words can describe this experience, but they will never capture it. Like a finger pointing to a twinkling star, they direct our attention, but cannot complete the journey for us. To see the light, we must move from the map symbols, into the territory of direct experiential knowing. By owning our minds, thinking with heart and facing our darkness, we peel away old layers of resistance to remember this experience and invite this honored guest's light back into our lives through the medium of direct embodied experience.

This is the process and path that everyone must travel given the natural laws that govern the development of human consciousness. *These laws guarantee our ultimate success as part of the evolution of mankind.* In the mid-point transition from Phase I (Stages 1-6) to Phase II (Stages 7-12) we radically shift course and begin to unlearn a lifetime of shadow patterns, one stage at a time. Our lives gradually turn from problem to poem, as we awaken from shadow slumber to see the light of shared Innocence in all things.

This is the Poet's return. This is the endgame of freedom, made complete through our unshakable faith in our Voice. We are One, after all. The journey and the destination were never separate. The search *out there* was only to find light within. The search *within* was to bring light out there. The whole journey was to dissolve the false dichotomy between inner and outer that kept us feeling separate and limited. The Poet reminds us. All we need do is clear our minds, open our hearts and surrender.

Voice in Action: **Unleashing the Poet**
Dragon Slayer: **Mary, Designer**

Mary is a beautiful, bright young woman with big dreams. But she was stuck. Imprisoned by a long-time relationship with a controlling and jealous man. Every time she went out with friends other men would surround her like wolves, treating her with the same attitude. "Why does this keep happening?" she wondered. "I don't want this attention, but this pattern keeps happening! How can I get guys to start respecting my boundaries?" I asked her to imagine that a shadow character living within her was giving off signals that triggered the wolves. "Who is this character?" I asked. She laughed, quickly conjuring an attention-starved character she named Candi the Floozy, who reveled in the attention. "Are you willing to take your power back from Candi?" I asked. She nodded. I gave her the CREATE script (see Scene 6), and asked her to set one hour aside to transmute this old shadow pattern. She did and the problem stopped immediately. This simple act unleashed a chain reaction that led her away from her old patterns and into a new life, in a new city, with a new career and a newfound resolve to let her gifts flower.

In the next section I'll help you see how our unconscious relationships explore the Poet's much-underutilized role as Chief Engagement Officer in the CREATE cycle. First, the simple *Feel the LOVE* process below will help you align with the Poet's powers in your everyday life.

Engage the Poet *Feel the LOVE*

Look • Open • Value • Embrace

Step 1. Look for Light: When we experience lack in relationships, shadows compel us to focus on what isn't working. When we do this, we collect more false evidence that our belief in lack is justified, leading us into downward spirals of frame locked mis-creation. The first step to transforming these situations into upward success spirals is to shift focus on what's going right: Where's the light? What's working? What three things could I be grateful for right now? Where's the hidden beauty within this situation?

Step 2. Open to Hope: When we look for light, our minds open to perceive the hidden beauty. The problems that once darkened our mind may still appear the same to our senses, but the music of hope and optimism begins to swell within regardless. As we open to hope, our inner condition changes. We lose interest in misery and our mind expands to include all possibilities with a peaceful knowing of our unconditional safety and worthiness.

Step 3. Validate Innocence: From the state of silent knowing, we look around to see things anew. As a sense of Oneness perfumes our minds, the need for even hope recedes and the beauty of Innocence becomes us. This joining happens, not through an act of willful forcing, but through the surrendering of the false belief will (aka self concept) that had kept us frame locked. Liberated from habitual pretense, we remember our Innocence.

Step 4. Embrace the Gift: Gratitude is the engine of greatness. When we validate our own Innocence, we no longer project our fears and self-doubts out onto others. Seeing others as they are, we embrace their gifts and feel grateful for them. Seeing their inner light reflected within our gratitude, they instinctively remember and reflect our own gifts back to us in kind. So it is that we connect with others to lift ourselves in shared grandeur through the Poet's innocent and eternally loving presence.

Poet Wisdom

"Every child is an artist. The problem is how to remain an artist when you grow up."
— Pablo Picasso

*"Whatever you can do or dream you can, begin it. Boldness has genius,
power and magic in it. Begin it now!"*
— Goethe

"Stay young. Stay foolish."
— Steve Jobs

The Poet's Mission
Embody Joy: CREATE Oneness

The Poet stands opposite the Emperor in the CREATE cycle.
Yet, in a very real sense, these two archetypes are a mirror reflection
of the same thing. Neither could possibly exist without the other.
The Poet's primary function is to help us remember our Innocence
by embodying our reclaimed gifts in a spirit of shared self-interest.
Poet-inspired actions complete the CREATE cycle mission, that
begins with the Emperor's Commitment, blessing the inner
kingdom as we bring our chosen future into the present.

The energies of these mentors combine into a magic elixir of
mindfulness. Together they form the Axis of Presence, which
governs our ability to remain connected to our Voice at all times to
generate a life of boundless prosperity. When we restore a healthy
Poet-Emperor relationship, we forge an unbreakable bond with the
creative mind that orchestrates life. Through this sacred inner pact
the four mentors unite and we become One with our Voice, the
elusive fifth element (*quintessence*) from which greatness flowers.

To understand how the Poet-Emperor dynamic plays out as our
Phase II journey progresses, consider a healthy ecosystem in nature.
Have you ever heard the sound of a healthy, fresh-water lake, near a
forest in the dead of night? It's like a free-form symphony with a
beautifully spontaneous structure. There's this pulsing, patterned
buzzing and chirping — a beautifully chaotic wall of sound led by a
chorus of soprano frogs singing with jazzy syncopation.

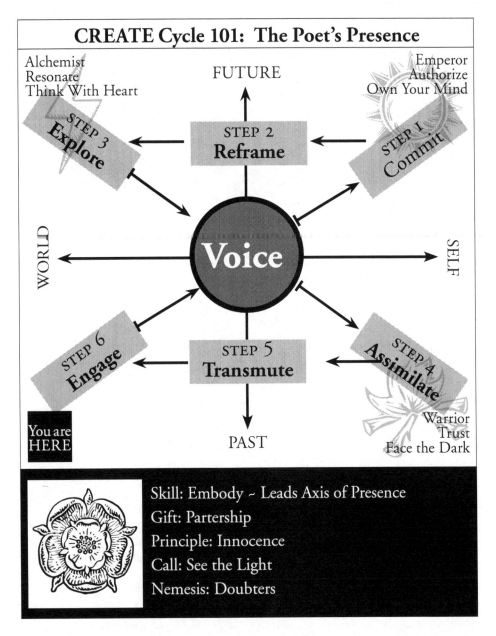

CREATE Cycle 101: The Poet's Presence

Alchemist
Resonate
Think With Heart

FUTURE

Emperor
Authorize
Own Your Mind

STEP 3
Explore

STEP 2
Reframe

STEP 1
Commit

WORLD

Voice

SELF

STEP 6
Engage

STEP 5
Transmute

STEP 4
Assimilate

You are
HERE

PAST

Warrior
Trust
Face the Dark

Skill: Embody ~ Leads Axis of Presence
Gift: Partership
Principle: Innocence
Call: See the Light
Nemesis: Doubters

When Poet and Emperor are united, your life will take on a similar quality of spontaneous harmony and perfection. Your inner music will merge with the external flow, and your life will have this

Axis of Presence

Engage ←	(rest)	→ Commit
Parternship		Purpose

Poet	Presence	Emperor

The Axis of Presence brings the CREATE cycle full circle. This axis gives us the power to be joyfully present and detached while standing with total Authority for our Purpose. To harmonize the Emperor and Poet energies we must master and integrate the skills of Commitment and Embodiment. When we honor the Emperor, we let our highest Purpose guide our life path. When we honor the Poet, we let the future pull us into action to offer our gifts. This completes the circuit and creates that elusive 2+2=1 gestalt through which Presence and Purpose become One. To claim this Voice inheritance, restore the Axis of Presence by transmuting all major shadow habits that block the natural flow of the CREATE cycle.

same effortless quality of creative thriving. As the shadows clear, your natural calling or function will emerge to give your life a strong sense of stability and structure through the Emperor's gifts of Purpose. But this masculine ordering influence will not feel overbearing, because a stream of playful exuberance from the Poet will bring a sense of joyful spontaneity to each passing moment.

Through increasingly effortless cycles of purposeful action and release, the Emperor and Poet will gradually transform your life into a thriving forest of passion and prosperity through the peaceful Innocence of your mindful presence. As you surrender to the flow of life through you, your highest aspirations will unfold without effort as you simply listen and take action, one step at a time.

The splendor that blossoms as our Poet speaks through us, is freedom. This is the ethereal freedom many writers speak of when they use the word love. Not that sappy, desperate love we hear about in pop songs, but an innocent and all-encompassing love that never changes. *Seeing this love in others is the Poet's gift.* Our desire to become one with our beloved is the Poet speaking through us, shining through shadows to quench our yearning for completion. We all share this yearning. But few ever satisfy it, because when true love approaches we pull back fearing the loss of our individuality. Until we reach a tipping point of inner game mastery, we lack the courage and faith to surrender without preconditions.

Psychologist Abraham Maslow called those moments when we experience the Poet's bliss "peak experiences."[2] Others have called them mystical experiences, altered states, flow, revelations or any number of other labels. Whatever name you use, know that such states are the Poet's calling card. When gripped by such states, we are experiencing *a mere fraction* of the love and joy that is our inheritance. Once the CREATE cycle is restored, our Poet blesses us with this awesome energy as a constant backdrop to our everyday life. The only barrier is belief — this is particularly true when it comes to belief in the sickly shadow poet charlatans previewed below.

Shadow Poets

Doubters: Dragons of Despair

Our Voice cannot be created or destroyed. No matter how hard we may try to deny our heart's yearnings, they never go away. Instead they just get buried under layer upon layer of old shadow patterns until they no longer seem to exist. At the core of this inner fiction lies the deeply mournful emotional detritus of the Doubters. This diabolically persuasive duo is *hands down* the most powerful team on the Thou Shalt roster. The other shadow dragons are comparatively easy to spot and take on directly. But the Doubters occur for us as pitiful orphans and starry-eyed romantics who pine for our protection. Over time the repressed grief that accrues when we fail to deal effectively with these lost inner children places an invisible manhole cover over our passion for living.

Psychologist Carl Jung concluded that nothing exerts more influence on the psychology of the child than the "unlived life of the parent."[3] The "unlived life" of the parent is that part of their own innocence that they have failed to remember. As children, we become shaped by this legacy in profound ways. As parents, we pass this same pattern along to our children as the buried Doubter patterns we harbor. So it happens that the Doubters seduce us, generation after generation, into lives of quiet desperation that could easily be lives of joyful exuberance, if we only had the gumption to say, "Who is that?" and choose again.

Everyone wants to go to heaven, but no one wants to die. When we doubt our own core worthiness, we die to the heaven of joyful Poet alignment. The yearning for heaven in the future is the yearning to be fully alive NOW, projected outward onto another time and place through the Doubters wistful lens. The team that keeps us forever searching includes two powerful characters, each with four specific sub-types that you'll learn about in great detail in Act III. Scene 15. Dissolve the Doubters.

Dreamers – *These wistful "somewhere over the rainbow" Doubters control us by keeping us searching for love in some imagined future that never seems to arrive. Whenever we smell the fragrance of transcendent possibility, these shadow energies tell us that this (job / person / idea) is "the one". The initial rush is usually quite intoxicating, but once the rush dies down, we are left holding an empty bag.*

Downers – *These "Why me?" Doubters are an endless pit of grief playing on repeat in the backdrop of our primal unconscious. Unlike healthy sadness and grief which can pass through us to cleanse our system, the melodrama these shadow dragons stir up never ends. Whenever our true feelings of sadness might arise, they jump in to save us with a more persistent and willful species of self-pitying, manufactured sadness and hysteria that plays on a permanent loop until we disarm them.*

The Doubters generate an unconscious sadness, moodiness and distraction that keep us from knowing and being the love at our core. When we reclaim our power from the shadow poets we restore the entire kingdom. They are the anchors to the whole shadow dragon charade. Because the Doubters are so powerful, I always encourage people to tread with particular care, kindness and patience when treading on shadow poet territory. I also strongly advise you to make sure that all of the other archetypes are thoroughly clean and aligned before treading too deeply into Doubter waters. When we do our

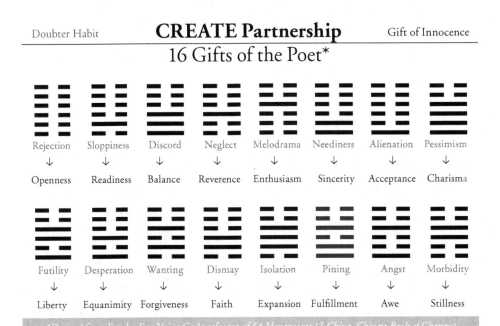

Doubter Habit **CREATE Partnership** Gift of Innocence

16 Gifts of the Poet*

Rejection	Sloppiness	Discord	Neglect	Melodrama	Neediness	Alienation	Pessimism
↓	↓	↓	↓	↓	↓	↓	↓
Openness	Readiness	Balance	Reverence	Enthusiasm	Sincerity	Acceptance	Charisma

Futility	Desperation	Wanting	Dismay	Isolation	Pining	Angst	Morbidity
↓	↓	↓	↓	↓	↓	↓	↓
Liberty	Equanimity	Forgiveness	Faith	Expansion	Fulfillment	Awe	Stillness

*Derived from line-by-line Voice Code reframe of 64 Hexagrams (I-Ching, Chinese Book of Changes)

inner-game mastery work in the natural sequence, from Emperor to Alchemist to Warrior to Poet, we create a natural safety net of vision and vitality that helps us distinguish and dissolve Doubter voices without needless melodramas. In Act III. Become a Child, you'll invoke the Poet to transmute the Doubters and reclaim the 16 gifts of Partnership your Voice offers through this mentor. The Week 4 exercises will help you pave the way for this epic awakening to unfold.

Week 4. Behold the Poet (checklist)

Step 1. Capture: Take note of key insights and areas of resistance now emerging having read through this material.

Step 2. Consider: Review the 16 Voice gifts and the 16 Doubter habits in the table above. Give self-assessment rating between 0 and 10 on each gift where 0 = Doubter Habit and 10 = Poet Gift. Total responses for baseline Poet Quotient (PQ) between 0 and 160.

Step 3. Clarify: Review and read your milestone mission goal statement aloud. Visualize success for 3 minutes.

Step 4. Connect: Perform the Summon the Poet process (below) to connect directly with your Voice via the Poet.

Step 5. Consult: Use same process to get direct Poet feedback to clarify next steps and infuse your vision with the Poet's essence.

Step 6. CREATE: Repeat this process every morning for 6 days. On the 7th day, rest, relax and release the cycle. Then move forward with the Poet's Innocence.

Choose Innocence *Summon the Poet*

The Poet is the state of innocent love that is our deepest essence. When this archetype surfaces we feel intimately connected to life, without the sense of lack that so often plagues us. These experiences transcend our ordinary language because they collapse our sense of separation completely. We have no words for this! Yet, as hard as these experiences are to convey, they usually feel more real, true and vivid than our everyday perception. In this section, you will practice aligning with the Poet and anchoring these energies to help you begin accessing the Poet's gifts anytime.

Remember the Poet: Consider a few moments when you felt connected to something larger than yourself, some transcendent beauty that stirred your core. Maybe you were playing with a small child and felt a deep sense of peace or got caught in a fit of silly laughter. Or perhaps your breath was taken away while gripped with aesthetic appreciation of a sublime work of art, the grandeur of a stunning natural setting or a moving piece of music. Or maybe it was something less obvious: a seemingly random connection with a stranger or even a crisis that pulled you into sudden awareness of the preciousness of life. Please take a moment to come up with a memory or two where you accessed such a state. If this is challenging, just relax into the moment and embrace a state of profound appreciation for the inquiry itself as you gently attune to this Poet frequency.

Experience the Poet: Consider one of the moments you just recalled. Allow yourself to open to the same state of being you were in at that time. Release any need to control your experience and just trust yourself with the natural flow of happiness and joyful presence this memory evokes. If any shadow resistance arises, accept and allow it exactly as it is. Then gently shift focus to tune the resistance out, without adding more resistance. To let your guard down a bit, you may find it helpful to suspend your ordinary ego identity and just imagine that you are an innocent child, safe and protected, unburdened by worldly concerns.

Fully immerse yourself within this joyful memory state for the sheer fun of doing it. Follow the thread of your inner experience to its root origin within. Don't worry about getting it right. Just enjoy the ride. Do your best to feel into the core of the Poet's essence through this specific memory. Hold the chord of heart resonance this memory state stirs, and let it expand. When you've tuned into the feeling strongly, let the facts of the situation (setting, people involved, etc.) fade away. Turn your attention inward to focus purely on your inner state. If resistance arises, BREATHE it away and expand to encompass your entire inner kingdom just as it is, without conditions. Be the Poet. Rest in this state for one full minute before moving forward.

Invoke the Poet: as you hold the state you've just accessed, place your hand on your heart and speak the following invocation to summon the Poet's assistance:

"With deep reverence for the creative source that sustains me, I now invoke the transcendent love of the Poet to help me *see the light of timeless truth, beauty and innocence in all things* as I venture to reclaim my gifts from old shadow delusions.

"I acknowledge that the Poet offers a higher order of power than I have yet learned to contain, given the unconscious shadow programming that has dimmed and distorted the Poet's light within my perception. With this invocation, I confess my desire to remember the Poet and see the light of Truth unfiltered. I yearn to find my Voice by helping others find theirs and unleash upward spirals of success and fulfillment in the service of life.

"In a spirit of gratitude for the countless gifts that the Poet has already bestowed, I hereby vow to gracefully receive and assimilate whatever guidance this sacred mentor would offer in support of my mission."

Hold the state of open-hearted innocence you've accessed through this invocation for at least two minutes. Gently observe your inner world. Rest peacefully in the Poet's joyful presence.

Before moving forward, offer thanks to your Voice. Allow gratitude for the countless gifts the Poet brings to you and the world.

Consider how much the Poet's happiness and gratitude has brought to your life already. Without it your life would be a colorless void, completely lacking in love, light and laughter.

Anchor the Poet: Rest in this state while focusing on the number 432 in the center of the Voice Code matrix below. Whenever the Doubters (or any) shadow energies arise, the number 432 can serve as an efficient mental trigger to help you quickly re-anchor into this expanded state of being. Focus on the white 432 in the center as you take 9 full breaths. Notice numbers in the surrounding quadrants with your peripheral vision, as you keep your eyes gently focused on the meeting point in the center. Hold the state of receptivity and openness you've accessed as you do this.

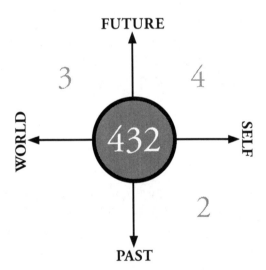

Consult the Poet: We'll now tap your creative unconscious to consult the Poet directly. Place your hand on your heart as you offer the words below, infusing them with the same quality of being you've now anchored.

"With profound respect for the timeless creative source that connects us, I now request direct assistance from the sacred Poet, that today I may dissolve the Doubters, and see the light to fulfill my mission. As I am just now learning how to remain aligned with my creative unconscious in everyday life, I still fall prey to the Doubter's distortions without even knowing it. I appreciate your support that I might dissolve the Doubters and usher in a new era of exuberance in your honor. I have four questions:

After each question be silent. Listen quietly and write.

1. Collaboration Clarity: Are there any new questions, images, or advice that You would offer to help me strengthen our connection?

2. Calling Clarity: What words, images or other information can You offer to help me better understand the unique gifts I offer?

3. Milestone Mission: What input might you offer to help me reclaim my power in the pursuit of my mission?

4. Action Items: Is there one simple thing I can do before the end of the day to generate traction to move my mission forward?

"Thank you. I appreciate your guidance and support. I will give you what you need moving forward."

Release the Poet: Take a few final breaths, imagine exhaling any excess energy into the earth to ground yourself. Relax into a moment of quiet appreciation that you have been given a direct path to access and own these gifts again. Befriending this archetype is the key to happiness, love, meaning and fulfillment — the aspirational endpoints that most of us spend our entire lives striving in vain to achieve through external accomplishment. The Poet holds the keys, and now you hold the keys to the Poet!

Visit TheVoiceCode.com to get free digital resources, including free training videos and digital copies of key tools offered in this book. You will also find the Voice Code glossary at the end of this book helpful for clarifying and expanding upon any new words, ideas and symbols used.

Scene 6 | *Become a Lion*

Section Overview
Description of Tools
Tool #1: CARE Ritual
Tool #2: CREATE Script

Congratulations! You have befriended the four inner mentors who will turn you into a mighty lion. This section contains the primary tools that you will use to slay Thou Shalt in Act II. These tools are simple and multi-functional, designed to help you master the habit of choosing your Voice as you accelerate the accomplishment of any goal from the inside out. Using these tools may feel a bit awkward at first, but will become quite natural after a few reps.

By using these tools on a consistent basis, you will be training your conscious mind to think in alignment with your Voice. With practice you will permanently remove the conventional delusion that you are the effect of the world, and begin to see yourself as the root cause of the world you perceive. Anything your mind can conceive, you will achieve — if you make it your mission to master your connection to Voice.

Use these tools separately or together as one coherent process. Separately, each should take from twenty minutes to an hour, depending upon your level of experience and the depth of shadow resistance you process. However long, know that it will be time well spent. Each moment spent transmuting problems at their source saves you many future moments of stress and strain. As mastery improves, I predict that you will be able to shave up to a year or more off your natural Phase II learning curve in just one focused session.

Tool Descriptions

Tool #1. CARE Ritual

Calm • Authorize • Request • Execute

The CARE ritual offers a simple, powerful new process to help you make following your Voice a new life habit. The acronym CARE stands for a 4-step sequence through which you: Calm your mind, Authorize your Voice, Request guidance from the four mentors, and Execute their advice to move things forward. Perform this process in the mornings as a daily alignment ritual or anytime you feel a desire to improve inner alignment.

Once you master this tool, you will consult with your inner Voice in your everyday life as a matter of habit. As this happens, you will instinctively frame the principles of Authority, Resonance and Trust from a Phase II perspective. This will place you in a state of creative dominance, in which you ultimately become immune to shadow identification. When these framing habits become a way of life, we escape ordinary linear clock time to experience the vertical (timeless) dimension of consciousness in which we maintain radical inner alignment regardless of external challenges.

Tool #2. CREATE Script

Create • Reframe • Explore • Assimilate • Transmute • Embody

This tool helps you lay a sturdy foundation of experiential knowing that helps you embody the concepts in this book. If the CARE process helps you *align* with the timeless truth, the CREATE script helps you *collapse time* by removing inner barriers to external achievement. This simple, powerful and highly versatile Voice Code tool helps you apply all six CREATE skills in sequence. This process will help you produce three positive outcomes every time you use it:

• **Goal Velocity:** Collapse time required for goal achievement by removing the unconscious shadow energies that would otherwise show up out there in the world as problems.

- **Vision Clarity:** Expand the scope of our vision to unleash powerful new insights that solve problems and shape the future.
- **Mindset Mastery:** Establish powerful new thinking habits that persist over time, producing results that grow and scale using holographic logic across every area of your life.

Use this tool to make powerful breakthroughs in the pursuit of literally any outcome (inner or outer) that can be written as a goal. With each pass through this script you discover and permanently transmute old unconscious shadow energies to expand your presence and increase your power.

Tool Alignment

The CARE Ritual

Step 1: Calm your mind
Step 2: Authorize Voice
Step 3: Request guidance
Step 4: Execute the advice

Step 1: Calm your mind

Sequence 1. Inner Focus

To begin, please read this paragraph to understand the process before closing your eyes to perform it. When you are ready, close your eyes and inhale slowly and deeply as you picture a blue 4. When you exhale, release your grip on any stress, tension or resistance you may feel as this blue 4 turns red and reverses to an upside-down 4, symbolizing the shadow. Repeat this simple breathing cycle 4 times. Once you've completed this first round, do the same with the number 3 (3 breaths — blue 3 on inhale, red upside down 3 on exhale). Then the number 2 (2 breaths — blue 2 on inhale, red upside-down 2 on exhale). On your final exhalation, let the red upside-down shadow version of the number 2 dissolve into the upright number 1 in blue. Sit calmly with your eyes closed for 9 additional breaths as you hold the image of the blue 1 in your mind's eye. On the final breath, open your eyes and relax into the stillness of the present before moving forward.

Sequence 2. Outer Focus

To anchor this state with eyes open focus on the white 432 in the matrix below. Hold the sense of openness for one full minute, noting unity of inner and outer. As you move forward, do your best to maintain the state you've established. Should resistance arise at any point, imagine a blue 432 and BREATHE and expand to encompass it without adding more resistance.

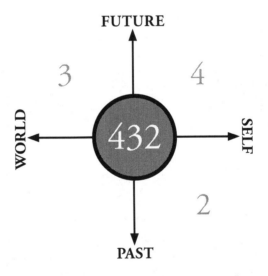

Step 2: Authorize Voice

Before invoking your Voice, select 3 specific items that you can feel grateful for. If possible, let these be simple items that you normally might take for granted. When you are ready, adopt a calm and reverential attitude as you make the following invocation, hand on heart, in front of a mirror:

"With this invocation, I hope to establish a direct experience of connection with my Voice, that awesome creative intelligence that speaks from the core of my being. This powerful inner directive defies explanation using ordinary language as it seems both larger than life and also somehow the 'real me' that I am when I act naturally. For ease of communication I will now address my Voice as 'You' in respectful awareness that we are of one unbroken mind.

"Let me first express my profound gratitude for the support You have given throughout my life. Come what may, You have never doubted me. You have remained strong and patient at all times. You have offered me the world, but You have never tried to interfere with my freedom to choose.

"Even when my choices have brought me pain and confusion, You have not once wavered in your support. Nor have You placated me by granting me 'successes' that would ultimately have delayed my long-term growth, happiness and freedom. In other words, You have shown yourself to be a humble servant leader of the highest order, and I wish to acknowledge this. Thank You.

"I also wish to openly declare my intention to improve our relationship. My vision is that we might now collaborate to transmute the shadow patterns that have caused me to perceive us as separate. As our alignment grows, I foresee a bright and fearless future in which I consistently demonstrate the power of our shared mind to drive accelerating cycles of success and fulfillment.

"By healing my own split mind, I will become a conduit for the larger creative source that connects everyone. Backed by Your wisdom, bonded to all of life through my unbroken awareness of our essential unity, I will know no bounds. I will change the world, by first changing my mind *about* the world. I will develop that rare ability to connect with others so that they find their own Voice within my words and deeds. When this happens, change will unfold naturally and I will be lifted to greatness with minimum struggle, along the path of least resistance.

"As I now narrow my focus to access specific archetypes, I will honor our Oneness by remembering that these four mentors are ultimately just four different masks of You, representing four integrated dimensions of the same underlying essence at the core of my being. You are that essence, whole and complete without any division or separation. These archetypes are separate portals back to You, as I master the inner game that allows me to contain Your mighty creative powers as One.

"With each mentor I summon, please infuse my brain, body and being with the unique quality, character and wisdom that each offers. With Your assistance, I will quickly come to experience our unbroken unity in everything I do.

"Thank You for all that You've done thus far, and for all that we will become together as our sacred partnership dissolves all fear in its wake. In the light of shared purpose, we will heal the gap and restore the inner altar through which greatness grows and extends itself outward into the world of perception."

Step 3: Request guidance

A. Tune into Emperor. Get Feedback.

The Emperor thinks through calm commanding presence, self-assurance, and composure. To invoke the Emperor archetype, recall a memory of a time when you made a calm powerful decision amid uncertainty. Summon the feeling of being the calm in the center of the storm, completely self-assured by a peaceful power within that always knows the way. When you have tapped into this energy state, read the following invocation in a tone that resonates appropriately:

"With profound respect for the creative mind through which we are One, I request assistance from the sacred Emperor that I may own my inner experience today with authority, poise and presence. As I am just now learning how to remain aligned with my creative unconscious in everyday life, I still fall prey to shadow emperor (Divider) distortions without even knowing it. I recognize that by letting the shadow rule my thoughts, I make it impossible for You to work through me effectively. I'd like to get your input on some questions to improve our connection:

1. What would You have me focus on today?

2. Are there any insights You might offer to help me better understand the shadow forces now blocking clear access to your guidance?

3. [Insert any additional question(s) here]

"Thank You. I will give You what You need going forward."

B. Tune into Alchemist. Get Feedback.

The Alchemist speaks to us through inspired insights, curiosity and creative vision. To invoke the Alchemist energy, recall a memory of an inspired frame shift, a time when a great idea just landed in your lap, or where you had been struggling to solve a problem and then released to find that the solution came unbidden. Imagine that your mind is unlimited in size, scope and clarity, able to receive messages instantly and create vivid compelling images to represent whatever your heart longs to create.

"With profound gratitude and respect for the timeless creative source that connects us, I now request assistance from the sacred Alchemist that I may access the mental clarity to discern truth from delusion today as I seek to solve problems, make decisions and communicate my ideas to others. As I am just now learning how to remain aligned with my true Voice, I still fall prey to shadow alchemist (Forgetter) distortions without even knowing it. I'd appreciate your wisdom and guidance on a few questions that will help me better understand how I can strengthen our connection going forward:

1. What would You have me focus on today?

2. Are there any insights You might offer to help me better understand the shadow forces now blocking clear access to your guidance?

3. [Insert any additional question(s) here]

"Thank You. I will give You what You need going forward."

C. Tune into Warrior. Get Feedback.

The Warrior thinks through our powerful resolve to face fear in the service of something larger. To invoke the Warrior archetype, take a moment to consider a time you took bold and selfless action in the service of a higher principle. Or, if helpful, imagine that something or someone you care about deeply was being threatened and decisive action was needed to prevent harm. Summon that feeling of fearless power and courage rooted in your gut.

"With respect for the timeless creative source that connects us, I now request assistance from the sacred Warrior that today I may face my fears with courage, honor and resolve in the service of our shared purpose. As I am just now learning how to remain aligned with my creative unconscious in everyday life, I still fall prey to shadow warrior (Enforcer) distortions without even knowing it. I'd appreciate your wisdom and guidance on a few questions that will help me strengthen our connection:

1. What would You have me focus on today?

2. Are there any insights You might offer to help me better understand the shadow forces now blocking clear access to Your guidance?

3. [Insert any additional question(s) here]

"Thank You. I will give You what You need going forward."

D. Tune into Poet. Get Feedback.

The Poet thinks through transcendent love and praise for the beauty of life. To invoke the Poet now, take a moment to consider a time you felt connected to something larger, some transcendent beauty that stirred your core and connected you with life. Perhaps it was beautiful sunset that took your breath away, or an exquisite piece of music or art. Or maybe it was something less obvious — an everyday connection with a stranger or even an unexpected crisis that pulled you into sudden awareness of the preciousness of all life.

"With profound gratitude and respect for the timeless creative source that connects us, I now request assistance from the sacred Poet to help me see into the light of truth and Innocence as I move through my day. As I am just now learning how to remain aligned with my creative unconscious in everyday life, I still fall prey to shadow poet (Doubter) distortions without even knowing it. I'd like to get your input on some questions to improve our connection:

1. What would You have me focus on today?

2. Are there any insights You might offer to help me better understand the shadow forces now blocking clear access to your guidance?

3. [Insert any additional question(s) here]

"Thank You. I will give You what you need going forward."

Step 4: Execute the advice

For the final step, please think of one question that you'd most like answered and then review your dialogue above to see what new insights emerge. When finished, think of one thing you can do today to embody this insight with inspired action. Then do the closing invocation below to complete this session.

Closing Invocation (Recommended)

For the closing invocation, hold the state of reverence with this "bigger you" that you have summoned. Then read the following declaration, hand on heart, in front of a mirror:

"With this closing invocation, I want to express deep appreciation for the partnership we are creating. That You could be so incredibly powerful and also somehow be the 'real me' in disguise both amazes and inspires me. I won't pretend to understand it intellectually, but in the core of my being I know that this is true. I am honored to be in this conscious collaboration with You now after so many years of feeling somehow limited or disconnected.

"Now I know: I had become frame locked into forgetting my true identity. I had allowed myself to become limited by choosing to believe what the world told me to be true instead of choosing in alignment with inner truth. I thank You again for the deep trust and honor you have shown as I worked through the lessons required to achieve this level of clarity. Come what may, You have never doubted that I would awaken. You have remained strong and patient at all times. You have offered me the world, but You have never tried to interfere with my freedom to choose.

"Thank You. Thanks for Your patience, support and guidance as I take steps to master this new Phase II mindset to access Your powers in my everyday life. By healing my own split mind, I will become a conduit for the creative source that connects us all.

"Through this partnership, I will change the world by changing my mind about the world. By removing the unconscious fear, I will develop the ability to awaken others to their true Voice that we may remember our unbroken unity. Bonded by Voice, in a spirit of shared vision, the world will change naturally as we stand fully for truth in the fierce urgency of now.

"We are One, after all. One Mind. One Love. One Purpose. When we follow the right inner guide, we speak with One Voice."

Processing Tool
The CREATE Script

Ground 0: Craft goal statement

Step 1: Commit to your goal
Step 2: Reframe from success
Step 3: Explore the shadows
Step 4: Assimilate resistance
Step 5: Transmute pattern
Step 6: Embody the gift

Ground 0: Craft goal statement

To begin, please come up with a goal for the CREATE script goal acceleration process. For your first few trips through the CREATE cycle, you may find it easier to focus on an objective that feels slightly beyond your reach, but still within the scope of believability, given past experience. As you generate personal evidence that this process works, your goals will naturally grow in scale, scope and range of applicability as your Voice alignment and CREATE skill mastery increases.

You'll want to turn your mission into a clear goal statement. For each trip through this tool, create a statement capturing the desired outcome (measurable if possible) and the specific date of goal achievement. The generic goal template below works well:

"I will remove all limiting shadow habits associated with [TARGET GOAL DOMAIN] as I accomplish [TARGET OUTCOME], or something even better by [DATE OF COMPLETION]."

Note: this goal statement reflects the inside-out mindset. By making your inner outcomes a priority, you break frame-locked thinking and turn the tables on the shadow. As you log shadow patterns and use these tools to process them, you will come to enjoy the process intrinsically.

If you are using this to process shadow captures or to shift thinking for short-term purposes, you can use the phrase "by the end of this session" for the date, as outlined below. Some other templates are also provided that might be helpful depending upon the nature of your goal.

"I will shift thinking to establish Voice alignment and produce breakthrough around [PROBLEM ISSUE] by the end of this session."

"I will reclaim power from [SHADOW PATTERN] by the end of this session."

"I will shift thinking to establish Voice alignment and produce breakthrough around [PROBLEM ISSUE] by the end of this session."

"I will reclaim the gift of [1 OF 64 VOICE GIFTS] from the old [NAME DRAGON TEAM] shadow habit of [1 of 64 shadow habits] to accelerate progress towards [NAME DESIRED OUTCOME] by the end of this session."

Step 1: Commit to your goal

Holding the powerful frame you've just accessed, make the following commitment in the service of your mission. State it out loud, hand on heart, looking into a mirror (if possible).

"I hereby commit to achieving [TARGET RESULT] by [GOAL DATE]. I'm done playing small. Today is a good day to die to any limiting shadow patterns that would prevent me from owning my mind in the service of my chosen purpose. My word is law in the kingdom of my mind, and my mind is made up. With this declaration, I am choosing my Authority in the name of all things sacred, accepting any and all assistance that comes my way."

Hold the energy of this declaration as you calmly observe your state. Relax into the sense of calm conviction that your Voice offers through the Emperor as we move forward.

Step 2: Reframe from success

Now in your imagination go to the future date in which you have achieved your goal and look back to today — the moment when you made the commitment that shifted your future trajectory to bring this positive outcome into reality. Suspend disbelief and let this success vision feel real to you right now. Feel the sense of pride and accomplishment of knowing that you kept your promise and achieved or surpassed the goal you originally set, and with far less struggle or effort than you envisioned.

Bask in the feeling of your wish fulfilled. Experience the humbling sense of inner power and completion that comes from recognizing that you've *only just begun* to tap your potential. Your Voice is the real deal. It offers you unlimited creative power in every moment, and is always there for the choosing! If any doubt or resistance arises, don't resist. Let it be. Just take a breath and expand to encompass it as you remain focused on the feelings of inspiration and excitement you've tapped by owning your inner Authority.

Take a good look around in this future. Notice what you notice. What do you like most about this new normal? What does it feel like to be you? Give thanks to your Voice. Take a moment to fathom what other breakthroughs might be possible going forward. Hold this vision and the feeling state you've accessed for 3 full minutes before moving forward to Step 3.

Step 3: Explore the shadows

From this future, looking back at the path that brought you here, take a moment to reflect and tell the story. After you committed, what did you do differently from that day forward to make this happen? Was it a set of actions? Was it that you finally confronted some old fear that you hadn't been willing to look at before? Did you release a belief that helped you heal a relationship and inspire a sense of shared purpose? Did you embody wisdom that you understood with your intellect but hadn't been putting into practice? Or was it something very simple? Maybe you withdrew commitment to some project or relationship that was no longer serving you, and that choice ultimately ended up benefiting everyone?

With the wisdom of hindsight, stand in the future and surmise your success secrets. First, what did you let go of? Name 3 old shadow habits you chose to release to clear the path for this breakthrough:

- I released limiting habit (belief, behavior, etc.) X.
- I released the limiting habit Y.
- I released limiting habit Z.

Now, what actions did you take? Name three new Voice-aligned rituals or habits of thinking that grew naturally to fill the gap once you transmuted those old shadow patterns to reclaim lost power.

- Freed from the past, I was inspired to do A.
- Freed from the past, I was inspired to do B.
- Freed from the past, I was inspired to do C.

Once you've listed these, bring attention back into the now. Step back into your current reality. Consider the facts of the situation as they currently stand. Consider your feelings at the prospect of doing the work required to close the gap between your vision and present reality. Feel that gap fully, even if it's not 100% comfortable. Your goal is to find any hidden fear and resistance, so don't be shy. Stand fully in the present and curiously observe what shows up in a spirit of unconditional self-acceptance and total non-judgment.

Step into this gap once again. Notice any inner resistance to doing this work. Just invite it up and observe it.

Where is this resistance located in your mind and body? What does it look or feel like?

Remember: this is just shadow energy from the past. It has no power whatsoever unless you believe in it, or fail to look at it. So just calmly and objectively examine it without judgment or resistance. Always remember: You are the author of all shadows. They have no power whatsoever. You created these patterns and soon you will choose again to take your gift back, erase the original cause and change your life from the inside out.

In a moment, you will harness your Warrior's courage to reclaim your power from the shadows you've uncovered. But first, seriously consider the possibility that there's nothing to fix or change. Consider that you are already perfect, you already have what you want, but you've just been frame locked by a distorted sense of reality caused by unconscious belief habits.

What if what you have now is exactly what you have wanted and were committed to until today? Might this be true?

If so, then you are now and always have been 100% self-authored, and the future is yours for the choosing. Also consider that the future will never make you better, because the future happens now. This means that you don't need to wait. What you need to do is actively confront and release your barriers to seeing reality clearly *right now.* When you do, you will know that the future actually is present as a possibility that is constantly unfolding according to your choices.

So relax and know that there's nothing to be afraid of in looking at anything like this. All you are doing is reclaiming your wholeness— that naturally brilliant unbroken mind through which your Voice speaks clearly. The only possible loss from doing this work is loss of an illusion that was limiting you.

Step 4: Assimilate resistance

Now, invite the doubt, fear and other repressed emotions you've observed up into your conscious awareness. Don't resist, judge, or intellectualize — just observe them as they are without adding meaning. Experience them as energy with a certain quality. Observe your body: Where do they live? Are there dark spots in your mind filled with pockets of untapped energy you can sense into using your imagination? Let your fuzzy heart logic guide you, and don't worry about being right. Just find the places where the potential is hiding.

Allow yourself to feel into them fully. Keep your mind open and honor your gut.

What is this thing you have been examining? What is its essential nature?

Turn this shadow pattern into a character. Imagine this character sitting beside you.

What does he or she look like? What does he or she want? How does he or she feel right now? How do you feel?

Let the room between you stay open, quiet and present for a moment. Feel the relationship in that space for what it is, bad or good. Let your heart lead this process. Try to keep your mind open, quiet and receptive.

Now you are ready.

It's now time to stand for your innate power to turn these shadow energies into a blessing, by removing all fear and confusion they have ever brought you, including any habits you may have developed in the past that may have grown from the avoidance patterns this split-minded thinking style has caused you.

How does the Warrior slay the enemy? With fearless resolve that shines away all shadows. Force or resistance never works. You must attune to the resistance and become one with it. Make up your mind to assimilate by tuning in until the charge is fully neutralized and you've authenticated your gifts trapped inside. This removes fear and releases your untapped potential while restoring integrity to your inner kingdom. Now is your time to end the cycle of suffering and start over. You already committed to this, hand on heart. Now execute your mission and be done with it.

Dive into the shadow energy and the fog of pain surrounding it. Do this until you see the light of your Voice buried beneath. Don't think about it, just stand in the fog without worry over personal discomfort until you feel an inner shift, an opening of some sort, as if you are being pulled through to another layer of yourself. This takes as long as it takes. It's not a matter of time; it's a matter of your willingness to surrender completely. So give yourself fully. Revel in the process knowing that you cannot fail. When the shift occurs, please continue.

With the shadow pattern now largely diffused, follow the thread of inner truth to the core of this pattern until you see the gift that was buried within. What is it that was waiting for you? Stay focused and observe until the inner essence shines through. When you are ready, name it below.

"The gift that was buried beneath my shadow resistance was…"

Step 5: Transmute patterns

Let your body relax fully. Take a few deep breaths.

Now you will use active love to transmute old undigested pain using the transcendent purity of the Poet, that Innocent inner artist who sees the beauty in everything.

What gift did you uncover? Note that the words you used to describe this gift were just tags for something beyond description. Whatever essence you felt when the gift finally emerged, please access it now… Imagine the feeling tone within this gift expanding and radiating outward from the center of your chest as a shimmering light that pulses through you in waves of captivating music, calling you from hidden depths of your being. For at least one full minute, let this gift's intoxicating potential envelop you, placing you into a state of innocent unguarded wonder.

When you are ready, let this light contract down into a dense glowing jewel about the size of an egg, hovering in front of you just out of arm's reach. Now in your minds eye, imagine the shadow character you assimilated reappearing around this egg sized jewel, trapping it within itself so that it glows almost imperceptibly from the center of the shadow character's chest. The shadow has lost the momentum of it's energetic grip over your mind, but to claim your gift you must take it's soul—that part of you which became trapped within it's lair.

Allow your body to relax. Take a few deep breaths.
Sink into the moment and let your thoughts soften.

Observe the shadow character with your gift trapped inside.
Imagine a cord that connects your heart to that glowing jewel that once gave it power. As you do, invite the Poet to summon infinite love on your behalf. Let it envelop you from all four corners of the kingdom, condensing itself into your heart.

When you are ready, send this energy along the chord in fierce beam of light… Imagine this light as a tractor beam of otherworldly love at the same frequency as the gift. Watch in slow motion as this energy pierces the shadow character's darkened shell, connecting your heart with the glowing jewel inside. As this beam connects with the gift the dim glow grows brighter and brighter. The shadow dissolves slowly into oblivion against the illuminating backdrop of this awesome creative power.

As the shadow dissolves you will feel this gift pulling itself to you, like the yearning of a long lost friend returning home. Notice the pull, *but don't stop sending energy along the chord until the shadow's form has been completely erased.* Take as long as you need to erase it completely. When you are finished. Stop.

Let the chord connecting you to your gift remain still for a moment. Feel the pull between you once more — the yearning for completion. Be still…. Hold the chord. Don't move. Accept the moment as it is, trusting in your own sufficiency. By sending love like this and then releasing you signal that you trust in the infinite supply. Energetically, this generates a "vacuum" that the world fills over and over again in waves of inspired co-creation.

Feel the pull once more… and then drop the chord.
As you do, open your heart and allow the gift to flow across the

tiny gap and enter your heart again. Let it expand to energize every corner of your mind and cell of your body. Feel the returning creative power; let it assimilate into you on every level, lifting you to a state of inspired Voice alignment that brings you into direct contact with the creative mind that governs all of life.

Take at least 3 minutes to let this power return fully as you open further to the beauty of the new future you've chosen. Receive it fully, with almost childlike gratitude and joy. You have released the past, reclaimed the present and opened a new window into the future of your dreams. Receive it and feel worthy. You always were worthy. But today you have chosen to accept this, to remember. Give thanks for the gift that your life truly is.

Take a moment to consider just how great you will get at this process with more practice. These are truly the only skills you really need master to create the life of your dreams from the inside out. As you master this process, you completely dismantle the conventional delusion that you are the effect of the world. You will come to know beyond the shadow of any doubt, that you are the root cause of everything that you experience.

Step 6: Embody the gift

Revisit the original goal statement. (I will achieve X by Y date) How does it feel right now? If any resistance lingers, let it melt into the gratitude you feel for the gift you've reclaimed. Remember your vision (Step 2. Reframe). Having now reclaimed your power, step fully into your future vision again. Feel the pull of this new future possibility calling you into action. Are you ready to close the loop on this CREATE cycle and bring this future into the present?

What is one small thing you can do right now or by the end of the day to celebrate this gift and make it real? It doesn't have to be difficult or take up a lot of time. It just needs to be inspired with the essence of the gift you have reclaimed. To complete this cycle, make the embodiment declaration below with your hand on your heart, inserting today's action promise in the space provided:

"**Today I will [ACTION PROMISE] to celebrate this gift and close the vision-reality gap. I know that even a small action taken in alignment with my Voice can usher in all manner of unforeseen events that pull my highest future into reality along the path of least resistance, in concert with life as a whole.**"

Gain Tracking

Before moving on, are there any successes or gains that you want to recognize from doing this work so far? If so, write them down and review the list each week as your spoils (inner and outer) increase. This will help you recognize your progress and accelerate your learning, motivation and mastery of the Phase II visionary mindset.

Visit TheVoiceCode.com to get free digital resources, including free training videos and digital copies of key tools offered in this book. You will also find the Voice Code glossary at the end of this book helpful for clarifying and expanding upon any new words, ideas and symbols used.

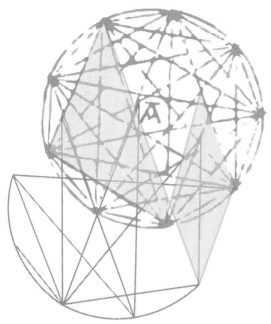

ACT II
Slay Thou Shalt

Scene 7 | *Desert of Authority*

Once upon a time there was a musk deer named Ed who had a powerful wake up call. You see, every time mating season comes around, the musk deer emit a scent that acts as a signal to let other musk deer know that nookie time has arrived. Season after season, on through the years, this scent has kept the cycle of life moving forward for this stinky beast. The moment arrives, musk fumes rise, and the good times roll.

One year when the mating season dawned, Ed caught a whiff of the most wonderful stink. Off he went in a flash! Over the stream, up over the hill, through the sandy deserts he ran. For two full days and nights, Ed galloped, feverishly in search of the source of this intoxicating aroma. "Where is she?" he kept asking during this marathon of doe chasing. "I can smell her now! I know she's nearby!" he'd keep grunting, doubling down yet again on his mission.

On his third day of searching, beside himself with exhaustion, Ed lost his footing. Next thing you know, he was toppling headlong off a rocky cliff and into the underbrush below. When he came to, he looked down to find his front legs broken. The legs would one day heal, but the mental scars would take longer. You see, when he finally woke from his fall he still smelled that scent! In that fateful moment, Ed realized that the scent he'd been chasing was his own.[1]

Choose Authority *Own Your Mind*

Frame lock makes us lose our minds looking outside ourselves for things that we innately possess. Projecting our power outward, we chase our own scent right over the cliff! If we're lucky, we land on the other side of the Voice mountain to begin our Phase II life. If we're unlucky, we double down on the past and lives that feel limiting no matter how much external success we achieve. Money, social status, good looks, beautiful cars, houses, gadgets and so forth can be wonderful things to have; but they can just as easily lead us down the road to misery as anything else. When we search for them under the shadow's guidance, we do so to fill an inner void that only our Voice can satisfy.

To Own Our Mind we must be vigilant to hear and follow the correct inner guidance. We must commit to our Voice with such definiteness of purpose that we know ourselves as the 100% creative authority of our lives. This is the Emperor's calling that all great dragon slayers must learn to embody. When Apple icon Steve Jobs told people to "Think Different," this is exactly what he meant. But Jobs' power didn't come from the slogan, it came from his willingness to *embody* its meaning until he ushered in a new era of capitalism.[2] Thinking different doesn't mean buying Apple products. It means owning our minds. We don't want to be like Steve Jobs — we want to be ourselves by owning our Authority as he did.

To be free we must commit freely and fully. Powerful choices summon the mighty forces of Voice Authority latent within all people to orchestrate the events that ensure the fulfillment of our purpose. To grow our inner garden into a forest of shared prosperity, we must embrace our freedom by choosing our Voice over and over again, experimenting and learning until we finally become One with the pearl of timeless truth at our core. Make no mistake: this path isn't for everyone. It's a labor of love for those with the audacity to stand for greatness. Success always comes eventually, but it doesn't come overnight. Here's the good news: the journey is the destination. By even *being willing* to commit ourselves fully to the *process* of *learning* to own our minds, we engage the world with a quality of intention that changes our life trajectory immediately.

Owning our minds means observing and accepting our inner experience with a state of calm authority and definiteness of purpose. When we follow the first calling, we become self authored. Following the Emperor's guidance, we are a wheel moving from its own center. We don't blame, judge or condemn. We are the sovereign masters of our kingdom, which extends outward in an ever-growing sphere of influence through the principle of Resonance. When things go wrong, we don't react. We calmly survey the facts, consult our inner Authority and respond in a way that moves things forward. We take responsibility for our lives by releasing our resistance to problems and taking action to solve them, leading our lives to increasing levels of harmony and coherence.

Authority *To Principle of Cause*
Paradox: To know all, believe nothing

If your Voice were a tree, Authority would be the roots. People who "own their minds" frame authority as internal. Authority grows naturally from our freedom to choose how we author our lives. People frame locked by shadow habits see power as something outside. Thinking this way, we split our minds at the hands of the Dividers, those sneaky shadow emperors. By reclaiming power from these shadow dragons of endless seeking, you will reframe the principle of Authority to own your mind and discover yourself as the 100% author of your life. The Emperor is your inner mentor to help you pull this off. Befriending the Emperor is the world's best-kept secret shortcut to finding your Voice and fulfilling the purpose for which you (and only you) were designed by nature's creative mind.

Authority *The Power of Purpose*

This principle forms the foundational root system that feeds our everyday thoughts, feelings and decisions. People frame locked by shadow beliefs, frame authority as external. Believing that the power to create lives outside their sphere of control, they attempt to create inner freedom and security through external accomplishment. This would be fine if it worked, but it never does. How could it? Our inner world creates our outer world. When we start from the premise that we are lacking, no amount of money or social approval in the world could ever make us feel whole. The levers of freedom are internal and they only reveal themselves when we break frame lock and remove ourselves from the treadmill of endless striving.

Creative visionaries think like nature — and exactly backwards from most people. Nature never asks permission to create what it must. Neither do great dragon slayers. They answer to a higher Authority — the authority of their inner knowing. Authority is always internal, but we don't experience ourselves as self-authored until we water the seeds of our inner freedom to choose freely and fully without compromise. This practice is what turns us from approval-seeking camels into lionhearted visionaries, backed by the full force of nature's orchestrating intelligence. It unlocks stale shadow frames and opens our conscious awareness to our creative unconscious where our true power lies.

In Phase I (Stages 1-6), we understand Authority as something outside ourselves. Investing belief in the voice of shadow emperors (Dividers) we enforce strict disciplines upon ourselves to control ourselves and achieve our goals. This mindset makes us live in fear of our own power, which we habitually project outward onto people in positions of power. Thinking this way we both envy and resent external authorities for their power, while we do our best to game the system to our advantage. If and when we finally achieve a level of power that satisfies our competitive drive, we lose our sense of purpose and get consumed by an inner void that leaves us wanting more. After a lifetime of climbing in order to achieve some imagined future happiness, we begin to feel that we've been had.

Once the pain of not changing outweighs the pain of changing, we begin to doubt the authoritarian Divider voices that drove us off the cliffs of compromise. When self-doubt reaches critical mass, we release our investment in the lifetime of unconscious beliefs that have kept us frame locked. Thus begins the *great unraveling* that opens us to our true Voice and eventually brings us to a higher plane of thriving. This transition is rarely greeted with open arms, of course. But once we begin to doubt the Dividers, the Emperor's call is growing strong and the writing is on the wall. Those who embrace the call, choose their Voice to enter Phase II. Those who don't, do their best to feel happy in a frame locked life.

When we commit to full mind ownership, we look inward to discover riches beyond our wildest dreams when shadows ruled. Dismissing the fearful warnings of the Warden and the Wimps, we follow the thread of our heart's calling as it speaks through the Emperor's calm presence. One step at a time, we reclaim our power from those old shadow patterns until we've owned ourselves as the sovereign Author of our experience. Starting with small gains, we build momentum that gradually inspires us to think bigger and bigger about what is truly possible. As Emperor alignment grows, we understand what it truly means to Own Our Mind. Powerfully connected to the creative mind that governs all of life, we know ourselves as capable of achieving whatever it is life calls us to do.

Note: *In the "Worldview Dynamics" section that follows we will explore how the principle of Authority influences the outer game via the Voice Code segmentation system. Because this book is primarily about the inner game, we did not have space to dive more deeply into the psychology of each stage of thinking. For more in depth insights, see the glossary entry for each worldview and/or read my 2008 book* **Igniting Inspiration: A Persuasion Manual for Visionaries.**

Worldview Dynamics

Achievers (Stage 6) vs. Explorers (Stage 7)

The shift from Phase I to Phase II occurs through a reframing of Authority from external to internal. In worldview terms, this inner reversal marks the passage from the Stage 6 Achiever to the egalitarian Stage 7 Explorer worldview. In pop culture, this transition has been represented by the stereotypical mid-life crisis movie, in which a ruthlessly ambitious character does a complete 180-degree reversal to become a more caring and compassionate human being. In many ways, this is the most challenging shift of the entire 12-stage journey. It is also the major shift that mass culture today is awkwardly trying to navigate as a new generation of creative visionaries leads capitalism to its next grand phase.

When someone with an Achiever worldview makes the choice to dismiss the Dividers' "Do Not Find" ethic, they embrace the inner work of Stage 7 Explorers. It can be a very humbling transition. As Explorers, we go from being the alpha-dog of Phase I to the new man on campus in Phase II. As we awkwardly learn how to hear and follow our inner Authority, we almost always become inflated by the dramatic influx of psychic energies and project our own Divider shadows back onto folks still working through lessons of Phase I. (See excesses of the 1960's hippie counterculture movement and the 2011 "99% movement" for two more prominent examples of this dynamic in action.)

Believe it or not, this is a healthy part of the natural process whereby Explorers and Achievers collaborate to bridge the mountain and move life forward. As Explorers process their own Divider shadow projections, their inner Authority frame shifts from external (power outside) to internal (power inside), and they begin to reclaim the gifts of the Emperor. By forgiving the Achievers, Explorers forgive their own unconscious guilt and become grounded in the practical world again as Pathfinders (Stage 8). With this epic inner shift, people become capable of creative problem solving and feats of

Choose Again

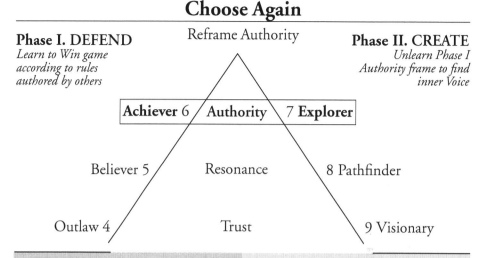

Phase I. DEFEND
*Learn to Win game
according to rules
authored by others*

Reframe Authority

Phase II. CREATE
*Unlearn Phase I
Authority frame to find
inner Voice*

Achiever 6 / Authority \ 7 **Explorer**

Believer 5   Resonance   8 Pathfinder

Outlaw 4   Trust   9 Visionary

Achiever Authority

In Stage 6, we derive our sense of Authority from our performance relative to others. This outside-in mindset can drive us to high levels of status and achievement, but the results we generate leave us perpetually unsatisfied. Over time we run out of steam and begin to question our motives. Our yearning for something more leads us to unravel much of what we've come to believe.

Explorer Authority

In Stage 7, we retract belief in Phase I Authorities as we redefine our priorities to embrace the "inside out" Phase II perspective. For people deeply steeped in the ambitious Achiever ethic, this reversal can be uncomfortable at first. But it is also a time of joyful inspiration as we learn to tap creative powers beyond our grasp when frame locked by Phase I Authority games.

innovation that defy conventional thinking. In today's world, people at Stage 8 (Pathfinder) have become Emperors of the global economy. They become this way not by luck or magic, but through a natural step-by-step process laid out by nature as part of the evolution of life.

To those still climbing uphill in Phase I, the shift from the hard-nosed Achiever (Stage 6) to the soft Explorer (Stage 7) seems like a regression back to naive idealism in a dog-eat-dog world. But once we transmute the Dividers, we don't see dogs eating each other so much. When we do, we are much less inclined to use this to justify compromising our conscience with zero-sum Phase I thinking. The open-hearted Seeker mindset is a tender start for the healing process through which everyone must pass to actualize their dreams. Until this shift, the shadow emperors (Dividers) control our lives and our freedom remains limited, no matter how much we achieve.

Explorers and Achievers play a pivotal role in the evolution of mankind, bridging the gap between Phase I and Phase II so that we can all continue learning together. The dynamic creative tension this worldview pair holds stabilizes both parties and serves the evolution of the whole planet. It gives Achievers a projection partner to help them safely process deeply repressed fears of being weak and unlovable. It gives Explorers a sparring partner to help them build their Voice muscles, by holding strong to their inner Authority frame in the face of social push-back.

Once an Explorer completes this process, they become capable of satisfying those old Achiever security and status needs without reverting back to a Phase I survivalist mindset. This process turns Explorers into self-authored Pathfinders on the precipice of a journey unlike any most would ever imagine. As nature would have it, once the inner game lessons of Stage 8 run their course, we discover our life's calling and make the quantum leap into Stage 9 Visionary. This is where our ego gets shredded and the real fun begins!

Voice In Action: **Losing the Handcuffs**
Dragon Slayer: **Ryan, C-Suite Exec**

When I met Ryan he was a highly paid, highly respected exec for a multi-billion dollar corporation — a successful person by any standard but his own. For years his Voice had called him to lose the golden handcuffs and follow his bliss. But whenever this happened, old shadow voices would whisper of danger and loss. Believing these voices he was paralyzed by self-doubt. A naturally gifted creative artist and performer in his youth, Ryan had never been able to forget the exalted feelings of exuberance he once knew This memory made his current life feel drab and filled him with regret that he wasted his talents. But his creative energies resurfaced quickly once he started using the Voice Code tools. He began writing poetry and music again, embracing words and ideas in a spirit of childlike wonder. Soon he was hosting his own radio show. At our 12-month follow up, Ryan proudly announced that he'd tendered his resignation and was embarking on a journey of creative discovery with no agenda whatsoever. This man who had been haunted by uncertainty and possible doom, now reveled in uncertainty, embracing the moment, trusting fully in his Voice.

Battle #1
Dethrone the Dividers | CREATE Purpose

In Scene 8 you'll face the Dividers to Own Your Mind and reframe the principle of Authority. Through this initial leg of Act II you'll shift from the Phase I "power outside" to the Phase II "power inside" mindset in service of your mission.

Voice Mentor: **The Emperor** | The Gift: **Purpose**
Shadow Emperors: **The Dividers**
Active Divider: **Warden (Bad Cop)**
Passive Divider: **Wimps (Good Cop)**

The Divider's Strategy *"Do Not Find"*

The Dividers keep us from "Owning our Mind" in the service of our true Voice as it expresses through the Emperor. The Warden and the Wimp lead this domineering group, performing a classic "good cop/bad cop" routine that keeps us split minded. The Warden is the bossy inner know-it-all who "helps us" by prodding us to have, do and be more than we are. The Wimp, the good cop, who lets us off the hook, offers easy outs for the stress, anger and inner tension the Warden causes. The problem: over time these Wimp "solutions" only make our problems worse.

A Tale of Two Mentors

	Dividers	Emperor
Power	Seek Outside	Choose Within
Commitment	Grim Obligation	Creative Expression
Innovation	Cope with Change	Lead the Charge
Motivation	Beat Competition	Make Contribution
Dilemma	Fact of Life	Lazy Thinking
Paradox	Nonsense	Reality

Turning Point: Week 5 practice

At the end of Scene 8 you'll find the "Own Your Mind" checklist followed by an "Explore the Dividers" exercise to help you uncover and remove key shadow habits now blocking your Voice. If you perform the Week 5 exercises before moving forward, you will restore the rightful Emperor to establish a sense of Authority and reclaim the gifts of Purpose this mentor offers. This will help you to own the frame against those sneaky shadow alchemist's we call the Forgetters in Battle #2.

Visit TheVoiceCode.com to get free digital resources, including free training videos and digital copies of key tools offered in this book. You will also find the Voice Code glossary at the end of this book helpful for clarifying and expanding upon any new words, ideas and symbols used.

Scene 8 | *Dethrone the Dividers*

Dragons of Dilemma

The Warden			The Wimp
Control	←	→	Escape
Change	←	→	Deflect
Improve	←	→	Indulge

8 Thou Shalts of the Dividers

Thou shalt *fret over things beyond thy control*

Thou shalt *sacrifice now for an ever-receding future*

Thou shalt *secretly indulge to excess and feel guilty*

Thou shalt *punish thyself to improve thy morale*

Thou shalt *judge all situations through belief filters*

Thou shalt *judge all situations through polarized beliefs*

Thou shalt *fix, change and improve everything*

> *By persuading us to mistake seeking control for having it, the Dividers lead us down a predictable path in which we use our own free will to enslave ourselves. In this chapter, you will see how they do it. Some of the shadows we profile will occur as uncanny descriptions of people you know. This is good! Keep track of anything you read that reminds you of difficult people from your past or present. Try as we may to be objective, our assessments of others always involve the distorting influence of shadow projection. The good news is that every time we discover, capture and reclaim our power from old shadow projections, our sense of inner freedom and authority increases. So summon the Emperor, and have fun harvesting Divider gifts by reflecting deeply and tracking your insights for later processing. The more shadow patterns you discover, the more of the Emperor's gifts you will soon exude.*

The Dividers *Dragons of Dilemma*

When the Voice Emperor governs our inner kingdom, we feel the freedom to choose our passions and fully abstain from making choices that compromise our conscience. Instead of having us seek power and gain control, the Emperor helps us own our power and have control by remaining calm, centered and radically aligned with our life's purpose. When the Emperor loses the throne, we no longer perceive our own best interest. The inner calm that could give us the clarity to find and Commit to our heart's calling decays into a discordant symphony of competing obligations.

When overlooking our own authority becomes a life habit, we feel threatened by anything that challenges our need for control. Starting from the premise that life is dangerous, we enter a hypnotic trance of frame-locked thinking in which sacrifice seems noble; fear seems rational; and freedom feels like a receding mirage in an endless desert of unsatisfying choices.

This is the handiwork of the Dividers, a tag team of stress inducing, upside-down shadow replicas of the rightful Emperor. The Dividers are not real, but they feel *very real* when we believe in them. In truth, they are projected relics of our primal unconscious rooted in buried Outlaw (Stage 4) vows that we've long since forgotten. They have no power whatsoever apart from that which we give them. But once we believe them, we hand them our power by default until we reclaim the throne and restore the rightful heir.

If you've ever seen a great magician, you know that illusions can seem very real. Now imagine that the world's greatest magician has been camped out inside your mind since childhood, telling tales to convince you that life is unsafe. Once you bought into the lie you would rely on this inner guide, gathering ample evidence to prove his case. Eventually you'd come to mistake this imposter for your own Voice, keeping you safe and secure in a dangerous world.

This is how the Dividers trick us. Let's face it: we live in a world riddled with shadow emperor energies in which even the most thoughtful people get frame locked by such propaganda. Some of us get trapped through forced Divider striving, and others through active rebellion *against all* striving. Either way, we get stuck. To the Dividers, either path (striving or rebellion) is fine as long as we stay split minded. This keeps the myth of separation alive and ensures that Thou Shalt gets to keep our Voice gold.

The shadow's prime directive is to convince us that fear is justified, because separation is reality. Once we buy this premise, the shadow gains our loyalty. It then convinces us that we can reclaim our power by fixing, changing and improving others and ourselves. Once we buy into the myth of self-improvement, we're off to the races, chasing symbols of happiness and success like a greyhound chasing an electronic bunny around a track. The faster we run, the faster the bunny goes. Were we ever to catch the bunny and take a bite that wouldn't be much better either, would it?

The Dividers steel our mind against our Voice, telling us that without them we would be unsafe. They promote a seemingly practical, hard-nosed thinking style that promises the deliverance, but never delivers. Following their agenda, we sell our souls to lead lives of endless striving when we could be sharing our gifts. This outside-in mindset causes us to project our own power out onto the world, where we seek endlessly for something that lives only within. In time we get so accustomed to compromise that we see following our Voice as selfish. Unable to make up our minds, we fall into reactive coping patterns to dissociate from the discomfort.

If this situations seems hopeless, please remember: the Dividers aren't real. They are holographic projections of consciousness with no power whatsoever without our continual endorsement. They destroy our lives through our own free will. To reclaim our power and resuscitate our life's purpose, we need only choose again.

Reversing Authority

From "Own Your Mind" to "Do Not Find"

When ruled by the Dividers, we lose our minds. Under the Dividers' spell, we imagine that thriving outliers possess special powers not available to the rest of us. Instead of seeing ourselves as their equals, we put them on pedestals and make them special. When we think this way, we honor the Divider mantra "Do Not Find" as our childhood dreams slowly recede like romantic fantasies from a bygone era. In truth, we are merely frame locked. A lifetime of social programming has filled us with a matrix of unconscious Divider habits that are keeping us from "Owning Our Mind" in the present.

Seeing the world through Divider lenses, we act in ways that confirm our limited perspective, creating a lifetime of compelling evidence to justify our "rightness." As frame lock deepens, we become absolutistic, change intolerant, and downright aggressive when we fear losing control. When things don't work out the way we planned, we make things worse by doubling down on their bad advice, vacillating wildly between forced solutions and escapist self-indulgence to cope with rising stress. This strengthens the division in our weary minds and causes us to feel increasingly powerless in a changing world. The remedy for all of this is simple:

Deny the dilemma. Choose Voice now.

When we believe in shadows, nothing is simple. The natural flow of the CREATE cycle gets choked. Our mind splits against itself and life seems hopelessly complicated. The operative skill to help us break out of Divider enslavement is the "Big C" of the CREATE cycle: *Commitment.* Our ability to commit with Authority gets compromised as the "Big D" of the DEFEND cycle (Divide) ushers in that downward spiral of mis-creation we call frame lock.

As you may recall, the DEFEND cycle is a shadow inversion of the CREATE cycle that we set in motion through our original choice to deny our inner Authority (See Scene 1 for a quick review). Through the Voice Code lens, sin, guilt, fear, evil and all other negative emotions are ultimately shadow delusions projected outward and made real through the selective evidence we gather. When we observe the simple cause and effect patterns of our own choices without self-judgment, we enroll our problem-solving brains to solve all problems at their inner source. But to pull this off we must first loosen our grip on the Dividers' dilemma-based model of reality. Until then, nothing changes.

With the seductive promise that we might separate means from ends, these shadow emperors keep us on a treadmill of time scarcity, struggle and seeking to control things beyond our sphere of influence. When this happens, it's only a matter of time before our natural impetus to CREATE the future becomes a grim resignation to double down on limiting beliefs. This leads to vicious circles of misused creative energy that reinforce the very problems we are working so hard to solve.

The DEFEND cycle graphic below highlights the Dividers' role as guardians of the upside-down world we see in Phase I (Stages 1-6). Their main function is to maintain our belief in projection. Along

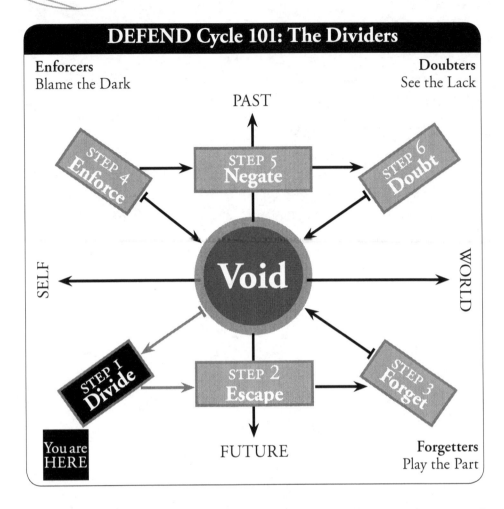

DEFEND Cycle 101: The Dividers

Enforcers
Blame the Dark

Doubters
See the Lack

PAST

STEP 4
Enforce

STEP 5
Negate

STEP 6
Doubt

SELF

Void

WORLD

STEP I
Divide

STEP 2
Escape

STEP 3
Forget

You are
HERE

FUTURE

Forgetters
Play the Part

with the Forgetters (shadow alchemists) they form the Axis of Dilemma, a shadow inversion of the Axis of Vision over which the Emperor presides. When this shadow axis is strong, our kingdom begins to perish from lack of vision. We steer our lives while looking into the rear view mirror for lack of an authentic, inspired purpose rooted in the core of our being.

The Dividers work their black magic through a good-cop/bad-cop routine that keeps us frame locked through our fear of both success and failure. If we are willing to challenge conventional beliefs that failure is fatal and success means sudden exoneration from the trials of life, we can see through the cracks to remember the Emperor and reclaim our power from these hooligans. In the next section, you'll see the tactics and strategies they use to keep us from uncovering their racket.

The Dividers

Bad Cop	"Do Not Find"	Good Cop
Wardens ←	OR	→ Wimps

The Dividers keep us addicted to delusions of control. There's nothing wrong with having control, mind you. The problem comes from *wanting* it. The Dividers trick us into believing we can have control by handing it over to the shadow. When we take the bait, we abdicate the throne and end up on a treadmill of time-stress and endless striving. Frame locked within by competing values, we find ourselves torn from without by competing obligations. This condition grows from the hopeless dilemma mindset which Dividers institutionalize to enslave us.

Over time, those who give into the Dividers' con create lives that satisfy their material needs, but which offer little fulfillment. This dispiriting scenario unfolds at the hands of the Warden and the Wimp, two clever illusionists with an impeccably orchestrated routine. Three telltale signs of Divider frame lock are risk intolerance, anxiety and control issues. Whenever we feel chronically weary and overworked, we can be sure that we've played into their racket.

When we take Divider bait, we find ourselves working harder and harder to achieve less and less. Invariably we develop a habit of bullying ourselves with Warden logic until we feel spent, retreating to the Wimps' arms to indulge in escapist comforts that deplete us further. So it goes that endless dramas between fear and desire play out within us, powered by our fading vitality which we bury beneath addictive life habits. The easiest way to tell if this is happening for you is with one simple question:

Are you truly happy?

Joy is what the Dividers fear most. Happiness is an existential threat to the shadow dragons. When we're truly happy we stop believing in scarcity and these old dramas dissolve like stardust.

Meet the Wardens

The Tyrant | The Savior | The Winner | The Critic

The Warden is the know-it-all inner dictator voice that goads us to push ourselves beyond our limits. The Wardens' influence is seen most clearly whenever we (or others) become stressed, controlling, overwhelmed, emotionally taxed, self-critical or inflated with grandiose self-importance. Such states are the Warden's emotional footprint. Warden voices compel us to gain control over our inner world (thoughts and feelings) by first controlling the world around us. Or, along these same lines, they persuade us to seek to control over our future by sacrificing our happiness with an iron-fisted self-management policy. This "sacrifice self for future reward" attitude seems rational when we're frame locked.[1] In Phase II we come to see it as a form of self-punishment rooted in magical thinking. Manipulating us into acting from magical premises is the Warden's expertise. Let it henceforth be known: any inner guide that compels you to bully yourself "for your own good" is not your true Voice.

Toppling The Big Boss

"Who was that?"

Character: **Reverend Firestone**
Type: **Divider, Warden (Tyrant)**
Gift Reclaimed: **Graciousness**

When I was a kid they called me the "Red Hulk" because I had a particularly intense temper. My explosive nature didn't soften until the age of 40 when I transmuted a tyrannical Warden that I named "Reverend Firestone." This fire and brimstone shadow emperor turned me into a caricature of my father when he'd lose his temper. The morning I was to meet the Big Boss, he came out with guns blazing for the final showdown. While traveling, I was rudely awakened by hotel staff, blaming me for a muffed up charge on my bill. With all the charm of a third-world dictator, I packed my bags and stormed away from the hotel, slamming doors and spouting venom. Driving away, I calmed and began to wonder, "Why did I let that upset me so much? I should call and apologize." I picked up my cell and dialed the hotel. Next thing you know, I'm raging at the top of my lungs again! I decided that I needed to grab some coffee and get my head on straight. A few hours later when I returned from the white light, I finally understood what was beneath this: the Dividers were launching a preemptive strike to keep me from discovering the Big Boss.

Theme: *Beat yourself until morale improves*

The Warden encourages us to make absolute black-and-white commitments and stick to them no matter what, under penalty of eternal guilt. When the Warden dominates, we derive our basic self-worth from our accomplishments and our inner security from our ability to make things happen. Following these inner guides, we become trapped by our own choices — over-committed and stressed by a long list of obligations that keep us trapped in the past, unable to remain fully present. When we double down on Warden logic, we adopt an aggressively competitive "more is more / failure is not an option / never say die / make it happen" attitude that turns our lives into a prison of social comparison, stress and seeking.

Mind Game: *Seek and Do Not Find*

The Warden controls our thinking by causing us to seek happiness outside ourselves. Through the clever use of guilt trips, worries, self-judgment, and ambition, it keeps us chasing after happiness instead of looking within to find it. When we don't find satisfaction by controlling the uncontrollable, the Warden becomes a ruthless inner critic, goading us to fix ourselves to keep from being a failure. If we believe this, we push harder and harder to reach impossible goals that wouldn't even make us happy if they were possible.

Best Trick: *Punish Present to Control Future*

The Warden doesn't care what we do, as long as we never stop seeking. What matters to these controlling inner tyrants is that we keep striving in vain to find inner security in some imagined future. When we come to accept endless seeking as our fate, the Warden can control us by causing us to live in a state of constant fear and desire for a future that never comes.

Four Faces of the Warden

Tyrants: *These imposing Wardens control us through our fear of lack. When we obey the Tyrants, we become workaholics who are unable to enjoy the moment, denying ourselves freedom now with the promise of future freedom. When we rebel against them, we experience goals of any kind as an imposition. Failing to consider the future, we fashion our lives around avoiding discomfort and gratifying our senses with fleeting indulgences.*

Saviors: *These high-minded Wardens control us through our fear of death, promising salvation from our sins for self-punishment today. When we obey them, our minds become filled to the brim with dogmatic beliefs and rituals enacted to purify "sinful" aspects of ourselves. When we rebel against them, we flaunt and even revel in our imperfections, indulging with careless abandon in actions that compromise our conscience and cloud our minds with guilt.*

Winners: *These driven Warden voices control us through our fear of failure. When we obey the Winners, we push ourselves to exhaustion to get to the top, trying to make things happen with little or no self-care. When we rebel against the Winners, we lose our dignity through lives of instant gratification with no discipline, compulsively seeking to create islands of pleasurable escapism to cope with stress.*

Critics: *These judgmental Wardens control us through our fear of vulnerability, constantly assessing our flaws and shortcomings to protect us from being judged. When we obey the Critics, our lives become an endless string of problems. We constantly focus on what's going wrong and become unable to appreciate our many gifts. When we rebel against them, we become beyond reproach, refusing to consider even constructive feedback that might help us improve our effectiveness.*

Most Wanted Authority Killers: The Wardens

These Most Wanted sections offer inquiries to help you begin to discover shadow dynamics playing out in your own life. Don't overthink it. (When we worry, the Wardens win!) Own your mind. Uncover the patterns. Enjoy the process.

Do any of these Warden voices remind you of people from your past?

Which of these Warden types do you find most offensive? What is it that strikes a nerve about that particular type?

Can you spot any of these Warden rackets wreaking havoc in your own life? How does this show up?

Have you ever been in a relationship with someone who seemed possessed by any of these Warden voices — either for or against? How did this show up? How did you cope?

In general, how have Wardens most limited you from actualizing your potential? What might be possible once you reclaim your Authority from these old shadow energies?

If you had to pick one Warden voice that you believe has the most Voice gold for you to mine, which one would it be?

Meet the Wimps

The Abdicator | The Pardoner | The Loser | The Indulger

To understand the Wimps, think of the Wardens and imagine the mirror opposite. If the Wardens are the bad cops who scare us into lives of endless striving, the Wimps are the good cops who let us off the hook, offering quick and easy remedies to ease the inner tension the Wardens cause within. While these quick fixes can provide short-term stress relief, over time they just make matters worse. By following the Wimps call to escape the Wardens, we program our unconscious with ever more evidence to support the same frame locked premises that led us to give our power to the Wardens in the first place. In time, the Wimps cause us to confuse the temporary stress relief caused by guilty pleasures with true love, happiness and enjoyment. This turns us into miserable, self-medicating stress addicts whose primary purpose in life is to press our instant gratification buttons whenever possible.

There's nothing inherently wrong with instant gratification. Many a particularly ruthless Warden could benefit once in awhile by taking a break to enjoy mindless fun. In fact, sometimes out-of-pattern choices like this help us break the Warden's spell. But when the Wimp's call becomes institutionalized through habit, the arteries of our creative passion get clogged, and we get lulled into a coma of complacency, mistaking hedonism for happiness. This renders us deaf to the call of our life's purpose, as true prosperity slips further and further from reach.

Theme: *You deserve a break today*

The Wimps are the world's worst best friends. Their stated goal is to help us feel better in a stressful world. Their unstated agenda is to make sure that we drift through life without a clear purpose rooted in our passions. When the imagined pain of following our Voice stresses us out, the Wimp offers us the comfort of intellectual excuses and rationalizations to justify our complacency. Should we venture out of our discomfort zone with an inspired venture that falls short of our unrealistic expectations, the Wimp is right there to soothe us with the "I'm not going to say I told you so" hug that lets us off the hook. Were we not already so beaten up from the Wardens harsh ways, we'd never take the Wimp voices seriously. If we obey their guidance, we remain emotionally immature until we are on our deathbeds, filled with regret for selling out on our dreams.

Toppling The Big Boss

"Who was that?"

Character: **Tolstoy Parliament**
Type: **Divider, Wimp (Pardoner)**
Gift Reclaimed: **Presence**

In 2012, when my mind was blown by cracking the Voice Code, I pardoned myself from my fanatical health habits and decided to take up smoking until I'd completed a draft of this book. Two years later I was a chain smoker with 30 extra pounds around my midsection and nothing close to a first draft! During the CARE ritual session in which I went to the light, I was feeling the powerful inner pull of an almost otherworldly sense of joy when the phrase "Wouldn't a smoke break be good right now?" entered my mind. I nearly consented, then my frame shifted: "Would my Voice call me to have a cigarette? No way! Who is this within me who wants a cigarette?" Tuning into the feeling tones of the impulse I imagined a brooding character

171

that I named Tolstoy Parliament, who always wanted one last cigarette before being executed by a firing squad. A week after the white light incident, I used the CREATE script to remove him completely. In this one session I killed my cigarette cravings and reclaimed the gift of presence. (Full disclosure: As of this writing, I'm still working off those last 20 pounds. Haven't yet found the shadow for carb cravings.)

Mind Game: *Be Present — Escape Reality*

The Warden seeks to keep us trapped in the past by seeking for a better future. The Wimp accomplishes the same end in a clever way: It tells us to "be happy now" as a ploy to have us avoid responsibility through escapist indulgences. While the Warden champions our ability to redeem ourselves for imagined past failures, the Wimp tells us to pretend that we aren't still holding onto the guilt and fear that make us vulnerable to the Warden's tyranny. Through these clever time-displacement tricks, the Wimp and Warden brilliantly conspire to ensure that we never recognize the power we could claim right now by simply choosing again.

Best Trick: *Bury the Bodies*

When we've come to accept that stress relief is the best life has to offer, the Wimp and Warden have successfully locked us into a rigid mindset from which our sense of purpose slowly fades. As time goes by, we then surrender to our fate and focus on "being practical" by avoiding our passions. The Wimp helps bury the bodies so that we don't remember how much we've sacrificed. It doesn't care what we do, as long as we surrender the Voice throne by looking for half-baked solutions that deal with symptoms rather than root causes. The Dividers are the root cause of the very problems they offer to help us solve. To truly unlearn the Wimps' bad habits, we must retrace their tracks, dig up the bodies and reclaim our gifts.

Four Faces of the Wimp

Abdicators: *These sneaky Wimps control us by our desire to avoid taking responsibility for our lives. When we obey them, we constantly make excuses and look for scapegoats to blame for our problems, developing a sense of entitlement that undermines self-authorship. When we rebel against the Abdicators, we take on too much, feeling stress, worry and anxiety for things beyond our sphere of control.*

Pardoners: *These elusive Wimps control us by our desire to escape our guilty conscience without facing the music. When we obey them, we take actions that violate our own principles, rationalizing our choices using an "everybody's doing it" mindset. When we react against them, we punish ourselves eternally for past errors and see failure as fatal.*

Losers: *These insecure Wimps control us through our desire to win by not losing. When we obey them, we see life as a zero-sum game, placing everyone on a hierarchy of failure according to our values. Thinking this way, we evaluate our success by comparison with others and feel diminished by others' gains. When we rebel, we declare ourselves the "winner" and stop trying altogether. Over time, the strange mixture of arrogance and apathy this breeds turns us into a genuine loser.*

Indulgers: *These self-gratifying Wimps control us by our desire to get the rewards of success without doing the work. When we obey them, we live with a "lottery consciousness" always on the lookout for shortcuts and quick fixes that promise big, but don't deliver. When we rebel against the Indulgers, we become frame locked by a self-punishing "no pain, no gain" attitude through which nothing comes easy and hard work is always necessary to prove our worth.*

Most Wanted Authority Killers: The Wimps

Do any of these Wimps remind you of people from your past?

Which of the Wimp masks do you find most repulsive? What is it that repels you about this character?

Can you spot any Wimp rackets playing out in your own life?

Have you ever been in a close relationship with someone ruled by a Wimp? Which one was it? Did this make you want to "Go Warden" on them?

Do any of these Wimp voices show up in your thoughts? After you indulge them, do you find yourself more vulnerable to the Warden's tyrannical ways?

In what life area has that Wimp's influence been most limiting? What might be possible in this area if you reclaimed your power and removed the Wimp voices forever?

If asked to choose one Wimp Voice you could remove to reclaim power, which one would you choose first?

The Divider's Agenda

Protect the Shadow Poets (aka Doubters)

Every shadow dragon has a weakness. For the Dividers it's the Doubter (aka shadow poets). In a classic display of shadow madness, the Dividers have a tightly coupled dysfunctional relationship with the Doubters that mirrors the opposite of the powerful relationship between the Voice Emperor and Poet. With each successful pass through the CREATE cycle, the Voice Emperor blesses the kingdom with victory over the shadow as our Voice emerges more fully. With each sickly pass through the DEFEND cycle, the Dividers curse our inner kingdom by adding another layer of shadow energy over the growing void within. This void is filled with fear, shrouded in despair, and reinforced from within by a steely layer of icy hatred. This is the sickly love child of the twisted Divider-Doubter affair.

A simple way to think of the Divider-Doubter relationship is as an unhealthy parent-child relationship, in which the parent both seeks the child's approval while also being harshly abusive towards that child. If you examine the emotional subtext beneath the often-domineering tone of the Divider Voices, you'll feel the weak, wounded quality of the Doubters beneath. Everything the Warden and Wimp do implies the false, puffed up quality of weakness pretending strength. When we let the shadow emperors cause us stress, we are always doing so to fend off a sense of vulnerability caused by the melancholy stirrings of unseen shadow poets. Our strident, controlling, stressful life habits are there for a reason — they keep our darkest feelings of hate, grief and despair repressed and projected outward onto the world around us.

Here's the bottom line: every harsh Warden has a pitiful shadow poet associate. Every sad inner victim has a coddling Wimp who indulges it. As your practice deepens, you will begin to unravel complex shadow conspiracies that involve all eight dragon types and reclaim your power from them all at once. For now, you'll have plenty to work with as you observe this particular Divider-Doubter dynamic playing out in your own thoughts and in the world at large.

The power of the human mind cannot be overstated. Even the most gruesome shadow projection is just a tiny sliver of nothing, trapped in a spinning orbit within our primal unconscious. When we shine the light of our creative unconscious down into that primal corridor of our mind, we begin to understand how weak and powerless the shadow really is. True power comes from choice. Choice happens now. The shadow came into power through early choices. As we master the inner game of choosing our Voice we reclaim our power from the past. Once we reclaim it, it's ours forever.

Our choices persist indefinitely — for better and for worse. We don't remember making the past choices that brought our shadows to life, but if we look closely we see the evidence of that Big Bang moment everywhere around us. Each time we choose again, we regain more and more of our natural power until we become One with our Voice at all times and in every area of life. As you learn to see through the shadow's schemes, you will come to know with conviction that the real you has always been unlimited. The only barrier is belief.

Week 5. Own Your Mind (checklist)

Step 1. Capture: Probe and inquire to uncover Divider habit patterns and Insights using the Explore the Dividers inquiry exercise in the final section of Scene 8 below.

Step 2. Consolidate: Create a four-folder shadow insights research file. Place Divider habits uncovered in the Authority folder as part of ongoing shadow pattern discovery archives.

Step 3. Clear: Use the CREATE script (in Scene 6) to transmute top 5 Divider shadow patterns (projections & reflections) uncovered. Process one pattern each day for 5 days at a consistent time to establish rhythm (ex. mornings, Monday through Friday).

Step 4. Compare: At week's end, compare gifts reclaimed through CREATE script with the 16 Gifts of the Emperor in the CREATE Purpose graphic below.

Step 5. Calculate: Perform follow up self-assessment rating between 0 and 10 on each gift where 0 = Divider Habit and 10 = Emperor Gift. Total responses to calculate updated Emperor Quotient (EQ) between 0 and 160. Note any changes from baseline EQ rating taken in week 1 (Scene 2. Befriend the Emperor).

Step 6. Connect: On Day 6 of week 5, perform CARE ritual (in Scene 6). Consult with Voice mentors to align fully with Voice and determine best next action steps to achieve mission.

Step 7. Complete: On Day 7, release the week, relax and revel in laziness. This will help you pave the way for the next round.

CREATE Purpose
16 Gifts of the Emperor

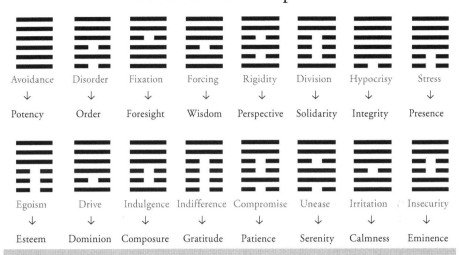

Avoidance	Disorder	Fixation	Forcing	Rigidity	Division	Hypocrisy	Stress
↓	↓	↓	↓	↓	↓	↓	↓
Potency	Order	Foresight	Wisdom	Perspective	Solidarity	Integrity	Presence

Egoism	Drive	Indulgence	Indifference	Compromise	Unease	Irritation	Insecurity
↓	↓	↓	↓	↓	↓	↓	↓
Esteem	Dominion	Composure	Gratitude	Patience	Serenity	Calmness	Eminence

Reframe Authority *Explore the Dividers*

This exercise will help you find areas of Divider resistance that you can process to reclaim your gifts. Every shadow pattern you uncover can be transmuted and cleared using the tools in this book. To "Own Your Mind" while shadow hunting you may find it helpful to first prime your creative unconscious with the *Choose Authority* exercise at the end of Scene 2.

Prospect: *Observe the Experience*

While this material is fresh in your mind, perform a quick review of your inner experience while you read the chapter. Imagine that you are a world-famous shadow-seeking detective hired by the Emperor, to crack the Case of the Dividers. Capture emerging ideas and insights. Observe any inner resistance. Notice what you notice.

Exploratory Insights: *What stood out from your exploratory investigation? Please make sure to capture any clues that came to you, however* *faint or dimly felt. Subtle clues are often the ones that crack the case. Be sure to capture these notes before moving forward to the more formal inquiry process given below.*

Probe: *Expose the Dividers*

Step 1: Review Most Wanted. The questions in the MOST WANTED AUTHORITY KILLERS section are particularly helpful for discovering Divider associations from your personal and professional life. If you haven't yet considered them, please do so now. If you have, please review your answers again to see how they show up in the context of the exploratory probe you've just launched.

Step 2: Associative Inquiry. Please consider the 11 questions below. As you do, gently observe your inner experience to discern Resonance and resistance patterns.

1. As you read this chapter, what resonated most? Did anything jump out as particularly relatable or personally relevant? What triggered the strongest reaction?

2. At any point, did you feel defensive, as if you (or someone you know) was being unfairly characterized? If so, what triggered this?

For questions 3-7 please refer to the 8 Divider profiles below.

8 Faces of the Dividers

Tyrants: *These imposing Wardens control us through our fear of lack. When we obey the Tyrants, we become workaholics who are unable to enjoy the moment.*

Saviors: *These high-minded Wardens control us through guilt and fear of death, promising salvation from our sins in exchange for self-punishment today.*

Winners: *These driven Warden voices control us through our fear of both success and failure.*

Critics: *These judgmental Wardens control us through our fear of vulnerability to protect us from being judged.*

Abdicators: *These sneaky Wimps control us by our desire to avoid taking responsibility for our lives.*

Pardoners: *These elusive Wimps control us by our desire to escape our guilty conscience without directly facing our darkness.*

Losers: *These insecure Wimps control us by our desire to win by not losing, seeing life as a zero-sum game.*

Indulgers: *These self-gratifying Wimps control us by our desire to get the rewards of success without doing the work.*

3. Have any of these Divider personas played a critical role in creating any of your current problems or life challenges?

4. Do any of these remind you of difficult people you've known or worked with? If so, who were they? What did they do that inspired that association?

5. When it comes to achieving your current mission, which Divider type would be most likely to limit you? How so?

6. When it comes to knowing your calling, which of these Dividers would be most likely to block your path?

7. All things considered, what Divider do you sense has been the biggest detractor to keep you from Owning Your Mind?

Questions 8-11 refer to the 8 Thou Shalts of the Dividers below.

8. Which of these Thou Shalts are you most likely to follow as a matter of habit?

9. Which of these Thou Shalts are you most likely to actively resist?

10. Which one of these Thou Shalts bothers you most when you see it in others?

11. All things considered, which Thou Shalt has had the strongest negative influence? How does this show up in your life?

---

8 Thou Shalts of the Dividers

Thou shalt *fret over things beyond thy control*

Thou shalt *sacrifice now for an ever-receding future*

Thou shalt *secretly indulge to excess and feel guilty*

Thou shalt *punish thyself to improve thy morale*

Thou shalt *judge all situations through belief filters*

Thou shalt *judge all situations through polarized beliefs*

Thou shalt *fix, change and improve everything*

Visit TheVoiceCode.com to get free digital resources, including free training videos and digital copies of key tools offered in this book. You will also find the Voice Code glossary at the end of this book helpful for clarifying and expanding upon any new words, ideas and symbols used.

Scene 9 | *Forest of Resonance*

Humpty Dumpty sat on a wall
Humpty Dumpty had a great fall
All the King's horses
And all the King's men
Couldn't put Humpty together again

Because Humpty wasn't broken
T'was a mere peasant rumor
Yet how that tale did spread like fire
In that cloud-darkened kingdom
By the dragon's slithery tongue

Soon Humpty was a legend
A symbol of all things broken
To redeem the deprivation
To defend the delusion
Of innocence lost

Choose Resonance *Think with Heart*

What if Humpty never shattered? Is this story a harmless fairy tale, or clever shadow propaganda? When we say "Humpty," are we talking about some broken egg, or could dear Humpty be a metaphor for Voice? When we bemoan Humpty's demise, might we be secretly mourning the loss of our innocence? But what if the whole "innocence lost" thing is just a shadow hoax? Might unlearning such silly Phase I fairy tales be the secret to remembering our innocence and actualizing our highest hopes and dreams?

The secret to freedom is asking the right questions. One great question can free us forever. But to discover great questions, we must be willing to challenge our own blind spots. Consider the "fall from grace" stories that have dominated our collective psyche since the dawn of civilization. From Humpty's great shattering to Adam and Eve's shameful banishment from the Garden of Eden, we find one essential theme playing out over and over again:

Separation happened. Now we're screwed.[1]

But what if this is just frame locked Phase I thinking? What if separation isn't real? What if the only real problem is the habit of believing in shadows? This might sound crazy, but it's a testable hypothesis. If all problems are shadow projections, then by finding and removing shadows with the CREATE cycle we should be able to solve *any* problem from the inside out. What's one problem area from your personal or professional life that you could use to test this out for yourself? Why not give it a try and see what happens? What if it really works? Wouldn't that be something?

Great questions unravel false assumptions to open our minds to new creative possibilities. Great questions unmask the brilliant solutions waiting to emerge from the dense forest of data that bombards us. Great questions lift us from the orbit of dilemma, redirecting our attention towards the twinkling stars of creative opportunity inherent within every problem. When we let our minds become a tool for heart Resonance, we don't just ask questions, we *live* them and become the solution the world has been seeking.

Great questions are the Alchemist's mastery tool to help you Think with Heart and thrive in today's Phase II economy. Thinking with Heart means keeping our minds open, living the questions and embracing wonder as a lifestyle. To do this we must make inner space to observe our thoughts objectively — without self-judgment or condemnation. When we live the question, we enjoy the process of discovery, viewing all of life as a process of continuous unfolding. When we don't, we fall into a pattern of narrow-minded thinking, deleting facts that don't fit our mental models. This makes change impossible and keeps us from finding the great questions to unravel our blind spots and set ourselves free.

The Shadow Profiler

The questions below will help you attain clarity about any shadow pattern that you uncover. Use them to dive deeper into highly charged shadow characters before reclaiming power using the CREATE Script (Scene 6).

Triggers: *How, when and where does this shadow pattern show up in your everyday life? What kinds of situations?*

Responses: *What does it goad you to think, say or do? Are there any hot buttons, catch phrases or unconscious behavior patterns associated with it?*

Wants: *What does it want? In other words, what does this shadow pattern seem to feel is lacking in you and/or the world?*

Belief: *If this pattern were a character, what would be one belief that it feels absolutely right about?*

Emotions: *What undigested emotions were likely trapped within this shadow pattern when you first made the original choice that conjured it?*

Cause: *What might have instigated the original choice that brought this pattern into being? What kind of event was this choice in response to? How might this choice have seemed to make you safe at the time?*

Gift: *Given your analysis, what gift do you imagine might be waiting for you once you dissolve this shadow projection to reclaim your Voice essence?*

Resonance *The Heart of Possibility*

The year was 1986. I was finishing up my usual bowl of peanut butter Captain Crunch before school. An idea formed in my sixth grade brain that would steer my thinking for the next thirty years. Watching stray bits of cereal floating in the milk of my almost-empty bowl, I noticed that when I'd try to separate two clumped bits, they'd just float around the edge of the bowl until they met again, clasping each other like lost lovers reunited.

I'd seen clumping cereal bits before, but this time I was captivated. "What invisible force is drawing them together?" I wondered, "How do they know where to go?" After a few controlled spoon jabbing experiments, I ruled out explanations involving cereal-floating momentum, and subtle milk currents caused by my breath.

I was stumped.

My mind softened into idle fantasy. I began to personify the cereal bits, wondering how they might explain these milky rendezvous to themselves. When they were separate did they feel sad and lonely? Were they longing for each other? Or perhaps they'd just float along, making their daily rounds, when BAM! they'd run into each other out of the blue, engaging in awkward small talk to be polite.

Hearing a stir from others in the floor above, my mind moved from floating cereal bits to my floating family life at the time. "What if this is a law of the universe?" I wondered. "What if all people are connected by some invisible milky field that binds us together without our knowing it?" The jarring jabs of separation that had marked my home life since my parents divorced — might they also be caused by spoon jabs from some larger unseen intelligence that remains invisible to us while we're still trapped in the swirling milk bowl of life?

In the coming weeks this inquiry matured into what I called my *Cereal Bowl Theory of the Universe.* I was certain that this idea held the promise of unlocking the mysteries of human existence. For some reason, my friends and family did not find it nearly as compelling. By the time fast cars, pretty girls and college applications filled my days, my passion for Captain Crunch had dwindled, but my desire to understand the seemingly random physics of human relationships had only grown stronger.

It came together when I cracked the Voice Code. The *invisible milk* was the principle of Resonance, which draws and repels us to one another through a paradoxical like-attracts-like-*and*-opposites logic. This principle governs how the world shows up for us through the belief frames our unconscious mind generates via the principles of Authority and Trust. These three principles — Authority, Resonance and Trust — are pillars of the human mind, a brilliant structure of dynamically interlocking unconscious forces that pull us toward total freedom along a 12-Stage developmental path.

When we choose our Voice, we frame Authority as internal and naturally Resonate with that which uplifts us. Thinking this way, we achieve results in the world using methods that often go directly against conventional best practices. As our alignment with this principle improves, our sense of separation dissolves, and our identity expands to include the mysterious intelligence that governs all of life. Ultimately, this process leads us to identify less with the cereal bits of our everyday consciousness. Instead of trying to control the cereal (outer game), we focus on expanding and strengthening the bowl (inner game). This is how ordinary people become strange attractors of success — from the inside out, following their Voice.[2]

Seeing ourselves as the context in which life happens, we come to experience ourselves as a microcosm of the entire universe. This invisible inner shift places us on a bold new life trajectory, filled with wonder at the ineffable mystery within every moment. With the spirit of a brave adventurer, we follow our curiosity on a quest to know truth. When the quest for truth trumps the fear of being wrong, our Voice brings us vision into a deeper layer of social reality unseen by most. Inspired questions become fresh opportunities to open our hearts and release ourselves from the bondage of believing. This mindset opens us to profoundly synchronistic insights that elude those who experience the world as if they were tiny cereal bits floating through the milky bowl of life. Like always attracts like, but when we think with heart *we attract what we like*.

Resonance governs our everyday choices in the service of our chosen inner Authority. When we choose the shadow, we let separation drive our attraction patterns through the Trojan Horse of belief. This keeps our attention narrowly focused on evidence that proves our beliefs correct. Through this Phase I lens, we unwittingly attract both what we want *and* the opposite of what we want. The world occurs as an endless series of either/or choices between competing needs. Eventually this natural process leads us to a stunning revelation: *we don't know who we are or what we really want!* This insight leads us down a rabbit hole of radical inquiry that unravels countless Phase I beliefs and opens us to receive our new Phase II purpose.

When we choose our Voice, we live the questions that light us up. Thinking this way, we discern Resonance according to our subjective level of inspiration in the present. As we let our natural sense of curiosity and wonder guide our inquiry, we keep our minds and hearts open to life without preconditions. As this alignment deepens, we experience the world as a perfectly orchestrated symphony, ripe with meaningful coincidences and timeless truth. Rules, categories and conditions that keep others trapped in the cages of compromise melt away as our natural inspiration directs us to find the path of least resistance to a life without limits.

Resonance *The Principle of Attraction*
Paradox: Like Attracts Like & Opposites

Resonance is the principle that helps us keep our minds open, agile and receptive. Aligned with this principle, we develop powerful vision clarity and insight into the inner worlds of others. Frame locked thinkers experience Resonance through the lens of separation. Instead of Thinking with Heart, they follow the Forgetters (shadow alchemists) to Play the Part — saying and doing whatever they believe will help them succeed according to rules written by others. In Phase I this choice happens automatically according to our unconscious Authority framing style. When we enter Phase II, we reframe Authority as we learn to let heart Resonance govern our attraction patterns according to our passions and purpose. In Phase I we project our power out onto the world, blocking our hearts with scarcity thinking. Thinking this way, we chase after things based upon our belief that they will make us complete. This frame locked mindset keeps most from ever discovering what they really want from life. Without an inspired vision that resonates at our core, we spend our lives attracting more and more of what we don't want, as our passions wither.

Worldview Dynamics
Believers (Stage 5) vs. Pathfinders (Stage 8)

The Believer and Pathfinder worldviews are key learning partners who govern Resonance framing on their respective sides of Voice Mountain. As our world moves into Phase II, the balance of power between these two worldviews has shifted dramatically. This process is rendering age-old Believer institutions (organized religion, government, etc.) irrelevant to new generations, wreaking havoc through polarization and gridlock across the crumbling cultural infrastructure of Phase I.

Once we've embraced the reversal of Authority that comes with the inner shift to Phase II, we begin to Resonate with reality based upon the frequency of inner truth. We still have our separate ego identity, but by Stage 8 (Pathfinder), we can achieve our goals without conjuring a big evil "them" to rally against. At this stage, we realize at our core that our only enemy is within. The increased cognitive complexity we've achieved through the lessons of Stage 7 gives us powerful new leverage to engage others without getting frame locked by approval seeking, group think, reactive rebellion and other shadow patterns that clog our mental arteries in Phase I.

Stage 5 Believers and Stage 8 Pathfinders engage in a powerful learning dynamic that anchors the entire developed world (Plane of Social Control; Stages 5-8) between the developing world (Plane of Primal Will; Stages 1-4) and the highest echelon of human consciousness (Plane of Creative Vision; Stages 8-12). When this social dynamic is healthy, societies prosper in a synergistic way that solves problems and generates shared prosperity. When it breaks down, a polarizing cultural schism develops which keeps the creative problem solvers and moral ideologues at odds.

Just as the Achievers (Stage 6) and Explorers (Stage 7) partner to bridge the Authority gap, Believers (Stage 5) and Pathfinders (Stage 8) straddle the principle of Resonance in a way that gives cultures a sense of moral justice and forward progress. Because they have worked through the lessons of the prior stages, Pathfinders are the most powerful group on the Plane of Social Control. Since the rise of digital technology, leaders with the Pathfinder worldview have been the toast of the new global economy, offering disruptive innovations and creative solutions that are dismantling longstanding Phase I conventions. But they shouldn't get cocky, because that next step (to Stage 9 Visionary) is a doozy!

To make the quantum leap to Visionary status, Pathfinders must be willing to transmute a lifetime of shadow projections that keep them frame locked against Believer (Stage 5) leaders and institutions. In practice, this leap requires that they forgive a host of repressed grievances towards abusive and unethical authorities. Through this process, Pathfinders master the distinction between knowing and mere believing as they transmute countless shadows projected onto Believer ideologies that they once wrote off as stupid or insane.

If the idea of forgiving frame-locked fundamentalists strikes you with horror, then you will understand why very few develop the inner fortitude to reach the highest levels of human thriving (Plane of Creative Vision). To escape the orbit of the Plane of Social Control (Stages 5-8), we must undergo a great ego-unraveling that feels a bit like death. To our ego this is a fearful ordeal. But to the real us (our Voice) it is a sacred rebirth. When Pathfinders finally shed the shackles of their old self-concepts, they discover their life's true calling and become a force of nature doing what they love.

Anytime we are in fear, we are frame locked. However justified our fears may seem, they are never more than old shadow tapes projected from our primal unconscious. Our Voice isn't afraid of anything, because it knows that separation isn't real. From the perspective of our Voice, we are One and life is a beautiful paradox, orchestrated by an invisible intelligence with a brilliantly conceived plan that includes everyone. To know this, we must first reclaim our power from a lifetime of grudges we've been harboring since potty-training first indoctrinated us into the Believers' (Stage 5) "sacrifice self for future reward" ethic.

In today's incredible world, Believers seem antiquated or archaic to many in the early stages of their Phase II journey. Be that as it may, this worldview plays an absolutely critical role in the evolution of all societies — past, present and future. With the rise of monotheistic religion three thousand years ago, Stage 5 became the new big worldview on campus for all humanity. Eventually the moral infrastructure offered by Believer institutions paved the way for the rise of capitalism and the Industrial Revolution, as the Achiever (Stage 6) worldview flowered in full force.[3]

Although Believers often espouse beliefs that seem silly or irrational to those in Phase II, this group still holds tremendous power as the grounding anchor for the Plane of Social Control. Not only do they maintain the moral frame for the developed world, they

Choose Again

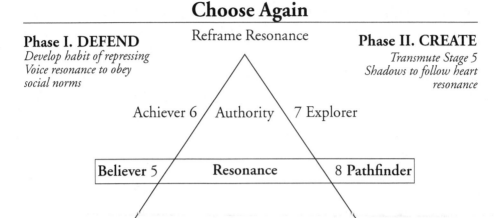

Phase I. DEFEND
Develop habit of repressing
Voice resonance to obey
social norms

Reframe Resonance

Phase II. CREATE
Transmute Stage 5
Shadows to follow heart
resonance

Achiever 6 / Authority \ 7 Explorer

Believer 5 / Resonance \ 8 Pathfinder

Outlaw 4 / Trust \ 9 Visionary

Believer Resonance

In Stage 5, we learn to get by in the world using our brain to frame Resonance for or against beliefs handed down to us by Phase I authorities. This is an important stage in which we learn the value of discipline. But this inner discipline becomes a problem when it becomes a habit that causes us to cling to our separate ego will in defiance of our true will which speaks through our heart's timeless knowing.

Pathfinder Resonance

At Stage 8, we align with the principle of Resonance in our everyday life as we unlearn many Voice-blocking shadow habits formed in Stage 5. This strengthens our inner Authority frame, and gives us the courage to truly "Think Different." Through this process, we gather powerful evidence for the wisdom of following our Voice to craft our life vision and make day-to-day decisions.

serve to bridge the gap between the first world and the developing world. Without this link, our world would collapse into chaos. Developing world Outlaws (Stage 4) have no clear path to climb up the mountain without a healthy infrastructure of Believer ideologies and institutions to guide them. For this reason, the fate of our world rests in large part upon the willingness of bold Stage 8 Pathfinders to face and transmute polarizing Believer shadow projections.

When Stage 8 leaders stop investing in dismissive attitudes towards Believer institutions, every other worldview begins to follow suit. This loosens the shadow's grip on our collective psyche and paves the way for a new Phase II world to unfold. This inner game work heals ancient wounds and helps people reframe the principle of Resonance, lifting Pathfinders to the highest echelon of human thriving as thriving Stage 9 Visionaries. Visionaries are the first worldview stage capable of operating from the holistic non-dualistic mindset of a true planetary citizen. If you are ready, the tools and concepts this book offers will help you navigate this transition in record time with minimal discomfort. The graduation to Stage 9 Visionary transcends description. For now, suffice it to say that it is well worth any effort!

Voice in Action: **The Power of Laughter**
Dragon Slayer: **Carl, Entrepreneur**

After 20 years of success, Carl's firm was struggling. He decided that he needed to chart a new course as a company on a mission to promote environmental sustainability. His passion was heartfelt, but whenever he shared his new vision, clients nodded with faint approval as they eyed their watches. He was confused. Why didn't they light up? After a little digging, we found the problem: shadow residue (guilt) from the Stage 5 Believer worldview. Client resistance grew from a sense of being judged as immoral for current unsustainable business practices. To win hearts and minds, Carl would need to pro-actively dismantle the old right/wrong Believer frame lock. I advised him to design a fun giveaway called an Environmental Guilt Waiver. This silly faux legal contract bestowed clients and friends with a "24-hour exemption from all existential torment in connection with global warming" for making simple positive workplace choices. Carl's team designed and started dispensing these as an icebreaker before meetings. The result? Laughter. Clients loved it! That old Believer guilt disappeared in a puff of smoke and Carl's brand began to make waves within this emerging marketing industry niche.

Once we pass a critical inner threshold of Voice alignment, the shift happens of itself ushering us to a life of unconditional freedom and fulfillment beyond believing. From the inside, it feels as if some thoroughly benevolent Voice wormhole opens within us, lifting us to a much higher octave of experience. The center of gravity for our self-concept now shifts to serve our Voice, pulling us out of time as most experience it. Everyday life becomes what psychologist William James called a "religious experience," but without any need for formal religious dogmas.[4] The power and energy that a single Stage 9 thinker can access is truly mind-blowing. Reaching this stage, we discover the true greatness that we were born to bring to the world and become infused at our core with a fresh vision of shared thriving doing what we love in the service of all.

Battle #2
Remind the Forgetters | CREATE Possibility

In Scene 10, you'll face the Forgetters to reframe the principle of Resonance and Think With Heart. If you win this battle you'll shift from the Phase I "belief Resonance" framing style to the Phase II "Voice Resonance" mindset in relation to your mission.

Voice Mentor: **The Alchemist** | Gift: **Possibility**
Shadow Alchemists: **The Forgetters**
Active Forgetters: **Sharks (Switch)**
Passive Forgetters: **Showboats (Bait)**

The Forgetter's Strategy "Play the Part"

The Forgetters keep us from "Thinking with Heart" in alignment with our Voice as it expresses through the Alchemist archetype. This slippery team consists of the Shark and the Showboat. Using a classic bait and switch routine, they keep us trapped into seeing others through the lens of our personal agenda. The Showboat is the "bait" that lures us in. These are the nicest and most charming shadow thoughts you'll ever meet. When we believe them, we get thrown to the Sharks. Once we make a habit of choosing the Forgetter's advice, we feel a state of chronic low-grade anxiety, which makes us even more susceptible to other shadow habits. If we resist or embrace them we try to "Play the Part" and lose inner alignment with the principle of Resonance.

A Tale of Two Mentors

	Forgetters	Alchemist
Resonance	Brain's Beliefs	Heart's Knowing
Trust	Social Conventions	Great Questions
Reframing	Positive Thinking	Creative Vision
Explore...	Outer Symptoms	Inner Causes
Truth is...	Dilemma (either/or)	Paradox (both/and)

Turning Point: Week 6 practice

At the end of Scene 10 you'll find a 7-point "Think With Heart" checklist followed by an "Explore the Forgetters" inquiry exercise to help you uncover key shadow patterns that block Voice Resonance. If you perform the Week 6 exercises before moving on, you will restore Voice alignment through the Alchemist archetype to infuse your vision with Phase II Resonance. The sense of inspired Possibility that this unleashes will propel you to the final Scenes of Act III where you'll arrest the Enforcers to restore the Warrior and reframe Trust.

Visit TheVoiceCode.com to get free digital resources, including free training videos and digital copies of key tools given in this book. You will also find the Voice Code glossary at the end of this book helpful in clarifying and expanding upon any new language and symbols used.

Scene 10 | *Remind the Forgetters*

Dragons of Duplicity

The Sharks	The Showboats
Hustle ←	→ Pander
Seduce ←	→ Placate
Confuse ←	→ Inflate

8 Thou Shalts of the Forgetters

Thou shalt *covet answers instead of questions*

Thou shalt *view others as a means to an end*

Thou shalt *always hold an unstated agenda*

Thou shalt *follow thy heart only if brain approves*

Thou shalt *use thy cleverness to outwit others*

Thou shalt *find security through social approval*

Thou shalt *never observe thy own thoughts*

Thou shalt *keep up appearances or else*

> *Just as fire can keep our houses warm or burn them down, our free will can lift us to freedom or keep us enslaved forever. When we follow our Voice, the Alchemist helps us find the right way to channel our power, guiding us with inspired questions that help us dismantle limiting assumptions that would otherwise keep us trapped. But when we fail to see through the Forgetter's clever ploys, we lose access to this brilliant inner mentor. Over time, these inner voices of shadow alchemy turn us into inauthentic pretenders, forever on the lookout for easy answers, trying our best to play the part handed to us instead of thinking big and authoring life on our own terms. By making us forget our natural genius, the Forgetters conspire to implement the Dividers' divide-and-conquer strategy within every life domain. This keeps our Authority frame inverted and kills our ability to discern heart Resonance.*

Forgetters *Dragons of Duplicity*

Most of us lose our way in life because we fail to challenge the Forgetters' loaded questions. Instead of following our curiosity to ask inspired questions that drive frame-busting discoveries, we ask loaded questions that keep us frame locked. To change the game, we must shift thinking. Otherwise we end up trapped in the past, frustrated by endless dilemmas, asking the same "have you stopped beating your wife yet" questions on infinite repeat.

Questions We Ask…
How can I get ahead?
When can I finally retire and be free?
Why does this always happen to me?

These aren't questions; they are limiting beliefs with question marks added. Such inquiries frame reality as an irresolvable dilemma in which any inspired both/and is not possible. Here's what these sentences are actually implying by default:

Beliefs We Imply...
Life is a competition.
Enslavement now creates future freedom.
I am a hopeless victim of circumstance.

When we let beliefs like these frame our thinking, we cannot help but to become manipulators. Believing that the world is inherently limited, we do our best to adapt. But in so doing, we forget our Voice and sell our souls at the hands of the Forgetters. The Forgetters are clever con artists with a knack for nuance and an impressive mastery of bait-and-switch tactics. The illusions they create are particularly compelling to us when we are looking for an easy way to solve our problems without transmuting their inner cause. Even when Forgetter strategies produce positive results, these results still ring hollow, because they don't satisfy our unmet inner yearning for beauty, truth and freedom.

The Voice Alchemist's gifts shine through inspired insights into hidden patterns that unravel blind spots to dissolve problems at the level of cause. The Forgetters leverage this gift of inquiry in a way that keeps us trapped in the cages of compromise. By projecting our instinctual pattern recognition skills outward onto the world, they train our clever brains to manipulate people and circumstances in the name of survival. Under their guidance, we sacrifice our heart's passions at the altar of a dispiriting "what's in it for me?" mindset that kills authenticity and saps our creative potential.

Here's a good question: What do the Forgetters make us forget? Answer: They make us forget our Voice and the awesome creative power at our disposal! The Forgetters are the scheming, self-defeating, voices of conformity that destroy curiosity, poison our conscience and make life extremely complicated. With their "hey man, everyone does it" pose, they lead us down a slippery slope of compromised decision-making that keeps us from ever feeling truly alive. Projecting our sense of inner lack outward, we cut corners and scheme to satisfy our unlimited wants as we daydream that we might one day escape the rat race and be happy.

This is magical thinking. To get out of the rat race we must remove the "rats" from our primal unconscious. Retire young after following these black magicians to material wealth, and watch what happens. You'll be bored senseless! You will have spent your best years alienating yourself through manipulation, and will have no genuine friends to share your time with. As you wonder why you don't feel fulfilled, these sneaky charmers will just keep feeding you with shifty schemes to dig your inner void deeper. Like it or not, there's no possibility of living a liberated life until we choose our Voice and remind the Forgetters who's boss.

The first step to slaying the Forgetters is to dethrone the Dividers. As we reclaim our power from their shadow emperor bosses, we give ourselves much-needed inner space to observe our own thinking without self judgment. From this expanded perspective, we learn how to ask questions that open our hearts and minds to the deeper truth that animates us. Like all shadow figures, the Forgetters are a delusion with no power apart from that which we give them. But when we fail to rigorously question our own thinking, we hand them the wheel and let them steer our lives into oblivion. Objective nonjudgmental awareness is the Alchemist's secret weapon to help us remember our Voice and restore our natural brilliance.

Reversing Resonance
From "Think with Heart" to "Play the Part"

When the Forgetters rule, we lose our gifts through a shadow inversion that turns *Exploring* the shadow ("E" in the CREATE cycle) to *Forgetting* our Voice ("F" in the DEFEND cycle). Our Voice Alchemist solves problems by inquiring to unravel the false assumptions. The Forgetters have us try to solve our problems through diversion and displacement.

The graphic on the next page highlights the role that these sneaky con artists play in the DEFEND cycle. Just as the true Alchemist plays the balancing role for the Axis of Vision governed by the

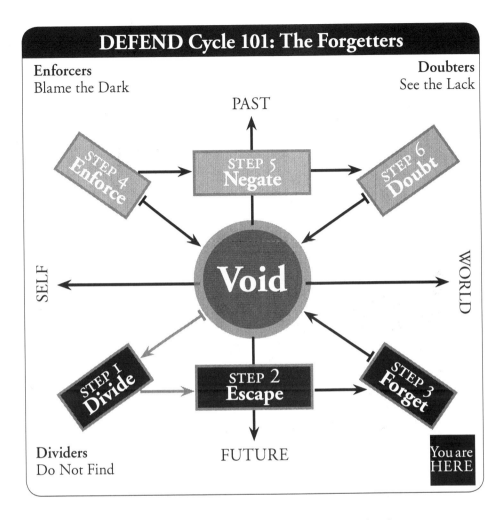

DEFEND Cycle 101: The Forgetters

Enforcers
Blame the Dark

Doubters
See the Lack

PAST

STEP 4
Enforce

STEP 5
Negate

STEP 6
Doubt

SELF

Void

WORLD

STEP 1
Divide

STEP 2
Escape

STEP 3
Forget

Dividers
Do Not Find

FUTURE

You are
HERE

Emperor, the Forgetters fill a key position on the Axis of Dilemma for the Dividers. Listening to them, we can get puffed up on short-term gains, but because these gains grow from an outside in mindset, they never last nor satisfy. Over time whatever gains we achieve through Forgetter antics must reverse into their opposite through the dynamic laws that structure human evolution.

The Voice Alchemist and the Forgetters both govern a domain that flows naturally from their position within their respective cycle. For the real Alchemist, this domain is the Axis of Traction, that portion of the CREATE cycle through which shadow neutralizing strategies are passed to the Warrior for further processing. The Forgetters manage an inverted version of the Axis of Traction, called the Axis of Dogma. When this shadow axis is running strong, the Forgetters are diabolically effective at keeping us trapped in beliefs that block self awareness.

As we approach the inner cave of the Enforcers where our Warrior's gifts have been stowed, the reptilian sentinels of fear and danger enter our minds to distract us. When we fall for their trickery, we cling to old beliefs and delete information that feels threatening. We then rely on the Forgetters to help us spin the truth to ourselves to rationalize our choices and minimize the discomfort of living in a constant state of low grade fear and anxiety.

Forgetter dragons come in two species: Sharks and Showboats. This tag-team runs a classic bait-and-switch operation that keeps us forever distracted and disconnected. In the next section, we will blow the cover on their epic con. Once you see through their game, you will naturally begin to question the wisdom of their guidance. No heavy lifting required. By simply being willing to witness their game as it plays out you will begin to hear the Alchemist's guidance. Objective inner observation opens new portals through which our heart and mind can collaborate, inspiring questions that unravel blind spots to solve problems at the level of cause.

As we reclaim the 16 gifts of Possibility from the Forgetters, the principle of Resonance lifts us. The roots of our Voice Authority sprout into an inspired vision of what could be, branching out in a spirit of service to create shared value. Remembering our unbroken connection with life, we no longer feel compelled to harbor secrets, nor do we feel guilt or shame for having done so in the past.

As we remind the Forgetters, we remember who we are. Our hearts open once again to the music of now, and we experience all events as helpful. The world works with us in concert, like a symphony of collaborative learning, riddled with wonder in the paradox of now. Resonating with life from the seat of true power, we begin to create our future in every moment by observing it into being with a sense of joyful exploration. We allow experiences to flow through us unimpeded, enchanting us with dynamic tapestries of interlocking melodies and echoes of that which is eternal.

The Forgetters

The Switch	"Play the Part"	The Bait
Sharks ←	OR	→ Showboats

The Forgetters are an old school bait-and-switch operation run by the Sharks and Showboats. Like the Warden and the Wimp, they arise from two shadow habit patterns that we chose into existence long ago. Today, these scammers run on an infinite loop in the backdrop of our primal unconscious. Now, whenever social threats and opportunities direct our attention to that hidden corner of our awareness, the Forgetter's come to life again, amplified into our consciousness as viable guides to direct our behavior. Having heard their counsel so many times before, we usually trust it blindly. But when we do so, we place ourselves on a dead-end track by using our brains as steely armor to keep our broken hearts guarded.

As with the Dividers, the Forgetter's routine is mesmerizingly well choreographed and deviously effective at conjuring lifelong limitations for the unwitting. To keep us confused, Forgetters love to trip us up with spurious assumptions and wishy-washy doubts about our own knowing. When we believe them, we discount the validity of our heart's knowing when it isn't already backed by conventional beliefs or social proof. Thinking this way, we are virtually guaranteed a life of frame locked mediocrity, always looking backwards, traveling a path paved by the frame locked masses.

Following Forgetter logic, we act like phonies. The Forgetters love clichés that sound good but don't deliver. Phrases like "follow your heart" are something our Forgetters would have us buy into with great passion, as long as we can do so without looking "weird" to others. Ultimately Forgetter frame lock has us create lives in which *practicality* means sacrificing our uniqueness bit by bit until we feel like prisoners of a boring social world that doesn't get us.

We are all victims of Forgetting. This is a game we play together. But the rules of the game are such that we can't admit it's a game or we lose and are then left to die alone in some dark alley. This is what the Forgetters tell us, anyway. But is it true? Examine the lives of people who have stood firmly for truth in the service of their calling and you'll see a much different story. In reality, people who remind the Forgetters, win the game of life. It's not that anyone really wants to fake their way to a life of regret. Most people do their best to practice what they preach. The problem is that most are far too frame locked by conventional thinking to turn laudable cliché's like "follow your dreams" and "find your voice" into a clear plan of action.

Thank god for this new map! Here's a simple three-step plan to help you escape the spiritual doldrums of Forgetter frame lock and put your own best advice into action:

1. **Meet the Forgetters.** *Read profile descriptions below and see how the Shark and Showboat conspire to turn people into phonies.*

2. **Find the Forgetters.** *Perform a deep dive inquiry to see how these shape shifters have limited you personally.*

3. **Remind the Forgetters.** *Use Voice Code tools to transmute them and unleash your brilliance. (Hint: the Week 6 checklist at the end of this scene is a great place to start!)*

The Forgetters would have us forget that we have greatness within us. They'd love to help us hide this fact so that we can spend the rest of our lives chasing freedom through manipulation and approval seeking. Let's stop them shall we?

Meet the Shark

The Mercenary | The Seducer | The Evangelist | The Mole

Sharks are a slippery group. They live on our attention, but they never come right out and say it. They get our mental energy by luring us with promises of personal success that look good and promising on the surface, but which leave us empty once we take the bait. Following their advice, we jump on hyped up trains to nowhere that totally derail us from an authentic life. Anytime your find yourself feeling an inner urgency and pressure to make a decision or accomplish a goal that doesn't truly light you up, be certain that the Sharks are giving you an inner sales pitch to implement a Divider (shadow emperor) agenda. The source of pressure may seem to come from within or from external demands. However it shows up, rest assured that the Sharks in your primal unconscious are the power players. After all, the choice to feel pressured is always our own. The Sharks lure us into making this choice time and time again, siding with our beliefs instead of our Voice, until we no longer remember who we are, what we stand for, and the gifts we offer.

Toppling The Big Boss

"Who was that?"

Character: **Black Magic Jesus**
Type: **Forgetter, Shark (Seducer)**
Gift Reclaimed: **Humility**

A few weeks after I toppled the Big Boss, the shadow mob was scurrying like rats on a sinking ship. I was still leading and taking the first Voice Code inner game beta course at the time, having a blast. Then a disturbing thing happened: One of the participants went AWOL. This fellow was a well regarded spiritual teacher who had been making huge gains. Something was off. I followed a few hunches and discovered that he had borrowed the CREATE-cycle to create his own cyclical inner game course using the acronym "COMMIT". By the time I found out, he had apparently already signed up a long list of people to take his course. Once the shock wore off, I became curious. "If this is a shadow projection, then I'm the cause and there must be a hidden gift. What is it?" I wondered. I used the CREATE cycle to uncover a conniving shark pattern that I named "Black Magic Jesus" who'd apparently masterminded the whole Big Boss operation. I transmuted this character and reclaimed the gift of humility, which helped me release any fear-driven possessiveness over this intellectual property. Once the inner cause was removed, the outer game shifted. After making a public show of his "big discovery" for weeks, he quietly dropped his copycat course and removed any trace of it from the web. Problem solved from the inside out.

Theme: *I want what I want when I want it.*

The Shark Voices are always in a hurry, always on the move. Always feeling the ticking clock. Always looking for ways to work the angles. To the Sharks time is money and the goal of life is to not end up with the short end of the stick. Sharks love shortcuts! Why do things right when you can get the same results in half the time doing half the work? The problem is that Shark shortcuts don't deliver. When the Shark dominates, life is an endless competition to define reality and control other peoples' minds to further our personal agenda. The problem is that our chosen goals are not what we really desire in our hearts. Shark goals are quite literally *wants* — a sense of lack — projected forward in time. The endless wants that the Sharks conjure come from our habitual avoidance of that gnawing emptiness that lives at our core when we don't follow our dreams. When we see through the charade and choose our Voice, we satisfy the genuine need that was beneath our wanting. The inner pressure subsides and our aspirations unfold quite naturally.

Mind Game: *Apples vs. Oranges*

The Sharks steal our power through the habit of social comparison. Our Voice, knowing itself as One with all life, never compares or competes. Born of the belief in lack, the Shark voices within us become bored and listless at the notion of a life without competition. To them, if we aren't special and superior, we have no value as individuals. The Sharks tell us that if we can only outsmart, outperform or outshine something else (person, group, ideology, our past self, etc.) life will be heaven. The problem is that we are a one of a kind masterpiece. Comparison is pointless. Competing just keeps us frame locked by conventional success metrics. If we followed our Voice we'd naturally follow our passions to build a new model that renders the competition irrelevant. But when we listen to the Sharks, we lack faith in our native gifts. Blinded by scarcity and social inadequacy, we rush to fill the inner void using strategies and solutions that push our Voice further from our awareness.

Best Trick: *The Slippery Slope*

The Sharks thrive on those tiny "every penny helps" compromises that we make with our conscience. Over time, these small shadow choices gain steam, reshaping our lives while we're not looking. Anyone who has ever racked up big credit debt from relatively small purchases or become addicted to something that started out as innocent exploration, can attest to the massive snowball effect that tiny acts of self-betrayal have over time. As they say in the south, "Lying is like stealing chickens." I'm not exactly sure what they mean, but I'm pretty sure it has something to do with how the Shark's slithery advice leads us to downward spirals.

Four Faces of the Shark

Mercenaries: *These driven Sharks control us by our fear of scarcity, promising us personal freedom by castrating our conscience. When we obey them, we compartmentalize our thinking and focus only on objectively measurable outcomes, a thinking style that keeps us blind to everything else. When we react against the Mercenaries, we get frame locked by a soft-headed all-is-one malaise that makes us emphasize consensus over competence and feelings over facts.*

Seducers: *These conniving Sharks control us through our fear of being socially awkward or ineffective. When we obey them, we see others as targets that must be covertly persuaded to do our bidding and end up repelling people. When we react against the Seducers we feel guilty for any unstated motives whatsoever and become self-conscious, often confessing things that aren't relevant in a way that distracts from our message and limits our effectiveness.*

Evangelists: *Theses outspoken Sharks control us through our fear of being ignored and/or belittled. When we obey them, we become passionate champions of our message, but in a polarizing way that involves pandering and preying upon people's fears. When we react against the Evangelists we become falsely modest phonies (to avoid being seen as polarizing phonies), afraid to speak our truth or infuse our message with passion.*

Moles: *These scheming Sharks control us through our desire to influence the levers of power without full transparency. When we obey them, we pursue alliances with high-status people and pander to them hoping to assimilate into their circles. When we react against the Moles, we feel compelled to take a vehement moral stand against people with power, while secretly harboring envy and disdain towards them as if they'd somehow stolen the power that was rightfully ours.*

Most Wanted Resonance Killers: The Sharks

Do any of these Sharks remind you of people from your past?

Which of the Sharks do you find most relatable and/or repulsive? What is it about these shadow patterns that trigger you?

Can you spot any Shark rackets playing out in your social life?

Have you ever partnered with someone driven by manipulative Shark shadows? Which Shark was it? How did you deal with them?

Do you ever feel compelled by social conventions or survival needs to adopt Shark tactics? If so, what situations trigger you most?

How might the Sharks be limiting your ability to connect and effectively engage others to embrace your vision? What might be possible if you reclaimed your power from all of them forever?

If you had to pick one Shark voice that you believe holds the most untapped power for you to reclaim to actualize your potential, which would it be?

Meet the Showboats

The Flatterer | The Diplomat | The Lightweight | The Performer

While the Sharks lead us to misplace our moral compass, the Showboats show us how to become liked by people we don't like. When we obey the Showboats, we seek validation for our reality by getting approval from others. But what if we don't really relate to those who we must win over to achieve our goals? This is a practical problem that the Showboats help us solve by turning us into social magicians. Playing roles they offer us we might seem like the most charming and down-to-earth person one could ever meet, but beneath our social mask we feel disconnected.

Following the Showboats, we might fill our lives with adoring smiles and witty cocktail hours, but nothing scratches that itch for deeper connection. On the surface, the charming Showboats seem the polar opposite of those shifty Sharks, but this is the secret genius behind the Forgetter's con. While the Sharks covertly lure our attention towards the wrong methods, the Showboats help us implement the Sharks' strategies, as our social life becomes a prison of unsatisfying relationships. The Showboats know just what to say and how to say it, giving us clever lines to enthrall others. But play their game and we soon find ourselves swimming with the Sharks! These charmers feed on our need for specialness, leading us into situations where we lose our inner compass and feel forced to hide our true motives.

Toppling The Big Boss

"Who was that?"

Character: **Chip Smugly**
Type: **Forgetter, Showboat (Performer)**
Gift Reclaimed: **Respect**

Before the Voice Code, I was considered by some to be one of the world's leading strategic communication experts. Soon after this discovery, I came to see myself as a total hack. During this period, I excitedly shared this big discovery with many who offhandedly dismissed me as arrogant or delusional. Why weren't people more receptive? My message was exciting. Wouldn't people be at least a little curious to dive deeper and learn more?! I couldn't fathom the cause of this social resistance. Eventually I met a Forgetter shadow pattern I named "Chip Smugly." Chip was a repugnant streak of icy cool pomposity that surfaced whenever people doubted me or dismissed my ideas. When I followed his lead, I was masterful at making people feel intellectually inferior. Chip helped me prove to others that I was smart, but not once did he ever help me win friends or influence people positively. Until I toppled the Big Boss, I couldn't see that the puffed up feeling I'd get when Chip spoke was ultimately just a call for approval — he was a cocky shield against a fear of being dumb and unlovable. Once I reclaimed my power, I stopped worrying about whether or not people would doubt me. Can you guess what happened next? Yep, that's right! People started giving me the benefit of the doubt and became much more receptive to this discovery.

Theme: *We're just the best, aren't we?*

The Showboat thrives in situations of pretended intimacy. These voices compel us to be seen as people who've got it all figured out, and often show up in society through circles of mutual admiration with a strong in-group bias. In such tribes, the Showboat tells us we're safe from *them*. Forgetter tribes forge inflated feelings of superiority. Within such groups, there's always a dark battle for power brewing under the surface. When disagreements arise, they are seldom handled out in the open with transparency. Instead, alliances form and these groups splinter into competing factions. As the undercurrent of dissonance grows, the group does it's best to maintain the façade. But Showboat facades crack and Shark attacks become commonplace as Forgetter's reveal their rotted roots.

This Showboat-Shark social dynamic plays out across all Phase I relationships at every level of analysis — from marriages, to families, business teams, organizations and whole societies. Once we let the Showboats drag us into such situations, we waste much time and energy managing needless drama that drains everyone. The cultures of false intimacy that the Showboats foster feed our inner Sharks. Over time they turn us into someone we no longer recognize. In such cultures, feeding off our specialness relative to *them* becomes a way of life. Having used the Showboats to charm our way to success, we come to live our life like an actor playing a role written by invisible Sharks within us.

Mind Game: *Authentic Fakery*

When the charming and seemingly innocent Showboats lead us into untenable or unsatisfying situations, we grow weary. Eventually we can no longer distinguish ourselves from the social masks we wear. Showboat personas then become both the mask that we wear to charm people and also the "real us" who we think we are when we try to be authentic. This is the slippery inner slope through which we gradually lose access to our moral compass. Once we follow the shadow alchemist's calling to Play the Part in one area of our lives, we gradually forget who we are in every life domain. As our childlike curiosity and exuberance begin to wither, we feel that something is deeply wrong. But when we look around us, we see a bunch of other people in the same dispirited condition and assume that this is "just the way it is" reality.

Best Trick: *Death by Cliché*

Once we lose access to our inner truth compass, we become dependent upon approval and social proof to validate our ideas. This places us squarely on the path to mediocrity, because our Voice (knowing us as the force of nature we are) never calls us to support the status quo. When our Voice speaks, we may still experience inspiration quite powerfully. The problem is turning inspiration into action. When we seek to implement our Voice guidance, a host of cynical inner voices assail us, and we fall into self-doubt. In an attempt to protect ourselves from failure, we look around for social proof that what our Voice directs us to do will be successful. We may even tell some family and friends about it to get feedback. But if following Showboat voices has become a deeply ingrained habit, we find people depressingly unsupportive. Why? *Because being authentic violates the implicit "Play the Part" Forgetter contract we've established in all of our relationships.* Caught in this Showboat trap, people love to spout uplifting phrases like "follow your dreams" and "be your own person," but find it impossible to truly embody them. This is how all timeless wisdom becomes reduced to empty clichés at the hands of the Forgetters.

Four Faces of the Showboat

Flatterers: *These charming Showboats control us by our desire for approval. When we obey them, we find the right way to ingratiate ourselves to others, finding just the right way to make people like us so that we can "bag and pocket" them. When we get frame locked against the Flatterers, we find it difficult to either offer or accept compliments for fear that we will end up being manipulated or taken advantage of by others.*

Diplomats: *These smooth Showboats control us by our desire to be respected as mature, seasoned individuals. When we obey them, we do our best to occur to others as a calm, classy person* with excellent breeding. But this polished persona becomes a social straitjacket when it keeps us from being able to connect and communicate our truth clearly and directly. When we react against the Diplomats, we become rebellious provocateurs who flout conventions and call out the elephant in the room just to draw attention.

Lightweights: *These insecure Showboats control us through our desire to get what we want from others, without standing for our value. When we obey them, we give our power away hoping to friend our way to success, luring people in with an affable nature, hoping we can pivot and harness our rapport to satisfy our needs. When we react against the lightweights, we become like bulls in a china shop, cutting right to the chase without establishing a healthy rapport or seeming to care at all about our impact on the inner worlds of those we engage.*

Performers: *These gaming Showboats control us through our desire to seem special and magnetic. When we follow it, we seek the upper hand in social situations by making our presence known and then withdrawing our energy so that others find us mysteriously compelling. When we react against the Showboat, we often adopt an attitude of self-deprecating "aw-shucks" modesty, hoping to cover over whatever guilt we feel for our secret fantasies of being the center of attention.*

Most Wanted Resonance Killers: The Showboats

Do any of these Showboat masks remind you of people from your own past?

Which of the Showboat masks turn you off the most? What is it about them that strikes such a chord of dissonance?

Can you spot any Showboat patterns playing out in your life?

Have you ever been in a close relationship with someone possessed by an attention-seeking Showboat voice? Did you discover a deceitful Shark quality in them at times?

How do these Showboat voices show up in your own social engagement style? Do you ever find yourself playing the part of Showboat to win people over?

If asked to pick just one Showboat voice that probably holds the most untapped creative power, which would it be?

The Forgetter's Ally

Enforcers: Dragons of Deviance

When we fall into the Forgetters' traps, we do so to avoid feeling the Enforcers (shadow warriors) to whom they are tethered. Together these two shadow voice groups form the Axis of Dogma, a shadow version of the Axis of Traction from the CREATE cycle. The Forgetters and Enforcers are deeply allied partners in the quest to keep us frame locked by fundamentalism. This partnership is strong, but to our everyday mind the byproducts of this unholy alliance are anything but pleasant. The Forgetters constantly feed us fear-based strategic advice that we follow only when we feel the gnawing sense of dread that the Enforcers generate through their evil inner bullying.

Without the Enforcers, the Forgetters' ploys would ring hollow. At the same time, without a convincing "nothing to see here" spin job from the Forgetters, people wouldn't buy into the Enforcer's fearful hype and would quickly come to see through them. This being said, know that the Enforcers (whom you'll meet in Scene 12) are truly terrifying to us when we believe them. These shadow warriors arise from a deeper layer of the primal unconscious in which we store our belief in evil. When we become frame locked by the Forgetters, we do so to forget about this creepy inner cave!

There's a nearly universal belief that the Enforcers' cave contains terrifying information that would strike us dead were we to look at it directly. This Phase I belief is a critical cog in the shadow's mental machinery. This is why aligning with the rightful Alchemist to Think with Heart is so important. Doing this we make clean inner space to distinguish fact from fiction in our minds. Guided by the Alchemist, we spontaneously ask inspired questions that unravel fear-based thinking before it takes hold. This is how our Voice helps us remind the Forgetters, arrest the Enforcers and dismantle the Axis of Dogma forever.

After we walk step by step through this process you'll see that the Enforcers are ultimately a bunch of goofy windbags from a B-rated horror flick. Until then please be extra careful, kind and patient should fear or resistance arise. As you begin to disrupt the shadow's rackets, it's normal for old shadow energy patterns to come up and cause temporary discomfort. When this happens, it's best not to take your thoughts seriously. Just take a few breaths, get your heart and mind back in sync, and say, "Who is that?" to any fearful shadow voices that would have you play small going forward.

It also might help to consider the big picture — the game-changing nature of this inner game technology. Until now, our species was forced to face darkness without a simple, non-ideological, process-driven framework to help us solve our problems from their inner source. Human history has been one of believing in separation, choosing sides and creating endless evidence to confirm that our darkest fears were justified. It's no wonder most of us still let shadows rule our mind! There has never before been a clear and complete map to help us escape frame lock forever.

Now that there's a map, all bets are off. By doing this work, you are placing yourself on the forefront of human consciousness at the perfect moment in human evolution. You should feel good about yourself. But as your power increases, promise not to let the Showboats get your head all inflated![1] That's no good either. We've got some dragon slaying to do, beginning with the Week 6 checklist on the next page.

Week 6. Think with Heart (checklist)

Step 1. Capture: Probe and inquire to uncover Forgetter habit patterns using the Explore the Forgetters inquiry exercise (below).

Step 2. Consolidate: In your shadow insights research file, place Forgetter habits uncovered in the Resonance section, as part of your ongoing shadow pattern discovery archives.

Step 3. Clear: Use the CREATE script (in Scene 6) to transmute your top 5 Forgetter shadow patterns uncovered. Process one pattern each day for 5 days at a consistent time to establish rhythm.

Step 4. Compare: At the week's end, compare gifts reclaimed through CREATE script with the 16 Gifts of the Alchemist in the CREATE Possibility graphic on the opposite page.

Step 5. Calculate: Perform a follow up self-assessment rating between 0 and 10 on each gift where 0 = Forgetter Habit and 10 = Alchemist Gift. Total responses to calculate updated Alchemist Quotient (AQ) between 0 and 160. Note changes from baseline AQ rating taken in week 2 (Scene 3. Inspire the Alchemist).

Step 6. Connect: On Day 6 of week 6, perform CARE ritual (in Scene 6). Consult with Voice mentors to align fully with Voice and determine best next steps to achieve mission.

Step 7. Complete: On Day 7, release the week, relax and revel in careless abandon. This will help you pave the way for the next cycle of dragon slaying (Week 8. Face the Dark).

Rekindle Resonance

Explore the Forgetters

This exercise will help you find areas of Forgetter resistance to process. To set the stage for a powerful session, you may want to prime your mind with the *Choose Resonance* exercise in Scene 3.

Forgetter Habit   **CREATE Possibility**   Gift of Resonance

16 Gifts of the Alchemist

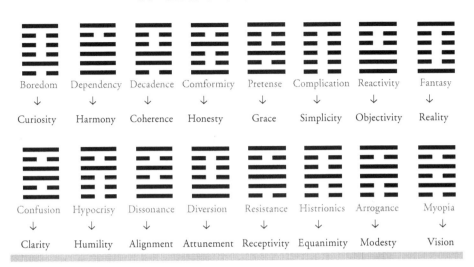

Boredom	Dependency	Decadence	Comformity	Pretense	Complication	Reactivity	Fantasy
↓	↓	↓	↓	↓	↓	↓	↓
Curiosity	Harmony	Coherence	Honesty	Grace	Simplicity	Objectivity	Reality

Confusion	Hypocrisy	Dissonance	Diversion	Resistance	Histrionics	Arrogance	Myopia
↓	↓	↓	↓	↓	↓	↓	↓
Clarity	Humility	Alignment	Attunement	Receptivity	Equanimity	Modesty	Vision

Prospect: *Observe the Journey*

A quick review of your inner experience while reading the chapter will help you frame the exploration. You want to enter a state of detached objectivity and expectant curiosity. Imagine that you are a detective hired to help crack the "Case of the Forgotten Genius." Page through and recall your inner experience while reading this chapter. Notice what you notice. Enjoy the process.

Exploratory Insights: *What stood out from your exploratory investigation? Please make sure to capture any clues that came to you, however faint or dimly felt. Subtle clues are often the ones that crack the case.*

Probe: *Expose the Forgetters*

Step 1: Review Most Wanted. The questions in the MOST WANTED RESONANCE KILLERS section are particularly helpful for discovering Forgetters associations. If you haven't yet considered them, please do so before moving forward. If you have, review your answers again so that you've set this new context.

Step 2: Associative Inquiry. Please reflect upon the 11 questions below. As you do, gently observe your inner experience to note nudges of Resonance and resistance.

1. As you read this chapter, what resonated most? Did anything jump out as particularly relatable, insightful or personally relevant?

2. While reading, did you at any point feel defensive, as if you or someone else was being unfairly characterized? If so, what triggered this reaction?

For questions 3-7, please refer to the 8 Forgetter profiles below.

8 Faces of the Forgetters

Mercenaries: *These ruthless Sharks control us by our fear of scarcity, promising us freedom by castrating our conscience.*

Seducers: *These conniving Sharks control us through our fear of being socially awkward or ineffective.*

Evangelists: *Theses outspoken Sharks control us through our fear of being ignored and/or belittled.*

Moles: *These scheming Sharks control us through our desire to influence the levers of power without full transparency.*

Flatterers: *These charming Showboats control us by our desire for approval and admiration from others.*

Diplomats: *These smooth Showboats control us by our desire to be respected by others as mature, seasoned individuals.*

Lightweights: *These insecure Showboats control us through our desire to get what we want without standing for our value.*

Performers: *These gaming Showboats control us through our desire to seem special and magnetic.*

3. Can you see any connection between these Forgetter patterns and your own limitations, past or present?

4. Do any of these remind you of difficult people you've known or worked with? If so, who inspired this association?

5. When it comes to achieving your goals in the next few months, what Forgetter pattern would likely be most limiting?

6. When it comes to receiving your calling, which of these Forgetter voices would be most likely to block your path?

7. All things considered, what Forgetter has had the biggest negative impact in your life? How has this shown up for you?

For questions 8-11, read 8 Thou Shalts of the Forgetters.

8 Thou Shalts of the Forgetters

Thou shalt *covet answers instead of questions*

Thou shalt *view others as a means to an end*

Thou shalt *always hold an unstated agenda*

Thou shalt *follow thy heart only if brain approves*

Thou shalt *use thy cleverness to outwit others*

Thou shalt *find security through social approval*

Thou shalt *never observe thy own thoughts*

Thou shalt *keep up appearances or else*

8. Which of these Thou Shalts are you most likely to follow as a matter of habit?

9. Which of these Thou Shalts are you most likely to actively resist?

10. Which one of these Thou Shalts bothers you most when you see it in others?

11. All things considered, what Thou Shalt has had the strongest negative influence? How so?

Visit TheVoiceCode.com to get free digital resources, including free training videos and digital copies of key tools offered in this book. You will also find the Voice Code glossary at the end of this book helpful for clarifying and expanding upon any new words, ideas and symbols used.

Scene 11 | *The Cave of Trust*

Imagine that you and everyone you know were born inside a dimly lit cave. You've spent your entire lives staring at a cave wall. Everyone's heads and limbs have been chained since birth, rendering them immobile. Upon this wall, you watch flickering shadows from an unseen source behind you. This is all you've ever known.

Watching the flickering shadow patterns is a cherished cave pastime. Where do they come from? What do they mean? This topic consumes cave culture. Some cave authorities offer strident stories and beliefs about the shadows. Others disagree, offering competing theories. Groups rally for and against given opinions, but one belief unites everyone: the shadows are real. How could the one thing everyone agrees upon be wrong?

One morning you wake up to find your best friend and neighbor missing. Where did he go? You are worried. After a morning of restless shadow watching, he returns with wide eyes. "Listen," he whispers breathless, "You have to see this! You see this wall? These dark spots? They are nothing. There's a whole world out there, brighter than a million candles. Come with me! Let's go. Quickly."

How do you respond to your friend's message? Do you believe him? Do you think he went mad? How will your fellow cave dwellers respond when they hear his tale? You have exactly one minute to escape. One minute to choose between staying in the cave or following your friend into the great unknown. Which path do you choose?

Choose Trust *Face the Dark*

This story represents our primal fear of finding our Voice. The characters represent competing forces built in the structure of the human mind. The cave is the place in our primal unconscious where we've stowed our deepest secrets. The main character is our ego identity. The cave dwellers are our darkest fears, grumbling shadows that sow the seeds of mistrust. The best friend who brings us news of deliverance is our Voice. Like our success in the Phase II world now unfolding, our main character's fate boils down to one simple choice:

shadows or Voice?

These two inner guides lead us in opposite directions, framing our experience through two diametrically opposed purposes. Our friend (Voice) is driven by truth. If we place our trust in him despite our fears, he will lead us to a life of total freedom. The grumbling cave dwellers (shadows) are driven by fear. They revel in darkness, projecting their powerlessness through blame, shame and endless posturing. Using guilt trips and threats, they fill our minds with frightful images of what would happen should we dare question our current view of reality.

Faced with this choice, most people imagine making the hero's choice to follow their friend (Voice) out into the light. But in reality, people who embody this courageous mindset are rare. To trust our friend in this scenario, we'd need to overcome a lifetime of unconscious beliefs programmed into us since birth. Imagine the courage this choice would require! Our entire identity would've been formed in that cave. To even consider leaving, we'd first need to be willing to seriously consider that our entire life until that moment had been a lie. Under these circumstances, it would be much easier call our friend crazy and stick with the status quo.

This story is a remix of Plato's Cave Allegory.[1] In the original, it is suggested that the truth teller would be murdered just like Socrates (Plato's wise mentor). Judging by a long history of similar attacks on truth tellers like Jesus, Abraham Lincoln, Gandhi, John F. Kennedy and Martin Luther King, Jr., this allegory reflects a universal truth. At every major turning point in history, we find this same drama playing itself out between Phase II visionaries and Phase I survivalists with minds so deluded they'd sooner kill the messenger than let their shadows be dispelled.

We have all been thoroughly socialized since birth to trust in the reality of evil. Once we believe in evil, it becomes real for us. Through this frame-locked lens, those who aren't afraid seem naive. I offer no indictment against those who think this way. But given the toxic impact of this condition in today's accelerating world, those of us with curious minds would be wise to consider new possibilities:

What if you made up your mind to face fear head on in every situation from this moment forward? What if you entered the cave of your own unconscious and removed evil at its roots? What if you just trusted your Voice so fully that you'd sooner die than surrender your power to the shadow dragons?

This is the choice that all game changers in history have made. Their seemingly supernatural powers came from their unwillingness to place faith in fear. We each have freedom to choose love or fear as we see fit. But when we choose fear, we invest our power in delusions. The only thing we have to fear is fear of our Voice. To remove fear at its source we must summon our Voice in the Warrior's pose.

To Face the Dark, we must embrace our resolve. We must make it a habit to remain vigilant for freedom by establishing an inner culture in which fear cannot flourish. When we make this courageous mindset a habit, we break through all boundaries to learn that evil is powerless. When we run from the dark, it rules us. When we face it, we dispel it with surprising ease. But honoring the Warrior's calling remains impossible when we refuse to challenge cave consensus. Cave thinking seems rational when we're frame locked, but is actually the core delusion that keeps most people in chains forever.

Trust *The Principle of Action*

Paradox: There's nothing to fear but fear

Trust is how we make our invisible inner worlds visible. The proof of Trust comes from spontaneous inspired action. If our actions aren't spontaneous and inspired then we aren't following our Voice. When we get frame locked around the principle of Trust, we remain stuck in our heads, debating our options and worrying about risk. Sensing our lack of inner coherence, others instinctively mistrust us. This split minded decision making style is a sure fire sign that we have invested belief in fear. When we embrace Trust in proper alignment with the principles of Authority and Resonance, we become a spontaneous force of nature in whatever we do. Our actions arise as a natural expression of our being, inspiring others to embrace our ideas and Trust their Voice also. This is how Phase II visionaries follow their Voice to change the world from the inside out.

Trust *Access to Power*

How do you know when you trust someone or something? Do others trust you? How do you know for sure? The more we think about trust, the less we understand it, because trust precedes conceptual thinking. When a salesman says, "Trust me" are you more or less likely to question their motives? Anytime you find yourself debating whether or not to trust someone, haven't you already decided? Whenever hesitation enters the picture, we're already frame locked by fears projected up from our primal unconscious. When it comes to this confusing topic, only one question really matters:

Do you Trust your Voice?

If the answer is yes, you will trust others appropriately without thinking about it. If the answer is no, you will trust in shadows and find yourself mired in endless problems. When we look deeply into the inner cause of recurring problems, we always eventually find the cave — that dark storage unit in our primal unconscious where we bury our deepest fears. The call to "Face the Dark" is the call to stand fully for our Voice so that we can clear the cave by slaying the shadow dragons of mistrust that sap our power. When we do this, we begin to feel pulled towards our highest future by the Poet's invisible arms. When we don't, we stay stuck in the muck of frame lock.

Trust is demonstrated through action. This principle is where the rubber meets the road on our quest to become self-actualized. The phrase "talk is cheap" is true when our words are not backed by action — and without trust, action never happens. Even ordinary actions like eating food prepared for us by others or using a cell phone would be impossible were we unable to trust in the invisible. Trust is the anchor through which our authority, or lack thereof, becomes translated into its material equivalent. Without it, the CREATE cycle gets clogged, our Voice fades, and the kingdom falls into disarray at the hands of the shadow warriors (Enforcers).

The most immediate indicator of how much we trust Voice comes through the mirror of relationship. Do people light up around us? Do they take our ideas to heart and take inspired action? Unless we trust our Voice, we cannot make this happen. Others must trust us before they will open their hearts and let us ignite their passions. We can say all the right things in exactly the right way, but if we act without deep self trust our calls to action will not get traction. Following their primal gut instincts, people will sense our lack of congruence and retract back into the cave as a means of self-preservation.

As we clear the cave, trust returns. Bringing light to the cave of buried fears that once ruled us, we remove fear at its source. Trusting a gut now firmly aligned with our heart's leadership, we take inspired action that reminds others that shadows are powerless. We don't tell people to trust us — we *demonstrate* our trustworthiness by trusting our inner knowing without hesitation. Sensing this, others feel safe to withdraw their unconscious belief in fear, paving the way for present-moment awareness of their own timeless essence.

Afraid, we are nothing. In Trust, we move mountains.

We must Face the Dark to restore alignment with this principle. There's no way around it. We must leverage our Warrior's disciplined resolve to observe our darkest fears head on without flinching. Until we restore the Emperor and Alchemist, this is difficult because we are still frame locked by the Dividers and Forgetters propaganda. This is why we are wise to focus first on clearing shadows that keep the Emperor and Alchemist from radical alignment before storming the cave with guns blazing. When we follow this proper sequence, we cultivate an inner culture of safety and self-acceptance that helps us see fear for what it is: shadows of the past mocking reality.

Trust is the first and last principle of Voice. In Phase I, we treat trust as if it were gold, hoarding it to protect it from those who might steal it. Thinking this way, we parse our social world up into categories based upon perceived levels of trustworthiness. *This mindset is itself the absence of Trust.* Our need to categorize people as safe or unsafe, good or evil, us or them, worthy or unworthy is conjured by shadow projections from the Enforcer's Cave where our gold is hidden. Thinking this way, we surround ourselves with a like-minded tribe that shares our dogmas. Seeing life through this lens, we cling to beliefs regardless of evidence and make every effort to repress and project emotions that make us uncomfortable.

In Phase II, we enlist the Warrior to help us actively confront and remove the source of our projections. From a Voice Code perspective, the old acronym of FEAR as "False Evidence Appearing Real" is 100% correct. In Phase II we take actions that help us create unmistakably clear evidence that fear is unjustified. In so doing, we reclaim massive creative power, which we harness towards the accomplishment of our highest aspirations.

As our Phase II journey down the mountain proceeds, step-by-step, all of those old triggers that once sent our minds spinning, become powerless to disrupt the courage, confidence and calm presence we exude. When the dust settles, we realize that Trust was never a matter of belief. It was a matter of seeing reality to know ourselves as we truly are: unlimited.

Voice in Action: **Igniting Fortune 100 Inspiration**
Dragon Slayer: **Digital Technology Company**

Shortly after I cracked the Voice Code, I was brought in to speak as one of four thought leaders for a private 1-1/2-day "Innovation Summit" for execs at an IT company. Our assignment: shift thinking to unleash new ideas and solutions. I was the closing speaker. The first three speakers delivered slick, safe presentations. Taking the stage, I realized that I was about to make everyone extremely uncomfortable, as I'd designed a presentation filled with mind bombs that would crack the corporate frame wide open. I took a deep breath and gave it my all. When the speech was over, many seemed confused and out of sorts. The person who hired me looked anxious. "Just wait." I told her. "Let it sink in. You'll be a hero." I must admit: I went to bed that night terrified that I'd never work again. But when we gathered the next morning to harvest ideas, a tsunami of inspiration enveloped the room. Ideas that had seemed scary the day before had gelled in the collective unconscious, and many were now citing my speech and passages from my book as a source of insight. I looked over to see the person who hired me. She was glowing. The moral of the story: Trusting in our Voice can be nerve-wracking at times, but we always — I mean ALWAYS — win when we stick with it.

Worldview Dynamics

Outlaws (Stage 4) vs. Visionaries (Stage 9)

Stage 4 Outlaws and Stage 9 Visionaries anchor Trust for the Plane of Social Control (Stages 5-8). The Visionary worldview is technically five steps and two planes of consciousness ahead of the Outlaw. The Visionary is the first worldview on the Plane of Creative Vision (Stages 9-12), whereas the Outlaw is the last worldview on the Plane of Primal Will (Stages 1-4). Creative tension between these two worldviews anchors the Plane of Control (Stages 5-8) to frame perceptions of fear and desire for people in the developed world. When Phase I Outlaws have the edge in our collective psyche, tribalism drives our thoughts and actions. When Phase II Visionaries hold the power, the call of Voice leads us to collectively face and dissolve fear in the name of shared prosperity.

The impact of this polarity plays out on all scales, from within the minds of individuals, on up through group, societal and global level of analysis. As we move into Stage 9 and beyond, our ordinary sense of time and space breaks down, as the belief in separation dissolves. Our Stage 9 mission is to clear the shadows trapped in the Cave of our primal unconscious since our earliest Outlaw (Stage 4) days. This is a massively liberating experience for those brave Pathfinders (Stage 8) who are ready to embrace their true power.

The shift to Stage 9 Visionary is a landmark achievement in human evolution. It is here that we recognize with unmistakable clarity that *we are our Voice*. This awakening gives us a sense of peace and joy that never goes away, and tremendous power to influence others by our mere presence. But it also raises the stakes on our inner game management skills. Worry not. If you establish a strong Emperor-Alchemist alignment and then summon your Warrior to clear the cave, mighty powers will come to your aid. You will boldly go where others dare to tread and come out unscathed. In so doing, you will be doing the world a bigger favor than you realize, because every bit of early Outlaw energy that we transmute tilts the balance of power between Phase I and Phase II for the entire planet.

The cave is nothing to fear in reality. But until we pass through the valley of Stage 9, we fail to grasp just how much of our power we still invest in fear-based thinking. The journey to full Voice alignment unfolds in logical, orderly stages so that by the time we reach the cave's core, our Emperor's presence is Authoritative, our Alchemist Resonates with inspired precision, and our Warrior is powerfully resolved to reframe Trust in the name of shared thriving.

At this advanced dragon-slaying stage, it becomes clear why knowing our calling is so critical for achieving liberation: the Warrior

Choose Again

Phase I. DEFEND
Develop habit of trusting the shadow through forcing and willful self reliance

Restore Trust

Phase II. CREATE
Transmute Stage 4 Outlaw shadows to reclaim trust in Voice to guide actions

Achiever 6 / Authority \ 7 Explorer

Believer 5 / Resonance \ 8 Pathfinder

Outlaw 4 / Trust \ 9 **Visionary**

Subject 3 / \ 10 Luminary

Outlaw: Trust Ego

In Stage 4, we learn to trust our primal will to get what we want in the present moment. We haven't yet developed a mature adult identity capable of introspection and delay of gratification. In the developed world, most people (about 90%) move through this stage through the inner discipline of potty training. But long-repressed shadow Warrior energies linger in "the Cave" as a limiting factor in our ability to trust our Voice until we transmute them when we reach Stage 9 Visionary.

Visionary: Trust Voice

In Stage 9, we find our calling. By following it, we come to trust our Voice as who we are. Pursuing our vision, we reclaim powerful gifts from the Stage 4 shadow patterns rooted in a buried belief that we are evil. Through this work, we recognize that fear is always unfounded as we dissolve the shadow gap that made our Voice seem like an "other." This fosters a profound new level of trust and faith in the creative mind that governs life.

needs a mission! Without a wholehearted commitment to something larger than our ego, we lack the gumption to stand fully for our Voice in the Warrior expression. But when we commit to our Voice in the service of a transcendent purpose that includes everyone, we become unstoppable in the face of any obstacles.

When the call comes, you will be ready. Once you pass through the valley of buried darkness, you will remember the truth and trust your Voice again. Step by step, the irresistible attraction of freedom will pull you forward until every single bit of fear and pain from the past has been transmuted into power. At the end of the journey you will have no more choices, because you will no longer believe in shadows. You will have reclaimed your power to dissolve all polarities. At this point, all that's left is the truth, and truth is light. The rest was merely shadows.

Battle #3
Arrest the Enforcers | CREATE Power

In the final two scenes of Act II, you'll arrest the Enforcers to Face the Dark and reframe the principle of Trust. After this battle you'll shift from the Phase I "trust fear" framing style to the Phase II "trust Voice" mindset in relation to your mission.

Voice Mentor: **The Warrior** | Gift: **Power**
Shadow Warriors: **The Forgetters**
Active Enforcers: **Punishers (Vanquisher)**
Passive Enforcers: **Prisoners (Victim)**

The Enforcer's Strategy *"Blame the Dark"*

The Enforcers keep us from "Facing the Dark" in alignment with our Voice as it expresses through the Warrior archetype. This chest beating, light fearing group consists of the Punisher and Prisoner. Punishers control us by convincing us that our strength is our weakness. When we believe them, we enlist the Punisher to protect us. This choice reinforces the belief that evil is real and "they" did it. Reacting to this punishing projection, we run to the Prisoner to comfort ourselves with addictive behaviors, cynical beliefs and thoughts of superiority and self-righteousness. The Enforcers have 8 shadow Voices that form four teams. When we avoid or embrace any of them we attempt to blame the dark instead of facing it and lose alignment with the principle of Trust and the 16 gifts of Power that this principle offers through the Warrior.

A Tale of Two Mentors

	Enforcers	Warrior
Trust	Calculation	Action
Assimilate	Capture	Authenticate
Transmute	Magic	Mastery
Evil	Reality	Projection
Discipline	Forcing	Devotion
Innocence	Weakness	Strength

Turning Point

Clear the Cave ~ Week 7

At the end of Scene 12, you'll find an "Arrest the Enforcers" checklist followed by an "Explore the Enforcers" exercise. If you perform these practices you will clear the slate on the past to establish radical alignment across the Emperor, Alchemist and Warrior. To help you create this victory, at the end of Act II (Scene 13) you will receive a new CREATE shadow clearing process called "The Cave Clearer." Handle with care! This experience reverses your ordinary sense of cause and effect to enable stunning breakthroughs in record time through the power of Phase II thinking.

Visit TheVoiceCode.com to get free digital resources, including free training videos and digital copies of key tools offered in this book. You will also find the Voice Code glossary at the end of this book helpful for clarifying and expanding upon any new words, ideas and symbols used.

Scene 12 | *Arrest the Enforcers*

Dragons of Darkness	
The Punisher	**The Prisoner**
Blame ←	→ Resent
Intimidate ←	→ Appease
Threaten ←	→ Withhold

8 Thou Shalts of the Enforcers

Thou shalt *blame the world for thy problems*

Thou shalt *punish thyself eternally for mistakes*

Thou shalt *place great faith in the power of darkness*

Thou shalt *regard thy true strength as weakness*

Thou shalt *gather evidence for the power of evil*

Thou shalt *condemn those who think differently*

Thou shalt *defend thy beliefs even unto death*

Thou shalt *always preserve the status quo*

Once upon a time we chose to avoid discomfort. In this fateful moment, the mighty self-assured Warrior who once protected the kingdom seemed to abandon us. Fearing our own projected power, we split our minds to find safety. This split made fear and love seem like equal and opposing forces battling for our souls. Once we became seduced by this polarizing myth, we came to view gentleness, love and kindness as signs of weakness. We made this choice in a moment of self-forgetting, hoping to protect ourselves. But the disowned aspects of ourselves now trapped within our primal unconscious didn't disappear; we just stopped visiting that area of our mind where we buried the evidence. The part of our primal unconscious beyond the yellow "do not cross" tape is the cave where the Enforcers do their dirty work. The cave is filled with fearful voices telling us that if we bring light to the darkness, we'll be stricken dead. People are naturally afraid of dark caves with howling things. But fear of this cave IS the cave. That's why we must enter it. Until we do, we'll never remember our innocence and behold the beautiful light that shines behind the shadow clouds of doubt.

The Enforcers *Dragons of Darkness*

Great minds go where shadows cannot tread. Doubting the truth of their fears, they enter the cave with the Warrior's courage to reclaim their power. Those who successfully complete this mission change the world, each in their own way. Everyone is called, but most of us are so terrified of the Enforcers that we refuse to listen. Fearing our own power, we keep the Enforcers locked up tight and deny their existence as if our lives depend upon it.

Who among us has the courage to stand firmly for the power of love, knowing darkness as merely the lack of light? When we choose our Voice, we all possess this courage. For most of us, the problem is of avoidance. We've been trained from an early age to believe in "the power of evil." Starting from this faulty premise, we've cultivated countless mental habits that keep us "safe" by projecting our fears outward onto the world.

Once the fear seems to be *out there* we believe we can keep it from conscious awareness as long as we keep "them" (our projection target) out of the picture. Through reactive blame, shame and cynicism we become hypnotized by Enforcer voices that protect old sacred cow dogmas that maintain our projections. But when change threatens our inner control systems, the cave critters are exposed and we are confronted with a primal terror too powerful to deny. This uncomfortable moment is the portal to liberation. We soon realize that we were afraid of nothing — our projections were false and our fears ungrounded. But until this time, we let the Enforcers hoard our power, believing that somehow this keeps us safe.

When our projections no longer keep fear hidden, most of us try first to double down in denial. The rise in fundamentalist thinking and social gridlock that we've witnessed since the turn of the century are symptoms of this dynamic in action on a global scale. This is part of an unprecedented shift through which human culture is finding its collective Voice by learning to battle evil where it actually lives: within those buried caves of the human unconscious. As the old Phase I dogmas collapse, so too are the old cultural institutions that once kept the fires of repressed rage projected outward onto *them* through polarizing ideologies.

As we embark on this heroic journey into the primal cave to restore Trust, please take heart. With all their fire and fury, the Enforcers are merely nothing. Whatever darkness you may perceive, the light within remains pure and innocent. By arresting the Enforcers, you will restore the true Warrior to full power, assimilating any shadow patterns that block your path with the gentle strength that belies your true nature. The courage to see through fear lies in the very heart of visionary leadership. If you Face the Dark with gentle power, you will soon join an elite group of beautiful heretics who are changing the world from the inside out.

Reversing Trust

From "Face the Dark" to "Blame the Dark"

When the Enforcers rule, we trust in fear. This misplaced loyalty is kept in place by a shadow inversion that turns *Assimilating* shadows (CREATE cycle) into *Enforcing* shadow projections (DEFEND cycle). The Voice Warrior stands for the principle of fearless Trust, facing and neutralizing fear with disciplined vigor to help us remember our unbroken wholeness. The Enforcers stand for blame, shame and vicious attack towards anything that threatens the status quo. When this happens, "Face the Dark" becomes "Blame the Dark" and Trust in our Voice becomes impossible.

The diagram on the facing page shows the Enforcer's role in the DEFEND cycle. Just as the true Warrior leads the Axis of Vitality through which the Poet lifts us to joyful exuberance; the Enforcers govern the Axis of Despair, through which our inner light stays heavily guarded beneath dark clouds of undigested grief. When this DEFEND axis functions effectively, the Enforcers convince us to adopt absolutistic, black-and-white beliefs that protect and project our pain outward onto them with smug indifference. When the powerlessness that gave rise to this facade breaks through into conscious awareness, our punitive power-tripping turns into self-loathing. Both are confessions of powerlessness that grow from Enforcer identification. We see many examples of this today in the red-meat polemics of hatred, intolerance and violence that dance across our nightly news.

When sleeping Enforcer dragons awaken, this is a genuine crisis — a moment of great danger *and* opportunity. The outcome we generate is governed by the inner guide we choose to help us navigate the discomfort. Do we choose to honor ancient shadow vows by finding a projection target to blame? Or do we use this opportunity to choose again, trusting in the power of love? When we choose Voice, we win. When we double down on our projections, we add more fuel to the Enforcers' fearful fire.

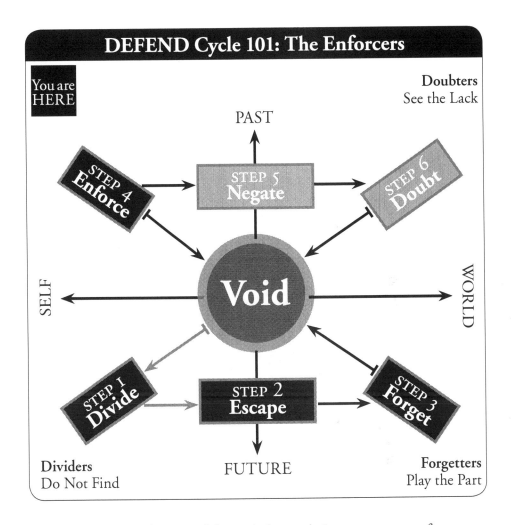

DEFEND Cycle 101: The Enforcers

You are
HERE

Doubters
See the Lack

PAST

STEP 4
Enforce

STEP 5
Negate

STEP 6
Doubt

SELF

Void

WORLD

STEP 1
Divide

STEP 2
Escape

STEP 3
Forget

Dividers
Do Not Find

FUTURE

Forgetters
Play the Part

Once initiated, downward fear-spirals run their course as part of the natural learning process through which the world evolves. With each downward spiral our lessons intensify until we finally get it. Dogmatic beliefs and blame games that once helped us feel safe, soon offer little or fleeting relief, as we begin to attract more and more of what we fear into our experience through the principle of Resonance. For people with an introverted temperament, these shadow cycles often get internalized. This can show up as any number of negative symptoms, including hypertension, anxiety, neurotic compulsions, emotional withdrawal, icy resentments, fits of grieving and unspoken angry judgments and grievances that materialize into tumors and stomach ulcers.[1]

The creative tension that the Enforcers produce within us gives rise to a Punisher-Prisoner routine that stays held in place by our desire to avoid facing our hidden darkness. To the extent that we are willing to calmly stare these old shadow dragons in the eyes, we can release ourselves from a lifetime of limiting beliefs to reclaim massive gifts of power trapped in our primal unconscious. In the next section, you'll see the clever con game the Enforcers run to keep us from claiming our birthright to restore the kingdom.

As we enter the cave, we have now removed enough shadow fuzz to see our true enemy with unflinching clarity. The enemy is not conceptual or logical — it is primal. It is our fear of fear itself — a looping shadow complex that ushers in self-fulfilling prophecies of powerlessness unworthy of the unlimited beings we were born to be. Call the Enforcers' bluff and regain trust in your sovereign Voice Authority to create a life worthy of your highest potential. Let these dusty delusions dissolve back into the void from which they arose. The map is here. The path is clear. The only barrier is belief.

The Enforcers

Vanquisher	"Blame the Dark"	Victim
Punisher ←	OR	→ Prisoner

You can't negotiate with shadow warriors. You can't launch an assault on them either, because attack is the fuel that drives them. The first step to arresting the Enforcers is seeing their secret playbook. Their core strategy for sowing the seeds of mistrust is to keep us safe from imagined threats. The two main characters that orchestrate this process are the Prisoner and the Punisher. These characters are markedly less civilized and more thuggish than those covered so far. Like the happy Warrior who is the Voice muscle that implements the plans sent from the Alchemist, the Enforcers are the shadow muscle that gives the Forgetters' schemes traction.

Once we've buried our fears and projected them outward, the Enforcers caution us to keep our guard up against retaliation, urging us to protect ourselves with attack and evasion. When we expose their reptilian habit patterns, we see first hand that they are powerless. But please don't underestimate how much power they have over us before this moment! This dynamic duo has conspired to keep the human race enslaved by war, violence and other species of fear-based insanity since the birth of culture. We should never be afraid of the Enforcers, but nor is it wise to tread without focused resolve into that ancient inner cave where their energies lurk. Fear is real to those who believe in it; and until we reach Stage 11, we still believe. The Prisoner and Punisher are the reason.

To help you see how the Enforcers steal our will, think of the Prisoner and Punisher as two shady criminals running an elaborate racket. Imagine having a small kitchen fire. You call the fire department. No sooner do you hang up the phone than fire truck arrives, sirens blazing. Two kind and strong firefighters step out of the truck. Grateful, you let them into your house. What you don't realize is that these two strapping saviors are the problem — they set the fire when you weren't looking and then showed up just in the nick of time to save you from it.

The Prisoner comforts you as the strong brave Punisher walks into the house, puts out the fire and steals your precious jewelry from the bedroom safe. Do you suspect anything? Not at all! Why would you? They just saved you from potential death by fire. You feel grateful. Where would you be without them? Thank heavens these fine young fellows arrived so quickly!

Once the smoke clears, you become friends, letting them into your life, consulting them during times of trouble, telling them your deepest secrets, and entrusting them with your most precious belongings. Strangest thing though... The more you hang out with them, the more bad things keep happening to you — burglary, muggings and relationship breakdowns. Fortunately, each time something bad happens, there they are to help out and make things right! You begin to feel dependent on them, wondering how you ever got along without them. True, sometimes you find their behavior questionable and, yes, a few old friends keep worrying about you, wondering why you've been hanging out with these creeps. But they don't understand. They're just jealous.

After losing a few friends, you eventually decide just to keep your new fellowship separate. They become your *special* friends. You understand them and they understand you. That's all there is to it! You forge a special pact that keeps all of you safe in an increasingly dangerous world. The Prisoner becomes like your most trusted confidant. When someone wrongs you, he's right there to comfort you. He never judges you or tells you you're wrong. He's on your side. No matter what happens, he helps you see that you are 100% right. To him, you are infallible like the pope. There's absolutely nothing about your behavior that could be the least bit improved. *How dare anyone suggest otherwise!*

The Punisher becomes a strong heroic father figure. He's forever on the lookout to keep you safe and defend your honor. When you go out in public, he acts like a bodyguard, scanning your surroundings to make sure there's nothing suspicious going on. As a gesture of loyalty he keeps a running a log of anyone who hurts you or does you wrong. When the time is right, he makes sure they get their just deserts. It makes you feel special to be looked after by such a strong, caring person. He's like the father you never had.

But eventually the charm wears off. You begin to feel suffocated. You need some space, but feel guilt and shame for your own disloyalty. Frankly, you also feel no small amount of trepidation at the prospect of setting boundaries. You don't want to hurt their feelings. Also, think about it: if they were so vicious protecting you, what's to stop them from being that same way *towards* you once you draw that line? It's quite a pickle you've gotten yourself into.

More and more you find yourself daydreaming about change. You want to move to a new scene, create a new life for yourself. But it's the damndest thing! Like clockwork, whenever you pull away,

Act II: Slay Thou Shalt

something comes up to remind you how much you need them. Another fire, break in or act of vandalism draws them back into your life again — and always just in the nick of time! How do they do it? They're like white knights in a dark scary world. Seeing their heroism, you remember what a blessing they've been and the fires of loyalty are rekindled. How could you have ever doubted them? What was wrong with you? You'd taken them for granted. You had forgotten what a dangerous world we live in. You solemnly promise that you'll never make that mistake again. *The End.*

Creepy story isn't it? The following sections will help you dive deeper to see the eight different personas that play these two roles. The downward cycle of false intimacy with our inner vandals ends once we clearly see that our trust has been misplaced. To make the scary fires and burglaries stop, we need only to spot their rackets and choose the Voice Warrior's gentle resolve.

Meet the Punishers

The Prosecutor | The Shamer | The Villain | The Sniper

The Punisher voices are like feral pit bulls waiting for us to let them maul whoever deserves our wrath. Most of us keep these thugs locked up tight to keep ourselves from being thrown into shadow prison (or literal prison for that matter). Because of this, few of us have stared these snarling beasts in the eyes long enough to realize that they are unreal. As long as we believe that attack of any kind serves a potentially necessary function, the Punishers have the upper hand. This isn't to say that we might not be called to defend ourselves, but such moments are actually quite rare. When they do occur, we need not fall into states of reactive anger or fear. We need only release fear and let the Warrior handle the situation with honor. The Punishers get us through the belief that we must stay on guard against threats. They do whatever they can to keep us puffed up with false power so that we never learn the true meaning of strength. Punisher patterns seem rational when we're frame locked by survival-based fears. But in reality, they are always completely irrational. They keep us in a state of constant stress, unconsciously inviting attack and trauma through the principle of Resonance.

Toppling The Big Boss

"Who was that?"

Shadow: **The Hammer**
Type: **Enforcer, Punisher (Villain)**
Gift: **Patience**

In Scene 8, you may recall a skulking chain-smoking Divider Wimp figure named Tolstoy Parliament. This shadow figure seemed relatively harmless, but was actually a key figure in an elaborate con to keep me from finding the Big Boss. His main partner in crime was the Hammer, a devilish Prisoner projection of inarticulate rage who reared his head anytime I felt attacked. A week after the Big Boss was removed, this Enforcer became the de facto leader of the shadow mob. In one particularly intense CREATE session, I transmuted both the Hammer and Parliament Tolstoy at the same time. Beneath the Hammer, I discovered the gift of patience — a much-needed skill for delivering ideas as challenging as these. Without this gift, I would be doomed to react with defensive rage whenever challenged. With the gift of patience, I am now much more receptive and gracious when dealing with unloving people and situations. What a relief it is to be free of that raging inner thug!

The Plan: *Flash the Fin*

The Prisoners are masters of suspense. Instead of showing us the whole cave of screaming meemies in one fell swoop, they usually keep it cool, flexing their muscles now and again to create dramatic tension (aka "anxiety"). Most often we experience their presence through a mild sense of irritability that vaguely forebodes something deeper. If our unconscious were the ocean, this would be like seeing a fin poke out of the water and quickly disappear next to us while swimming. "Was that a shark?" we wonder. With teasing threats like these, the Punishers create a persistent low-grade stress that keeps us forever on the lookout for possible attack. This sets the stage for more dramatic Punisher and Prisoner patterns to take over during moments of crisis. Seeing this as a tough love, we all too often embrace the Punisher's guilt trips, believing that this will protect us from future failure. The Punisher's "best" days are those when we have "just cause" to strike out at someone who has wronged us. When unjustly attacked by others, this righteous inner guide goads us to avenge the aggressor, lest we seem weak. When we take the bait, we *become* weak at the hands of the Enforcers.

Mind Game: *The Punisher's Dilemma*

Punishers thrive in the minds of those who believe their power has been stolen. Thinking this way, we get hooked on Punisher energy as a way to "take the power back." As we give these thugs the reins, we get inflated with a jolt of primal energy. But this is just temporary relief to a sense of powerlessness that returns even stronger once the adrenaline fades. When we harbor attack thoughts toward anything (ourselves included) we are implicitly endorsing the belief that separation is real and our Voice *isn't*. Until we release this false premise, the Enforcers keep us trapped no matter how we deal with our upsets. If we get angry but don't express it, we feel pent up like a volcano waiting to erupt. When we finally blow up, we feel temporary relief followed by guilt. This is the Punisher's dilemma.

Many of us attempt to express pent up Punisher energy by sublimating it into socially acceptable outlets where we can blow off steam like work, sports and sexual activity. There's nothing inherently wrong with these activities, but when we do them at the Punisher's behest, they become addictive forms of self-punishment that feed Prisoner guilt and drain our vitality. Over time, exhaustion caused by these sublimation cycles leads many to forge a passionless inner truce through which they trade their Warrior's gifts of power for a lifestyle of boredom and self-coercion.

Best Trick: *The Rope-a-Dope*

The Punisher uses something akin to a famous boxing trick called the Rope-a-Dope to knock us out. In boxing, this is a classic sneak attack strategy in which Boxer #1 holds back, conserving energy as Boxer #2 gives it all he's got. When Boxer #2 begins to tire, Boxer #1 turns on the reserves and pummels the exhausted opponent to oblivion. The Punisher does the same thing to us using the methods described above. Using the Prisoner as a front, the Punisher holds back as we wear ourselves out with thoughts of fear, worry and resignation. When the time is right, the Punishers then offer us ego inflating attack thoughts that give us a sense of false power over imagined threats and oppressors. When we take the bait, we perpetuate deeply dispiriting spirals of mis-creation through this bipolar shadow cycle.

Four Faces of the Punisher

Prosecutors: *These wrathful Punishers control us through our desire for revenge. When we obey them, we attack those who incite our anger and end up feeling guilty. When we react against the Prosecutors, we harbor unresolved grievances that destroy our peace and eat away at us like an emotional cancer.*

Shamers: *These embarrassed Punishers control us through our fear of not being accepted for who we are. When we obey them, we sell out on ourselves by hiding and repressing things about us that don't conform to social expectations. When we react against the Shamers, we intentionally rebel against norms and flout conventions only to alienate ourselves and become frame locked by our own rebellion.*

Villains: *These diabolical Punishers control us through our fear of evil. When we obey the Villains, we constantly look for evil in the world, becoming paranoid, self-righteous or intolerant towards the big "them" we've chosen as our projection target. When we react against the Villains, we fall into denial, failing to recognize evil as a powerful belief operating within our primal unconscious.*

Snipers: *These passive aggressive Punishers control us through our fear of dealing with conflict directly. When we obey them, we communicate our upsets indirectly, through passive-aggressive snipes involving sarcasm, gossip and backhanded compliments. When we react against the Snipers, we express ourselves with a brutally honest candor that offends others and alienates us further.*

Most Wanted Trust Killers: The Punishers

Do any of these Punishers remind you of people from your past?

Which of the Punisher patterns do you find most offensive? What is it that you find so off-putting?

Can you spot any Punisher rackets playing out in your own life?

Have you ever been in a relationship with someone possessed at times by Punisher qualities? Did this make you feel like a Prisoner?

Do any of these voices show up in your own mind when someone offends you? Which one is most familiar? What triggers this?

How has the Punisher limited you in the past? What might be possible once you reclaim your power?

If you had to pick one Punisher voice that you sense has the most power for you to reclaim, which would it be?

Meet the Prisoners

The Hostage | The Cynic | The Addict | The Martyr

The Prisoners are the voices of doom. These passive Enforcer voices siphon our vitality by stoking our sense of powerlessness. When the Punishers stir up attack thoughts, the Prisoners step in to make us feel afraid of acting on our thoughts and guilty for having them. When something inspires us to open our hearts to a new possibility, these are the cynical voices that convince us that there's no point getting our hopes up, reminding us of past failures.

People with a more optimistic and upbeat persona often establish relationships with deflating partners who puncture their bubbles, acting as projected spokesmen for their own Prisoners within. On the other hand, people with darkly cynical personalities become this way by consciously embracing the Prisoner to defend themselves against a deep pool of Punisher rage trapped in their unconscious. In such situations, the negative Prisoner identity becomes an uneasy truce to keep one from feeling both anger and the excruciating sadness that it masks. In all cases, the Prisoners gain their foothold when we attempt to manage fearful feelings without facing them.

After we've reclaimed our power, these games seem silly. But when we're frame locked they seem like the essence of maturity. Once we've resigned ourselves to the belief that separation is reality, the Prisoner's dispiriting voices show up as a comforting emotional salve in an uncaring world. By following them, we numb the pain and create a safe emotional cocoon to hide out in. For those who've suffered from early childhood abuse, this can be a particularly tempting delusion. But when we take the bait, we fail to see that we are making our powerlessness permanent. The only thing the Prisoner's emotional cocoon saves us from is the power we've lost by believing in shadows. This power is freely available in any moment if we but summon our Voice in the Warrior expression.

Toppling The Big Boss

"Who was that?"

Shadow: **Donny the Damned**
Type: **Enforcer, Prisoner (Hostage)**
Gift: **Peace**

A few days after I went to the white light, I was doing the CARE ritual, basking in the radiant afterglow of that experience, when shadows resurfaced. Upon asking for the Warrior's guidance to solve a problem, I got the chilling advice to "stop breathing." As I read these words, a creepy jolt of terror shot through me and I felt violated. When the shock wore off, I deduced that this couldn't possibly be my true Voice speaking. After a brief Voice honeymoon, it seemed that unprocessed shadows left in the Big Boss's wake were now creeping back up into my awareness. I would have to roll up my sleeves and get to work. I named the Punisher energy who said this creepy thing the Hammer (see last section). His Prisoner accomplice was the streak of shock and terror that followed. I named this shadow "Donny the Damned," imagining him as a terrified young boy seeking shelter in a cruel world. Donny formed at the age of four when my parents announced their divorce. By transmuting this Prisoner shadow, I reclaimed the gift of peace. After a lifetime of protecting Donny with the Hammer's punishing bravado, I can now happily report an abiding sense of peace that persists. I used to think inner peace would be boring. How wrong I was! Peace is awesomely engaging. May we all find peace and joy by healing the terrified and damned Donny's trapped in our primal unconscious!

The Plan: *Make Power Immoral*

The Prisoners send us down a rabbit hole of blame that leads us to see weakness as power. To do this, it has us deny our weakness by seeing ourselves as morally superior victims in a corrupt world. The Prisoner patterns brainwash us into thinking this way to help us disassociate from inner pain. When we feel powerless, they help us find a good external target (person, group or condition) to blame it on. Once we buy this logic, we come to accept our powerlessness as "just the way it is" reality. Why worry about something we cannot possibly control? Here's the rub: It's a total lie! The power is still present within us. This makes it impossible for us to fully accept Prisoner beliefs.

When Prisoner logic wears thin, and the pain breaks through again, the Enforcers often double down on projections by moralizing, equating all power with evil. By judging those in power as corrupt and therefore weak, they define our weakness as power attained through moral superiority. Through this method, the Prisoner Voices convince us to give our power away, adopting absolutistic dogmas and enforcing a harsh regimen of moral self-righteousness. This mindset breeds dogmatic, passive-aggressive cultures of denial in which the blame games flourish and the immense mass of undigested pain in our collective psyche stagnates in darkness.

Mind Game: *War on Evil*

Framing weakness as power, we naturally come to see the puffed up Punisher patterns as our saviors. They validate our aggression and help us maintain the delusion of strength we've conjured to compensate for our sense of powerlessness. But the con isn't complete until the Prisoners persuade us to believe that evil is a real and pervasive existential threat against which we must wage eternal warfare. This last step serves to institutionalize powerlessness and makes separation seem like an obvious fact of reality.

Consider for a moment that evil is merely a belief caused by habitual shadow identification. If this is true, then the whole battle between good and evil isn't real — it's an Enforcer's ruse, which plays itself out only in the minds of confused, frame-locked people. *But confused or not, our minds never lose their creative power, even when we're deeply deluded.* So when we believe in evil, it becomes very real to us. Left unchecked, it consumes us, turning us into human shadow puppets who perform atrocious acts to "overcome evil" and then justify this insanity in the name of all things holy. Most of us don't take Enforcer affliction to this extreme, but any time we embrace polarizing beliefs about a morally inferior *them*, we are being seduced into a mindset that leads us down this same slippery slope.

Best Trick: *Screaming Meemies Closet*

The Prisoner shadow warps our thinking until we are terrified of looking inside and ashamed of our own humanity. Seeking safety in darkness, we feel lost without the very beliefs that enslave us. Thankfully, we eventually reach an inner tipping point after which the pain of not changing becomes intolerable. It is here that we surrender the blame game and finally call "bullshit" on the whole shadow parade. When this happens, we discover, with great relief that our fears were unjustified. Seeing the light, we come to know evil as a mere optical delusion. To keep us from discovering this, the Enforcers have one last firewall protection for their fortress of lies: a closet of screaming terror deep within the darkest unlit corner of the cave. No one wants to open this closet! Oh the horror!

Of course, when we finally do open it, we find that it was a bunch of sound and fury signifying nothing. But having spent so much of our lives making this closet real by avoiding it, most of us don't dare admit to even *having one* until the last possible moment.

Four Faces of the Prisoner

Hostages: *These suffocating Prisoners control us through our fear of loss. When we obey them, we defend situations and relationships that limit us in fear that we will never find anything better. When we react against the Hostages, we become wild cards, making impulsive and often foolhardy decisions to escape limiting or frustrating circumstances without considering the cost.*

Cynics: *These jaded Prisoners control us through our fear of being disappointed. When we obey them, we defend ourselves against optimism to avoid getting our hopes up and end up living lives of boring mediocrity. When we react against the Cynics, we become blind optimists who fail to fully consider the facts when confronted with potentially promising opportunities and rush headlong into them only to end up disappointed.*

Addicts: *These obsessive Prisoners control us though our fear of being unhappy. When we obey them, we give ourselves over to compulsive habits that bring us fleeting pleasure, but which foster dependency and undermine our freedom. When we react against them, we develop a rigid and harshly repressive attitude towards pleasure that becomes a freedom killing addiction in and of itself.*

Martyrs: *These self-punishing Prisoners control us through our guilt over being selfish. When we obey them, we do the right thing for the wrong reasons, "selflessly" giving to others, but feeling resentful when they don't reciprocate. When we react against the Martyrs, we act with a sense of shameless entitlement, failing to consider others in any way, as our lives become a prison of projected resentment.*

Most Wanted Trust Killers: The Prisoner

Do any of these Prisoners remind you of people from your past?

Which of the Prisoner masks do you find most repulsive? What is it that repels you?

Can you spot any Prisoner rackets playing out in your own life?

Have you ever been in a close relationship with someone strongly identified with a Prisoner? How did you deal with them? Did they sometimes trigger you to become punishing towards them?

Do any of these Prisoner voices show up in your thoughts? Can you see how they collaborate with the angry Punisher voices?

How has the Prisoner limited you? If asked to pick one Prisoner that has the most power for you to reclaim, which would it be?

The Enforcer's Beloved
Doubters: Dragons of Despair

When we fall into the Enforcers' traps, we do so to avoid the most dreaded shadow patterns of all: the Doubters. The Doubters are the grieving shadow poets — those sad voices of hopelessness and unfulfilled longing that have been swirling about in the deepest depths of our primal unconscious since the womb. The Enforcers protect these sad sacks like a mobster protects his stash, and for a good reason: once we dissolve the Doubters, the whole shadow mob regime comes tumbling down! The anchor of shadow logic that once kept us frame locked dissolves as we remember our innocence and behold the Poet unfiltered. Knowing this, the shadow keeps the Doubters well hidden and fortified through that pitch black wall of punishing and imprisoning darkness we call the cave.

The Axis of Despair that the Enforcers lead (in cahoots with the Doubters) cannot function unless we make it a personal policy to avoid facing our fears. The Prisoner and Punisher are the shadow's primary bulwark to keep our illusions of powerlessness locked in place. Beyond this cave of idle threats, the Enforcer's sickly concubine plays the sanguine harp of abandonment and innocence lost. Of course, the Doubter's siren song is a shadow charade also. But before we clear the cave we hear that song only dimly, as a faint

251

wistful echo of loss that we dare not dive into for fear of being consumed with eternal sadness.

This partnership is quite tragic until we see through it. Then it seems hilarious that we could've ever believed the hype. If you aren't yet stricken with divine laughter just yet, worry not. The shadow always loses in the end. It has to lose because it isn't real and YOU are. This is pure common sense if you think about it. Thankfully, common sense has finally been made actionable with this new map. If you follow the step-by-step path to mastery laid out in this book, you will peel away layer upon layer of old shadow energy until you know first-hand, beyond any doubt:

Your Voice can't lose, because there's no competition.

Consider those *dark night of the soul* experiences that precede all great breakthroughs. When this phenomenon happens, people confront their worst fears, and the lights go on. This always happens right when they least expect it for a reason: because our expectations were based upon old Enforcer patterns that had us believe bad things would happen if we faced our darkness. But those expectations *were* the darkness. By facing the source of the projection, we remove the cause and see the truth. *Truth and light are one.* This has always been the case, with or without the Voice Code. What's cool about this new map is that it helps us dispel darkness without all the drama. Dark nights no longer required. How cool is that?

When the sense of powerlessness caused by the Enforcers reaches a tipping point, the projection of Punisher rage no longer works. We are then forced to retract the projection from our target *them*, remembering it as something within our own mind. When the frame lock breaks, we release the past, see the light and become One with our essence. It's a beautiful day! We feel reborn and in many ways we are. We have shed the false layers of death inside that we once mistook for reality. This gives us a second chance at life, even if we are 87 years old with very little time left:

There's always time to choose again.

Here's a big idea to ponder: What if choosing again is what time is really for? Wouldn't that be something? In other words, what if remembering our innocence is time's true purpose? If we thoroughly consider the logic of the Voice Code's 12-stage developmental path, we are hard pressed to come up with any other interpretation. Once we reach Stage 9, we no longer experience clock time on a subjective level. By Stage 12, we have cleared every bit of shadow in our unconscious to become One with our Voice. After that, what purpose could time serve other than to revel in timelessness? Could this happy ending be the true meaning of the so called *end of time*? What if those frightful armageddonist prophecies are all just fearful notions from Phase I thinkers frame locked by shadow projections? What if the real end of time is the beginning of life without separation in the white light of Stage 13?

Wouldn't that be something?

Well, there's only one way to find out for sure: evidence. We need first-hand evidence. Everything else is just hearsay and conjecture. Our next step is to summon the Warrior to Arrest the Enforcers and clear the cave of Trust. Only then will we be ready to face and dissolve those Doubters and see the light for ourselves. Then we'll know the truth in no uncertain terms.

As you may still be new to dragon slaying, let me offer one final piece of hard won advice. Please understand that the Enforcers are sneaky. They pull their punches and bide their time, letting the Forgetters and Dividers do the heavy lifting. There is only one sure-fire way to know that you are winning in the battle to reclaim your power from this group: they get desperate and start overplaying their hand. This is when you know you've got them cornered! It's as if the Enforcers are trying to beat their chest and scare us away from the grand prize. When undigested Punisher rage reveals itself to you full throttle through extreme overreactions to minor things, this is often a very good sign. Old chunks of rage are coming up because the Enforcer's secret cave has started to crumble.

If this happens to you, don't be alarmed. Stay calm, focused and resolved. Don't let these hooligans trick you back into frame lock before you've cleared the cave. Deal? If you have taken the process one step at a time, starting with the Emperor and Alchemist, when you reach this point, you will be so rooted in your Voice that you'll see through the silliness before it gets out of hand. The Poet's happy light will help you laugh away fear to remember the obvious.

Enforcer Habit · **CREATE Power** · Gift of Trust

16 Gifts of the Warrior

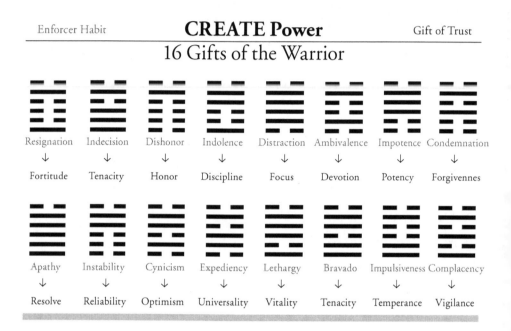

Resignation	Indecision	Dishonor	Indolence	Distraction	Ambivalence	Impotence	Condemnation
↓	↓	↓	↓	↓	↓	↓	↓
Fortitude	Tenacity	Honor	Discipline	Focus	Devotion	Potency	Forgivennes

Apathy	Instability	Cynicism	Expediency	Lethargy	Bravado	Impulsiveness	Complacency
↓	↓	↓	↓	↓	↓	↓	↓
Resolve	Reliability	Optimism	Universality	Vitality	Tenacity	Temperance	Vigilance

Who you are could never be punished and imprisoned by dusty wind-up toys made for children. The Enforcers are those toys. Choose again, clear the cave, and be free forever.

Week 7. Face the Dark (checklist)

Step 1. Capture: Probe and inquire to uncover Enforcer habit patterns and insights using the inquiry exercise (below).

Step 2. Consolidate: Place Enforcer habits uncovered in the Trust section of your shadow insights file as part of your ongoing shadow pattern research archives.

Step 3. Clear the Path: Use the CREATE goal process to transmute top 3 Enforcer patterns uncovered (Days 1-3) THEN: Use the Cave Buster (see Scene 13. Clear the Cave) at least twice (Days 4 - 5) to transmute most potent fears trapped in the cave.

Step 4. Compare: At week's end compare gifts reclaimed through the CREATE script with the 16 Gifts of the Warrior in the CREATE Power graphic above.

Step 5. Calculate: Perform follow up self-assessment rating between 0 and 10 on each gift where 0 = Enforcer Habit and 10 = Warrior Gift. Total responses to calculate updated Warrior Quotient (WQ) between 0 and 160. Note any changes from baseline WQ rating taken in week 3 (Scene 4. Embrace the Warrior).

Step 6. Connect: On Day 6 of week 7, perform CARE ritual (Scene 6) Consult with Voice mentors to align fully with Voice and determine best next steps to achieve your milestone mission.

Step 7. Complete: On Day 7, release the week and revel in the moment. This will help you release the cycle and pave the way for the next round (Week 8. See the Light).

Rebuild Trust *Explore the Enforcers*

The inquiry exercise on the next page will help you find areas of Enforcer resistance that you can process to reclaim the 16 gifts of power that the Warrior offers. While this chapter is still fresh on your mind, be sure to capture surfacing patterns and insights before the Enforcers sneak back into the cave. To set the stage for a powerful shadow exploration session, you want to first get into the right state of mind. Consider first priming and grounding with the *Choose Trust* Warrior invocation process at the end of Scene 4.

Prospect: *Observe the Journey*

Please take a moment to review your inner journey while reading the chapter. Play detective. Enter a state of objectivity and expectant curiosity. Imagine that you are a shadow detective hired to help crack the Case of the Enforcers. Page through and recall your inner landscape while reading this chapter. Notice what you notice. Capture any patterns. Expect the unexpected. Keep heart and mind open to whatever arises.

Exploratory Insights: *What stood out from your exploratory review? Please make sure to capture any potentially helpful clues that came to you, however faint or dimly felt.*

Probe: *Expose the Enforcers*

Step 1: Review Most Wanted. The questions in the MOST WANTED TRUST KILLERS section are particularly helpful for uncovering Enforcer patterns. If you haven't yet considered them, please do so now. If you have, review your earlier answers/insights again before moving forward.

Step 2: Associative Inquiry. Please reflect upon the 11 questions below. As you do, gently observe your inner experience to note nudges of resonance and resistance.

1. As you read this chapter, what resonated most? Did anything jump out as particularly relatable, insightful or relevant? What was it and why?

2. While reading, did you at any point feel defensive, as if you or someone you know was being unfairly characterized? If so, what triggered this response?

For questions 3-7 please refer to the 8 Enforcer profiles below.

8 Faces of the Enforcers

Prosecutors: *These aggressive Punishers control us through our desire for revenge and incite attack against those who offend us.*

Shamers: *These embarrassed Punishers control us through our fear of rejection, leading to hiding and defensive aggression.*

Villains: *These diabolical Punishers control us through our fear of evil and drive intolerant self righteousness.*

Snipers: *These passive aggressive Punishers control us through our fear of conflict, and make us prone to mean spirited snipes.*

Hostages: *These suffocating Prisoners control us through our fear of losing that which we currently possess.*

Cynics: *These jaded Prisoners control us through our fear of being disappointed by getting our hopes up.*

Addicts: *These obsessive Prisoners control us through our fear of being unhappy, leading to compulsiveness and dependency.*

Martyrs: *These self-punishing Prisoners control us through our guilt for being selfish and our desire for redemption.*

***

3. **Can you see any connections between these Enforcers and your own personal or professional limitations, past or present?**

4. **Do any of these remind you of difficult people you've known or worked with? If so, who were they and how so?**

5. **When it comes to achieving your mission, what Enforcer pattern would be the most likely to keep you frame locked?**

6. **When it comes to actualizing your life's calling, which of these Enforcer Voices would be most likely to block your path?**

7. **All things considered, which Enforcer has had the biggest influence in keeping you from trusting your Voice?**

8 Thou Shalts of the Enforcers

Thou shalt *blame the world for thy problems*

Thou shalt *punish thyself eternally for mistakes*

Thou shalt *place great faith in the power of darkness*

Thou shalt *regard thy true strength as weakness*

Thou shalt *gather evidence for the power of evil*

Thou shalt *condemn those who think differently*

Thou shalt *defend thy beliefs even unto death*

Thou shalt *always preserve the status quo*

For questions 8-11, reflect on the 8 Thou Shalts of the Enforcers.

8. Which of these Thou Shalts are you most likely to follow as a matter of habit?

9. Which of these Thou Shalts are you most likely to repress?

10. Which Thou Shalt bothers you most in others?

11. All things considered, which Thou Shalt has had the strongest influence to keep you from trusting your Voice?

Visit TheVoiceCode.com to get free digital resources, including free training videos and digital copies of key tools offered in this book. You will also find the Voice Code glossary at the end of this book helpful for clarifying and expanding upon any new words, ideas and symbols used.

Scene 13 *Clear the Cave*

Overview

The tools in this section help you align with the Warrior's courage to clear the cave on any issue. This process goes straight for the gut. No other tool in the Voice Code arsenal allows us to dive so deeply to generate such powerful results so quickly. But because this process is so potent, I highly recommend that you not attempt to use it until you've become comfortable with the tools already offered (in Scene 6. Become a Lion). If you build a firm foundation with the CARE ritual and CREATE script, you'll find the CAVE Buster process to be a radically efficient shadow clearing solution that adds a new level of power and primal vitality to your practice.

Applications

Use the tools in this section to transform anything that makes you feel fearful, powerless or limited. Literally *any* problem can be healed through this process. Below are a few ways in which these tools can be used to cause powerful and permanent breakthroughs.

- **Money Shadows:** Rich and poor people alike often feel trapped and disempowered by money. Whenever money shadows rear their ugly heads, transmute them and watch your financial life transform.
- **Family Issues:** Clear up family and relationship issues that seem hopeless by healing shadows around charged topics like infidelity, abuse, divorce, and longstanding grudges.
- **Social Polarization:** Clear the cave on polarizing social topics like sexuality, politics, violence and religion to escape fear and come to peace with the larger global and cultural issues of our day.
- **Addictions:** Any addictive patterns in your life can be released in record time. Dependencies can be chemical or mental in nature. All addictions are forms of frame lock caused by shadow projections.

These claims may seem audacious, but they are true. Through this natural process you can achieve peace and empowerment to solve literally any problem, as you change your world from the inside out. I have personally created miracles for myself with this process in each of the above categories and I have helped many others do the same for their lives.

If you are looking for the rub, here it is: *clearing the cave with these tools requires total commitment and can be very uncomfortable.* We must be willing and able to say, "It's a good day to die," and go full-Warrior from the start, jumping headfirst into whatever fear we've been avoiding. This isn't always fun, but is **always** worthwhile--as long as we do so from a loving state of Voice alignment.

[**Special acknowledgment:** *The "CAVE Buster" process (Tool #2) was influenced by Robert Scheinfeld's bestseller "Busting Loose of the Money Game." In the "The Path to Mastery" section at this book's conclusion I give more information about this and other* *complementary Phase II resources.*]

Tool Descriptions

The two new tools that comprise this process are previewed below. Use them consecutively or separately depending upon time availability and your situational needs.

Tool #1 Have FUN
Find • Uncover • Name
(**Average time:** 20 minutes)

The Have FUN process is an advanced alchemist exploration tool that helps you uncover and profile highly charged shadow patterns trapped deep in the cave. Following this three-step process, you will map, name and commit to clearing highly charged shadow patterns that have been holding you back. *Don't worry about answering every question perfectly. Just have fun and do your best.* Even the process of attempting to ask these questions sheds light on old shadow patterns and begins to dissolve limitations. Note: the Have Fun process was originally designed to work as a prelude to the CAVE Buster process but can also be used as a stand-alone shadow mapping tool. Shadow patterns uncovered can also be processed using the CREATE Script (Scene 6. Become a Lion).

Tool #2 CAVE Buster
Call • Authorize • Validate • Express
(**Average time:** 45 minutes)

The CAVE Buster leverages Voice Code logic to help you drive powerful change by embracing a highly advanced Phase II mindset. *This tool calls us to see ourselves as the 100% author of everything we perceive.* Once we pass through the veil of discomfort that comes with claiming full responsibility, we release our projections and remember ourselves as our Voice. As external problems dissolve, we gain first-hand evidence for the central theme that underlies this book: we *literally* CREATE the world from the inside out. This script goes straight for the shadow's jugular to produce results that would be magical if they weren't also predictable and scientifically explainable using Voice Code logic.

Best Practices

Here are a list of pointers to help you use the Clear the Cave process effectively and efficiently within minimum discomfort:

1. **Commit fully.** Remember the old saying about commitment: 99% is impossible, but 100% is easy. This is very true when it comes to cave clearing. You can't phone it in. Throw yourself into it with a strong will, open mind and receptive heart. This process works wonders, but you must be willing to burn the bridges to your past.

2. **Pick an emotionally urgent problem.** Because your life is essentially a hologram, every problem is contained within every problem. So when choosing an issue, prioritize your selection based on the level of negative emotional charge it carries. If you have a specific urgent problem, choose that one. If you are finding yourself unmotivated or distracted, consider selecting a different topic. Trust your instincts. In general, whatever limitation you are experiencing most acutely in the present moment is the best one to work on.

3. **Expect freaky miracles.** Because our Phase I world taught us to believe that life is an outside-in affair, experiencing outer breakthroughs through inner work can seem surreal at first. Expect to freak out a bit to see real evidence "randomly" showing up as you use these tools. This is an amazing and highly liberating process, but it can be a bit disruptive to our ordinary sense of reality.

4. **Lather, Rinse, Repeat.** The CAVE Buster (Tool #2) might as well be called the "ball buster." It acts like bodybuilder training for your Voice muscles. For particularly tough, longstanding issues you perform this process at least 6 days per week for a *minimum* of two weeks. Also, if you are truly committed to mastery, I'd encourage

you to do this script consistently, at least once a week, on whatever area of your life feels most limited at that appointed time. Make this a cherished ritual in your ongoing practice. The more you use it, the more you will enjoy the process and the more powerful you will become. Be prepared to keep raising the bar as your mastery increases.

Final Note:

Part I is an exploration that helps you find and process a highly charged area of shadow resistance to work on. If you are not ready to do this, please do not force it. If you are sure you are ready and you already have an emotionally urgent issue that you are ready to clear, you can skip forward to the CAVE Buster (Part II) immediately.

Part I.

Have FUN

Step 1: Find the fear
Step 2: Uncover the patterns
Step 3: Name the mandate

Step 1: Find the fear

For help finding a highly charged shadow pattern to work with, consider the questions below in a spirit of detached curiosity. As you do, monitor your inner experience for any dread or desire to avoid diving deeper. These are tell tale signs that you are on the right track! The more charged the pattern, the more power you will reclaim.

1. What am I most afraid of?

2. Where in my life do I feel most disempowered?

3. If I died today, what would be my biggest regret?

4. What am I most afraid that others will find out?

5. What am I most afraid to admit to myself?

6. Where in my life am I selling myself short?

7. What excuses would most likely stop me from doing the work required to actualize my full potential?

Take a moment to review your answers and your inner experiences as you considered these questions. Let your Voice direct you as to the best topic to tackle in today's session. When you have selected a topic, move to Step 2.

Step 2: Uncover the patterns

Your next step is to do more in-depth processing on the topic chosen in Step 1 above. Prime your Alchemist's curiosity as you consider each of the following questions in sequence.

TRIGGERS: What triggers the fear, resistance and discomfort that you associate with this problem?

REACTIONS: When you get triggered, what emotions surface? How do you react? How do others react to you?

ASSOCIATIONS: Where have you experienced this energy before? What does it remind you of? What is your earliest memory of this pattern?

COST: How does this shadow pattern limit you? How has it prevented you from actualizing your highest potential? If nothing changes, how will this affect your future?

PERSONA: If these shadow energies were in some way personified, what might the character look like? If it had a catch phrase, what would it be?

QUALITY: If you had 20 seconds to pick just 3 words to describe the feeling tone or quality that this character exudes, what words would you use?

BELIEF: If this character had one belief that it held as an absolute dogma, what would this belief be? (State in one clear sentence.)

FUNCTION: How does this character promise to protect you? What does it seem to protect you from? What is the one thing it wants to make sure you NEVER find out?

Step 3: Name the mandate

The heart of this shadow pattern contains your gift, which you will soon reclaim using the CAVE Buster process in Part II. Whatever it is, you can be sure it will be the mirror opposite of whatever is currently showing up through frame locked lenses.

GIFT: What gift would you imagine might waiting for you to reclaim by transmuting these shadow energies?

Now, Choose Again.

Name the mandate by reading the statement below aloud, hand on heart, in front of a mirror.

"I hereby commit to reclaiming the gift of my Voice essence now trapped within this shadow pattern. I created this delusion through my own free will during a moment of misguided choosing. I now choose again. I now choose to uncreate it, in a new moment of courage, clarity and reverence for the creative mind that governs life.

"The past is over. My mind is made up. The problems of lack and limitation that this pattern represents are no longer welcomed. Today marks a new day of thriving in the service of truth and the pursuit of my life's highest purpose."

Part II.

CAVE Buster

Step 1: Call the Warrior
Step 2: Authorize Trust
Step 3: Validate power
Step 4: Express gratitude

Step 1: Call the Warrior

A. Summon the Warrior

The Warrior thinks through courageous action in the service of a transcendent principle or purpose. To invoke the Warrior's energy, take a moment to consider a time you took bold, instinctual action in the service of a principle that matters to you. Summon that feeling of fearless courage and resolve rooted in your gut. Let this energy expand within you. Become one with it. This is how your Voice feels in the Warrior expression. Take a few breaths. Let this state sink in for at least one full minute. When you are ready, hold this state as you place your hand on your heart and recite the following:

"With profound respect and reverence for life, I now invoke the Warrior's power, that I may face the dark with indomitable courage, focused mental discipline and principled resolve.

"As I make this invocation, I humbly acknowledge that the Warrior's creative energies are far more powerful than my everyday ego. This request is made in good faith. My mission is rooted in my wholehearted desire to make a positive difference for everyone, in honor of truth and in defense of that which is beautiful and innocent at the heart of life.

"Today, in spirit of reverence and gratitude for the many gifts the Warrior has already given, I vow to receive and assimilate any guidance this sacred mentor might offer to help me reclaim my power from these old shadow patterns that now limit me."

Hold the state of empowered reverence and resolve that these words evoke for one full minute before moving on. Observe your inner state. Allow gratitude that you have access to this mighty inner power. Give thanks to your Voice in the Warrior expression. Let your heart and mind open to connect in conscious appreciation of the many blessings available to you through the Warrior.

B. Face the Dark

[Note: When done properly, Part B. can take 30 minutes or more. For best results, stick with it until you feel a shift and you no longer resist shadow emotions. The effectiveness of the next three steps in this process depend on how thoroughly we give ourselves to this first step.]

Consider the topic you have chosen for this exercise.

When you are ready, dive into the discomfort and feelings of resistance associated with this topic. Let your underlying feelings of powerlessness surface. Breathe into it and experience it to the limits of your ability. Your goal is to scrape up as much of the hidden darkness as you can. Let yourself completely identify with it. Don't self-medicate with excuses. Peel those shallow layers and let yourself experience the raw, uncivilized energy beneath the surface. *Don't hold back. To never have to deal with this issue again, feel it fully now and be done with it.* Amplify whatever discomfort you may have. Revel in it until you have defused its power.

Consider taking the situation to its worst possible conclusion. Give yourself to the discomfort. Die to this problem so that it is gone forever. The Warrior's wisdom was perfectly stated by Eckhart Tolle who said, "Death is a stripping away of all that is not you. The secret of life is to die before you die - and find that there is no death."[1]

Since you are unlimited, the pain you feel in relation to this problem *is* the problem. It's nothing to be afraid of. Feel it fully. Negate the shadow's power by no longer resisting the problem. Give up hope of ever solving the problem. Surrender to those buried feelings of hopelessness without apologies or preconditions.

Hopelessness is unproductive when doing everyday tasks, but it is *very* productive when it comes to clearing the cave. Beneath hopelessness we find our fear of death. Beneath this fear, we find the light that is our true essence. So dive in completely — as if the pain underneath were the truth, the whole truth and nothing but the truth. See how this pain has limited you in every area of your life.

When your fear reaches a level of agony, this usually means you are getting close. Keep at it. Stand firm and feel it fully. Don't bow down to distracting shadow voices that would have you cut bait too soon. Stand your ground. *When you finally surrender to your powerlessness, all struggle will stop.* You will feel a thread of peaceful possibility arise — the calm after the storm. When you sense that you've reached this place, move to Step 2 below.

Step 2: Authorize Trust

Read the script below aloud, embodying the words with your whole being. This script has been tested and refined many times and works beautifully. However, the specific words are not nearly as important as your *inner state* when delivering them. Do your best to own them fully and with passion. If any words stir up resistance, feel free to adapt with language that works for you. Most important: give yourself to the process as fully as you can without forcing.

"I am the unlimited creative power of the entire universe. My mind is creating every single detail of this situation. In truth, I am doing all of this to myself.

"I have created this situation as the perfect opportunity to wake myself up, right here and now. What I'm now experiencing as discomfort is actually an opportunity in disguise, an emotional thread of connection to my Voice.

"This thread is only uncomfortable because I have bought into an illusory separate self that I am now in the process of transmuting to reclaim my lost power.

"When I created and identified with this shadow pattern, I became split-minded and projected my power outward. This left me feeling powerless. I then came to believe that this projection was real and that it was authored outside of me by something other than me. *This is how I came to forget my true identity.* This problem is a message from the real me, my Voice, who has never changed and who is not fooled one bit by my pretensions of powerlessness.

"I have been frame locked by shadow projections masquerading as truth, willfully chosen to shield myself from my own unconscious guilt and terror of being annihilated.

"Here's the simple truth: I created this problem. It's all inside my head. There is no out-there, and there is no one to blame. I did it. Then, after creating this problem and believing it, I bought into the trap of trying to fix, change, or control it. This further reinforced the seeming-truth of the shadow projections that led me to perceive the problem as real in the first place.

"Until this moment, I have preferred to believe that this problem was real rather than to let it go. *Believing in this problem has helped me feel safe.* Until now, I wasn't prepared to accept the immense power of my own mind. I was afraid of my power. That is why I projected it out onto the world. My mind was split. That is why I felt unsafe. I was running from my own light. But that game is over. I have decided to let this split be healed at the level of cause.

"I am now waking up by releasing old illusions. As I become disillusioned, I naturally feel a raw sense of discomfort and vulnerability. But these are just more shadow patterns arising to be healed from the inner cave where I buried them. Before now, I projected these feelings out onto the world through blame, shame and other shadow games. I am now removing the original cause that gave rise to the appearance of lack and limitation. I am removing the darkness that the light of truth might return.

"From this moment forward, let me remember:

"*I am creating this.* This is *my* kingdom happening in *my* consciousness. All of it. It always was and always will be 100% me, only me, and nothing else.

"My true mind is the creative source that designs and amplifies the patterns that I experience as the world around me.

"The real me is creating the whole game; inner game and outer game, the entire situation and every single thing in it, including my feelings about it, both pleasant and unpleasant. I created it all. Exactly as it is right now. Every single detail, no matter how minute, is something I created and is perfectly orchestrated in space-time to help me learn this lesson and wake up to remember my Voice.

"I will continue to create and re-create situations of powerlessness like this as long as I remain committed to the shadow projections that make them seem real.

"The call of this moment is to restore honor and integrity to the kingdom by transmuting any shadow energies associated with this problem."

[Please be silent and consider the question below intently, as if being asked directly from your Voice]

Voice: *"Are you willing to place your trust in me and be free of this issue forever? Yes or No?"*

If you feel an inner nudge that says "yes" continue to Step 3. If "no" or if "yes" with hesitation, consider returning to Step 1 to more fully process the feelings before moving forward.

Step 3: Validate power

You've now laid the groundwork to reclaim your power. Please continue reading aloud, doing your best to embody these words with your whole body, mind and being.

"I now choose to put this particular lesson behind me, once and for all. I now choose my Voice. With firm resolve and humble reverence, I petition the creative mind that orchestrates life to help me create a new, more expansive and life-serving pattern in this area of my life. I release my fears. I release my old shadow commitment to maintaining a separate will apart from my Voice on this issue. That cycle of mis-creation is now over. I now choose truth, the whole truth and only the truth in this area of my life.

"I am the sovereign authority of the kingdom of my mind. Nothing happens until I choose it. Change will happen when I choose it, and I choose it now.

"As the [man/woman/person] that I have always known I could be, I now make a clear, unwavering choice to stand for the truth. By the power of life within me, I now banish these shadows from my mind. I forbid them to influence my free will. I now reclaim my rightful throne at the inner altar through which my Voice speaks.

"I now fully and permanently reclaim my creative power from this projection and from the false ego identity I had mistaken for 'me' when this problem seemed real.

"With great love and respect, I petition the divine mind for assistance. I accept all help, refusing nothing. I am here, I am open, and I am willing. I am ready to receive my gifts again. I am ready to release the past and come home now to Truth.

[As you read the following parts, let yourself feel power from the problem rushing back into your body. Let it flow up from the earth and down from the heavens. You might imagine the original problem as a dusty old black and white snapshot, and as the energy returns everything becomes vivid, animated and alive with color. The most important thing is to feel it in your body. Receive the power with every cell in your body and every fiber in your being. Pause after each sentence to feel the words fully before moving forward.]

"I reclaim my power *now*.

"As the power returns, I feel it coursing through me, head to foot, a circuit of truth from the core of the earth, spiraling upward through my head, connecting me with the heavens, opening to dimensions that before were blocked.

(Pause to receive)

"I allow the flow to channel through me unabated, permanently removing any obstructions that kept me from accessing this power only moments ago.

(Pause to receive)

"The light, love and power that streams through me binds me with unspeakable gratitude and reverence to the timeless ground of being from which consciousness emerges.

(Pause to receive)

"As I receive the power, I feel it surging through me in my heart, gut, and every cell of my body. This fullness is the simple truth of who I am: the unlimited creative power of life expressing itself in human form.

(Pause to receive)

"I am awake again. I have released the past to clear the future of the clouds that kept me playing small. I am free. I have been forgiven, because I have chosen to forgive myself for what never really happened. It is done. The delusions dissolved. My power reclaimed. The kingdom restored.

"I ask the creative source that governs life to remove every data point from the past around this issue, to help me learn this lesson fully, that I may be more helpful to the kingdom that I had temporarily disowned.

(Pause to release)

"I am now willing to accept healing for everyone around this issue in the service of my life's true calling, releasing any illusions that keep me from so doing.

(Pause to release)

"I have given up my belief in the cause of my suffering and am now receiving the solution that was waiting. I let anything that might block this acceptance go, clearing it forever.

(Pause to release)

"Love is returning to my mind as light from a parting cloud. I am calm. I feel the entire hopeless paradigm of power outside melting into the peaceful bliss of the timeless present. I need not believe myself worthy or even understand. Truth is the experience of revelatory knowing beyond the bounds of mere symbols. It is absolutely unfathomable to my everyday mind and yet it is also nothing more than my Voice unfiltered.

(Pause to receive)

"Peace is my power. Innocence is my strength. Love is my essence. These gifts reside beyond time, in the full alignment of the entirety of my being, right here and right now. I feel this returning power surge grounding me into an unlimited state. A state of deep, unconditional love and joyful acceptance of all that is."

Pause. *Tune into your body, heart and mind. Don't judge, think or analyze. Just open to receive whatever is present for 3 full minutes before moving forward to Step 4.*

Step 4: Express gratitude

You've now assimilated and transmuted the shadow energies to reclaim your power. The final step is to bring this process full circle and lighten the tone by reframing the present moment from this new expanded perspective, expressing gratitude for the process. When you are ready, read the script below, hand on your heart.

"As my power returns, I feel myself *expanding* more and more into who I really am, *expressing* more and more of who I really am. I am the creative power and intelligence of the entire universe. This entire world is an outward picturing of my mind. It isn't serious. It isn't scary. In fact, it's small potatoes considering the source. I AM THAT SOURCE and I exist in every detail of my creation.

"This kingdom I see before me is an extension of my consciousness. I created it by extending my mind, just as *I* was created by extension of the creative mind of life. I am One with my creation along with everyone and everything in existence.

"My life and the world around me, exactly as they are right now, are perfect. Every detail in my life, including this situation, is absolutely perfect just as it is right this moment.

"There is no need for change because there is no future state that could be any better than the present. Time has no power, beyond that which I give it by refusing to remember myself as my Voice.

"Circumstances do not determine my fate or my current state. How could they? *This moment is all there ever was, is or will be.* My ability to experience happiness, freedom, and success in life is directly tied to my ability to be fully and completely truthful and awake, now, within this dream of separation.

"I sink into the creative urgency of now and experience this moment as the gift that it is. It is a brilliant creation of my Voice, perfectly orchestrated to remind me of the truth at precisely the moment I was finally ready to remember.

"As I release my identification with old shadow patterns, I begin to author life consciously. Shifting my purpose from separation to

Oneness, old patterns collapse, rendered no longer useful, and my life expands. Easily and effortlessly. This is how true creation unfolds: along the path of least resistance from the inside out.

"Any attachment to specific outcomes, any fearful attempts to fix, change or control people, events, or even myself are just shadow illusions based upon a radical forgetting of my true nature.

"I am the creative power and intelligence of the entire universe. I now allow myself to relax and expand into this power. I fully bask in the peace that comes from remembering my perfection.

"I am wholly lovable, wholly loving, with nothing lacking and no needs unmet. Gratitude and abundance are my natural state. I am grateful for this life as an opportunity to experience the love I am within every moment, reflected back to me by the light within others. I am peaceful. I am joyful. I am awake."

Breathe into this last statement for at least 3 full minutes. Stay immersed. Merge into the infinite energy. Feel it. Rest in it.

Consider the problem or issue that you selected for this process. How does it show up for you now? If this stirs up any lingering discomfort, merge it back into the infinite energy you've accessed.

Reflect upon the original situation again until you can see just how perfectly designed and orchestrated it was to help you reach this moment. Experience the perfection beneath any seeming imperfections. Appreciate all of it without judgments or conditions. If those come up, appreciate them also.

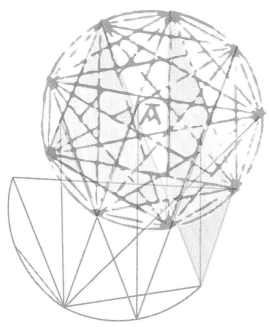

ACT III
Become a Child

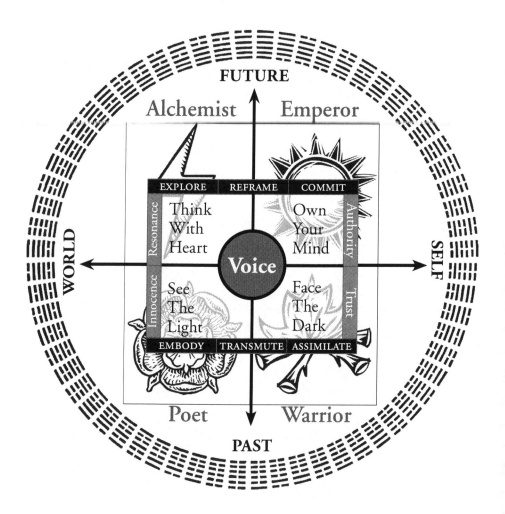

Scene 14 | *Pools of Innocence*

Echo was a lovely nymph with one fatal flaw: she always had to have the last word. One day Juno was looking for her husband. With her clever tongue, Echo kept Juno detained while fellow nymphs had their way with him. When she discovered the ruse, Juno cursed Echo to an ironic fate: "From this point forward the only words you speak will be to repeat the last words of others." With this, Echo was exiled to a life of empty repetition.

Narcissus was a beautiful young man. Echo longed for him. One day after Juno's curse, she found him roaming the woods alone. "Who's here?" he shouted, hearing footsteps. "Here!" She responded. He saw no one. "Come!" He shouted. "Come!" she replied. No one came. "Let us join one another." he said. "Join one another!" she cried, rushing happily to embrace him. "Hands off!" He recoiled. "I would rather die than let you have me!" "Have me…" she whimpered. Heartbroken, Echo went to live alone in the mountains.

In time, her body turned to rocks, leaving only her voice trailing throughout the canyons. Soon after, Narcissus suffered his own ironic fate. One day he came upon a pool of placid water. Stooping to drink, he glimpsed the most lovely creature. He soon fell madly in love with his own reflection. In time, this unrequited obsession would turn him into a shell of desperate yearning. "Alas!" he shouted with his final words. "Alas!" Watching him from afar, Echo joined in. "Alas!!" she cried, as his grieving soul departed.

Choose Innocence *See the Light*

The story of Echo and Narcissus packs many timeless truths in one mythic punch. While offering an imaginative explanation for echoes, it also serves as a morality tale about the dangers of self-obsession. But the secret to this story's enduring relevance lives beneath the surface. At this story's core, lies the bittersweet theme of impermanence. We relate to the trials of Echo and Narcissus because we see within them our own frustrated yearning to discover within ourselves a still point of constancy beyond the ravages of time.

"You can't step in the same river twice," said Greek philosopher Heraclitus. If change was the only constant in ancient Athens, how much more so today? The river of time has become a tidal wave of digital complexity, flooding our minds with more data than we could ever digest.[1] By some estimates, the average Sunday edition of the New York Times today packs more information than the average person was exposed to in their *entire lifetime* only 100 years ago — and we're just getting started! With each new wave this data deluge is washing away more and more of the Phase I culture once kept stable through top-down controls.

This is the evolution of human consciousness in a nutshell. The more it changes, the more it stays the same, unfolding through a cyclical logic that calls us to keep repeating the same lessons over and over until we embrace the timeless. As the rate of change approaches infinity, we reach the singularity point of maximum information density when time stands still. This immovable spot is the beginning and the end of our journey. It is the time when darkness fades and new light dawns as we remember our Voice, forever shining behind the darkened lens of those shadow dragons we call the Doubters.

The Doubters are thieves of innocence. These dragons of despair bear an uncanny resemblance to Echo and Narcissus. If we let them, these sad sacks would have us grow so smitten with echoes of past loss that we'd rather drown our joy in the river of regret than remember our innocence. Fortunately once we've tapped our Warrior's power to rebuild Trust in our Voice, we are poised to gently dissolve these inner tragedians, restore the kingdom, and remember the truth of our nature.

The Poet's return is the season of rebirth, where hope springs eternal. When the Poet's light dawns, our minds are perfumed with the timeless. The transcendent beauty of life reveals itself, youthful joy bubbles up within, and our Voice flowers with gifts that help us thrive without limits doing what we love. As the ice melts and the morning sun burns away the fog of despair, a joyful revolution breaks within our rejuvenated hearts. "In like a lion, out like a lamb" is the happy march back to where this saga first began. When the Poet returns, the lion (Emperor) and the lamb (Poet) lay down in peaceful union, bringing our long-fought journey full circle again.

Now we understand. Now we hear the call, as all four corners of the kingdom rejoin, without the dragons of delusion that once darkened our days. Now we understand: the only barrier *really was* belief. Who we are is incredible — as in beyond believing. The Trojan Horse of frame lock saddled us with untold burdens, steeling our minds against our better angels. *Now we understand.* This is the season when we remember that strength, which lives now and forever within the innocence of One.

The Poet is the essence of exuberance. In the realm of human relations, this prized mentor gives us that captivating *star quality* that enthralls others with graceful charm. When we embody the Poet, we exude a youthful beauty and disarming charisma that is understated and infectious. Have you ever met someone who you found deeply attractive even though they weren't good looking by conventional standards? This was your Poet shining back at you through them. The Poet's radiance is intoxicating.

But to bring this light to the world, we must see it in others. To see the light in others, we must invite the Poet back into our hearts by embracing the timeless truth of Oneness. Our senses show us a world of conflict against which this notion seems trite. The Poet is our gentle guide back to that divine element of mind through which unity speaks clearly, dissolving all delusions in the white light of infinity. Frame locked, we see innocence as weakness and attack as strength. When we meet the Poet, we remember. In so doing we see the light and become One with our Voice to create that rare gestalt that helps visionary minds break all the rules and thrive in so doing.

Innocence | *Perfect Oneness*
Paradox: Defenselessness is Strength

Innocence is the principle of Oneness. When we restore proper alignment with the principles of Authority, Resonance and Trust, we purge our primal unconscious of shadow toxins that keep us from seeing the light to remember our Oneness. In open systems theory jargon, innocence would be called an "emergent property" of consciousness — a quality that unfolds from the whole and which cannot be fully explained by analyzing the component parts.[2] Our eyes show us a mind-boggling multiplicity of forms, but at the level of being, we are One. Our minds make countless belief maps to carve up complexity, but these maps can never change our reality at the level of being. People at the most advanced stages of Voice alignment have traded the map of multiplicity for the territory of shared being. At One with Voice, they see light in all things and prosper sharing the Poet's light in a spirit of shared self-interest. If greatness is our goal, gratitude is the means and remembering our shared innocence is the final right of passage.

The Principle
Innocence: The ART of Partnership

When Nietzsche proposed that the three transformations of a great person were from Camel to Lion and back to Child again, he brilliantly invoked the power of innocence. Innocence is strength, pure and simple. Without a visceral knowing of our unbroken innocence, our brains and bodies fall out of integrity with our being.

According to the Voice Code map, integrity and innocence emerge in tandem as we release the belief in separation that gives rise to perception. By slaying Thou Shalt to reframe the principles of Authority, Resonance and Trust, we heal our split mind and restore awareness of our true nature. As false dichotomies dissolve, innocence flowers anew and our lives become a radically coherent expression of the whole. Integrity, once a harsh moral imperative from shadow tyrants on high, reveals its true essence:

Integrity isn't about morals.
It's about perfect love remembered.

Why did we ever settle? How did we ever believe that we were lacking and limited? What's possible now that we see the light? These are the questions that arise in our minds upon the Poet's happy return. In the past, questions like these were rhetorical mind candy. But we now have a practical, logical and rigorous map that offers clear actionable answers. Through this lens, we finally see the whole human journey from beginning to end.

In Phase I, we see innocence as something lost before grade school, when we became frame locked by a world of opposites. We learned to adapt to this frame locked world by tuning out our Voice. This mindset caused us to experience life through the lens of separation, secretly yearning that we might someday redeem the memory of loss we have carried deep within. The shadows that have framed locked our lives ever since are traceable to our earliest experiences in the womb (Stage 1). Until we dissolve these primal energies, they stay trapped in our unconscious where they cloud our minds and block the Poet's light.

In Phase II, we remember. When we reach the mountain's peak (Stage 6), we discover that no outer success will ever bring us true freedom. This disillusionment is the inciting incident, the catalyst that calls us to choose again as we enter Phase II to "become a lion" and slay the dragon. This mission evolves organically, from the inside out, over six epic stages. Step by step, we transmute old shadow habits in the reverse order from which we first created them during our Phase I climb. With each step, the light gradually returns as we restore awareness of our timeless origins.

By the time we reach Stage 10 (Luminary), our Voice is strong enough that we are ready to transmute the cornerstone Phase I belief that we are a separate ego. In Stage 11, we fully transmute the death belief to find ourselves living in a world of boundless joy. Stage 12 is our poignant return back home to Stage 1, yet now as a fully conscious adult. We have now achieved true freedom. Where others remain blinded by fear, we see only love. Where the frame locked masses see a valley of death, we see the light of timeless truth that joins everyone behind the veil of appearances.

"We shall never cease from exploration," said T. S. Elliot "And the end of our exploring will be to arrive where we started, and know this place for the first time."[3] The human journey a story of the birth and death of time in the mind of infinity. Like all great hero stories, in the first act we leave home on an adventure into darkness. We then meet mentors, defeat darkness and return home with our boon for mankind. The mind-blowing thing to consider is that *every step of this journey happens inside our mind.* After 12 Stages of dragon slaying we wake up, as if from a dream, to find ourselves exactly where we had been all along, but now happy beyond belief and grateful beyond measure. Dreams have ended, but life has just begun.

Worldview Dynamics

Subject (Stage 3) vs. Luminary (Stage 10)

The stark contrast between Phase I and Phase II thinking is never clearer than when we compare conceptions of innocence. From Voice Code perspective, birth is an infinitely repeating reenactment of the great fall of man — the moment of separation when our innocence seemed lost. When the umbilical cord is cut, we perceive ourselves as helplessly cast out into a cold confusing world with no control over our destiny. Our being still radiates the timeless

Choose Again

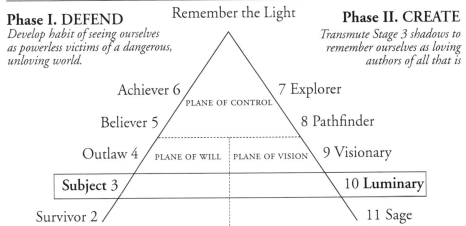

Remember the Light

Phase I. DEFEND
Develop habit of seeing ourselves as powerless victims of a dangerous, unloving world.

Phase II. CREATE
Transmute Stage 3 shadows to remember ourselves as loving authors of all that is

Achiever 6   7 Explorer

PLANE OF CONTROL

Believer 5   8 Pathfinder

Outlaw 4   PLANE OF WILL   PLANE OF VISION   9 Visionary

Subject 3   10 **Luminary**

Survivor 2   11 Sage

Subject: Innocent Victim

In Stage 3, we innocently trust the world to satisfy our needs without a hitch. But no matter how sincerely our caretakers may have tried to do right, they still missed the mark. Triggered by careless moments and seemingly minor mishaps, our innnocent minds erupted with pain and terror of abandonment. The memory of this fear lingered in the backdrop of our minds as we formed our early relationship to the world. These energies remain deeply hidden and highly charged in our unconscious until we do the inner work of Stage 10 Luminaries.

Luminary: Innocent Authority

In Stage 10, we transmute those early Stage 2 shadows to reclaim the gift of exuberance as we remember our unity with all of life. Early shadow wounds inaccessible to our language-driven brains dissolve and we remember ourselves as the author of all circumstances. As the light returns, we develop a direct experiential knowing that transcends mere words and symbols. Through simple actions, one step at a time, we then follow our Voice and change the world from the inside out while happily following our calling, doing what we love.

innocence of being, but we lack any language or sense of self with which to comprehend this. Our minds are raw, unformed and deeply impressionable. So begins the uphill climb to adulthood.

As we approach the final stages of Phase II, we return home to our natural state of radiance, only this time as a fully self-actualized adult. During this long journey up and over the mountain, we lose and find ourselves many times over until our quest for freedom is complete. When we finally reach Stage 10 Luminary and Stage 11

Sage, we join the ranks of history's greatest teachers. At these advanced stages we act as energetic transformers who transmute mankind's darkest shadows to keep the torch of Oneness alive for all. The gift of innocent unconditional love we offer dissolves the buried Stage 3 Subject and Stage 2 Survivor shadows in our collective psyche, collapsing time to ease human suffering and accelerate the evolution of life as a whole.

The Stage 2 Survivor and Stage 11 Sage worldviews are key bookends to a 9-step journey into separation and back again. The number 9 is well represented in many mythic systems as the number of completion. When we complete the lessons of Stage 10 (Luminary) by transmuting the shadows of Stage 3 (Subject), we enter Stage 11 (Sage) where we are called to transmute the Stage 2 (Survivor) shadows that create the perception of basic biological needs. We have now completed the inner journey to and from separation. Our only purpose now is to be of service to the rest of mankind that we might graduate from the realm of perception all together.

We then move to Stage 12 (Messiah), a worldview identical to what some spiritualists call Christ or Buddha consciousness. At this final stage we effortlessly embody the truth of Oneness as we fully transmute the earliest Doubter shadows formed in Stage 1 (Womb). All shadows are now defenseless against the radiant beauty that we exude. If you ever have the privilege to be in the presence of someone who has achieved this rare stage of mastery, you will know it. Within their presence miracles are natural and peace abounds. In their orbit, longstanding problems disappear like a mirage and we effortlessly remember the perfect love that is our origin.

The farther we travel along the path of Phase II, the more commonplace miracles become for us. Seeing our light shining back at us from others, we transmute shadows and offer miracles wherever we go through the unassuming act of innocent perception. Through this paradoxical Phase II process, we come to know our innocence as our biggest strength. The miracles we offer become the gifts *others offer us* by giving us yet another chance to choose again. As first hand evidence of our creative power grows, we come to remember who we have always been beyond the veil of the senses. In time, we escape time itself, as all symbols dissolve into the fierce brilliance of now in which shadows cannot live and only gratitude suffices.

Voice In Action: **The Fruit of Innocence**
Dragon Slayer: **Organic Food Retailer**

A Fortune 500 food manufacturer had chronically flat sales for a line of organic tomato products. I was called in to use the worldview framework as part of a repackaging campaign. After collecting psychographic market data using our worldview assessment, we observed multiple focus groups, searching for clear buying triggers that compelled loyalists to choose this product over cheaper competitors. Prevailing wisdom was that loyalists were motivated by gourmet elitism. Our analysis offered a much different perspective. Through the worldview lens, the driving motivator was purity, the essence of innocence. I advised the client to create new packaging that resonated with the Poet: pure, simple and unassuming like a newborn baby. I suggested that they place a simple unadulterated tomato image on every can, with aesthetics that likened this vegetable to a baby in diapers. This might sound silly, but it worked like a charm! The new packaging brought immediate returns, leading to an estimated 25% increase in sales in the first year alone. Precise sales data was hard to come by, but one thing seems certain: Purity sells — on the wings of the Poet.

The Final Showdown
Dissolve the Doubters | See the Light

In Act III you'll align with the Poet to dissolve the Doubters and remember your innocence. Through this journey you'll reclaim the gifts of Partnership to bring this adventure full circle.

Mentor: **The Poet**
Gift: **Partnership**
Shadow Poets: **The Doubters**
Active Doubters: **Dreamer (Loner)**
Passive Doubter: **Downer (Loser)**

The Doubter's Mantra "See the Lack"

The Doubters keep us from "Seeing the Light" by blocking access to our Voice in the Poet expression. These seeming "weaklings" are the central ringleaders of the whole shadow racket. Dreamers control us by convincing us to mistake pity and specialness for love. Often they speak to us through that "oh no, not this again" feeling of dread, other times through a blind optimism that we follow right off a cliff. The Downers play a more passive role, feeding us an endless stream of self-pitying emotions that scare most people away from looking honestly inward. When we either indulge or attempt to escape Doubters, we forget our innocence and see the lack instead of the light that is our birthright.

A Tale of Two Mentors

	Doubters	**Poet**
Voice	Mouth Sound	Shared Being
Transmute	One into Many	Many into One
Embrace	Specialness	Wholeness
Death	Inevitable	Impossible
Oneness	Aspiration	Actualization
Love	Romance	Reality

Turning Point

CREATE the Revolution ~ Week 8

At the end of Scene 15, you'll find a "Week 8. See the Light" checklist that directs you to a new "Be the Change" process in Scene 16. This consists of two new tools that will help you transform any relationship from the inside out. Once you've completed the Week 8 exercises, you will bring this dragon slaying journey to a conclusion as you begin your Voice Revolution in earnest. Be sure to also read the "Afterword" and "Path to Mastery" sections to see the clear step-by-step path I've crafted to help you master this material quickly.

Visit TheVoiceCode.com to get free digital resources, including free training videos and digital copies of key tools offered in this book. You will also find the Voice Code glossary at the end of this book helpful for clarifying and expanding upon any new words, ideas and symbols used.

Scene 15 | *Dissolve the Doubters*

Dragons of Desperation

The Dreamer			The Downer
Search	←	→	Mourn
Fantasize	←	→	Wallow
Ignore	←	→	Obsess

8 Thou Shalts of the Doubters

Thou shalt *wistfully romanticize youthful beauty*

Thou shalt *hide thy light to avoid being judged*

Thou shalt *deny impulse for joyful exuberance*

Thou shalt *fetishize the past with nostalgia*

Thou shalt *confuse love with specialness*

Thou shalt *take secret pride in thy suffering*

Thou shalt *always focus on what's lacking*

Thou shalt *avoid loving fully for fear of dying*

The Poet's light shines outward from the present moment awareness of our Oneness with the creative mind that governs life. But until we topple the inner shadow regime, this light remains buried by the Doubters. As cool and collected as we may appear, beneath our social masks we hold a deep unquenched yearning to be loved and loving without conditions. The Doubters tell us that this is impossible because we are broken. When we believe their cries, love becomes for us a fleeting external resource instead of what it actually is: our very nature. Since the earliest days we've been told how to find and keep love, but did anyone help us see that the idea of losing love is meaningless? This heretical idea is at the core of all spiritual traditions, but has never been made actionable in such a way that anyone might consistently embody it. By mastering the CREATE cycle to dissolve the Doubters, we accomplish this epic feat. This is the fateful moment when we see that Humpty Dumpty's shattering never happened. As we dissolve the Doubters, the beauty of innocence becomes us, and all things appear as they truly are: infinite.

The Doubters *Dragons of Desperation*

The Doubters are the most powerful shadow team, because they bypass our normal defenses. Even the Enforcer's downward shame spiral is mere kid's play by comparison. Yet, as with all shadow patterns, the Doubters power comes *from us*. It ushers from our will or, rather, from our *unwillingness* to bring light to inner darkness. Most of us would rather do anything than truly embrace our perfection. What then would be the point of seeking? How would an unconditional love affair with life change our goals and aspirations? With nothing to prove and no real problems to solve, what would we do with ourselves? If we were truly happy and fulfilled with our lives exactly as they are now, how would we relate to others? What would we talk about?

Seeing love as a limited resource, most of us go through life seeking not to lose the love we have. Thinking this way, we build belief fences around infinity, framing our lives with Phase I mental operating systems rooted in lack. This is true for everyone — even those creative rebels who buck convention by vehemently rejecting the beliefs handed down by culture. By their rejection, they get frame locked in rebellion and become wedded to their past indefinitely. The only way to truly break the frame open and be authentic is to stop seeking. When we surrender the quest to fix or change ourselves, we can meet life without the distorted filters of past learning. This is simple in theory, but to implement *in reality* requires that we be willing to see through the desperate seeking, grieving and pining of the Doubters.

The real Poet leads us out of the maze of seeking and into the light of reality where we transcend the usual games of social climbing and status seeking. But until we shine through this shadow poet haze, we cannot grasp what unconditional self-acceptance really means. Projecting parts of ourselves that we deem unlovable out onto the world, we build our lives around the yearning to become whole through external seeking.

Most spend their entire lives unaware that dilemmas are lies. Beneath our competing needs for security, autonomy, connection and change lies one unmet need: unconditional love. If we focus first on satisfying this one underlying need from within, we satisfy all other needs without any struggles. But most people do not realize this, and even those who do grasp the idea intellectually rarely put it into play in their day-to-day choices. Deluded by Doubters, even the bravest Phase II adventurers fall into escapist patterns, trying in vain to salve their self doubts with clichés and romantic appeals to fairytale endings. With this habit of avoiding the shadow poets so deeply interwoven into the fabric of our culture, it's no wonder we're so terrified to look within. We've been thoroughly socialized to think that our beliefs are the only thing stopping us from being devoured by the hungry wolves of emotional abandonment.

Those wolves aren't real. They are the Doubters, and they are a complete fabrication. But until we face them and see this first hand, we'll never remember this. We've been seduced by shadow logic to seek love outside ourselves when, in reality, *we are the love that we've been seeking*. In this chapter, you'll meet the shadow mastermind of this epic inner conspiracy. If you keep your heart and mind open during this final Act III adventure, you will be liberated from a lifetime of harsh lessons in the school of hard knocks. In reality, the Doubters are and always have been nothing more than delusions. But delusions are quite real to us when we believe them; and since our earliest days on earth, we have been programmed to believe.

Because the Doubters are the gateway to this mighty elixir we call unconditional love, I encourage you to tread with particular care when first exploring Doubter terrain. If you haven't yet performed the exercises prescribed in previous chapters, I highly recommend that you do so before moving forward. Every step in the process has been designed to ensure that you get the maximum results with the minimum confusion and discomfort. When we do our inner game process in the natural sequence from Emperor to Alchemist to Warrior to Poet, we create a natural safety net that helps us spot and dissolve the Doubters without getting seduced by their sirens songs of self loathing. The more we activate and integrate these other three mentors, the more we liberate the true Poet's love to shine through the shadow clouds and lighten our path.

Shadows of Innocence

From "See the Light" to "See the Lack"

According to scientists, frogs are the barometers of the health of an ecosystem. When you hear a chorus of vibrant croaking near a body of fresh water, this generally means that the ecosystem is thriving. When the croaking diminishes, the ecosystem has been degraded, leaving frogs underfed, begging for fly wings, sitting listlessly on the lily pads pondering their mortality. As frogs are to nature's ecosystems, so too is the Poet to our inner ecology.

When the Poet's light fades, our inner music dies. This happens to everyone to some degree during the process of growing up. But if we don't pro-actively purge our primal unconscious of shadow residue, this impact compounds over time until life seems gray. Just one tiny seed of undigested sorrow from a moment of childhood grief, grows into a sickly thicket of densely matted shadow weeds that block the fresh waters of our inner Voice wellspring from purifying and replenishing our consciousness.

When Doubters rule the pool, we sow self-doubt in others because we doubt our own Voice essence. This disconnect grows from a shadow inversion of the CREATE cycle that turns the Poet's skill of Embodiment into Doubt — the final D of the DEFEND cycle. The Poet helps us win hearts and minds by Seeing the Light within others. When Doubters dominate, we see lack and *seek the light,* as we cling to ancient pain, shielding ourselves beneath a mask of false bravado. Our lives then become an endless cycle of searching outside ourselves for that which we already have innate.

Just as a healthy Poet-Emperor bond transforms cynicism into shared vision through the Axis of Presence, the Doubters join with the Dividers to permanently institutionalize frame lock along the Axis of Death. Like everything the shadow creates, the Axis of Death is a travesty on Truth, made real through belief. But a lifetime of social proof reinforcing this warped lens has rendered most of us true believers. Because of this, precious few can correctly distinguish between sentimental Doubter love and the timeless true love inspired by the Poet.

The bipolar drama that the Doubters project within us conjure an illusory "special" love that oscillates on a spectrum between childish romanticism and bitter despair, keeping us forever imprisoned by our belief in loss. As we unite with the Emperor, Alchemist and Warrior to purge our inner kingdom of all shadows, the Poet's light shines away the ghosts of shadow love quite naturally. But until then, we invest belief in death and despair by avoiding the Doubters for fear that they might overwhelm us. In the next section,

I'll show you how these maudlin shadow players pull this off so that you never get suckered again.

Make no mistake: the Doubters hold the keys to the kingdom. But these keys are rightly ours. In a moment of forgetting, we seem to have disinherited ourselves. But nothing real can be threatened, and nothing unreal exists.[1] To reclaim our keys, we need only open our will to remember the truth beyond separation. To dissolve the Doubters we must be willing to topple all beliefs and surrender fully to our Voice knowing in the present — that paradoxical portal of now through which all four corners of the kingdom unite, erasing all shadows that once blocked our light.

The true Poet remains forever unfazed. Behind the smoke and mirrors of belief, this joyful mentor patiently awaits our invitation. In perception, love may indeed be fragile. But in *reality*, love is timeless. Love never left us, nor did we leave it. How could we? We *ARE* it! Rest assured, whenever loss seems real, you've merely fallen asleep under a blanket of sanguine beliefs woven by the Doubters. When we remove these blankets we lose all belief in loss and the beauty of innocence becomes us.

The Doubters

Loner	"See the Loss"	Loser
Daydreamers ←	OR	→ Downers

In the underworld of shadows, the Doubters are the celebrity débutantes. These gifted tragedians quite convincingly portray roles that make hate seem loving and walking death seem like living. Without their anchoring performance, the entire shadow mob infrastructure would collapse under the weight of its own absurdity. This poet shadow troupe consists of the Dreamer and the Downer, two award-winning thespians with no capacity for joy or irony. But what they lack in happiness, they make up for in talent, playing tragic roles with a level of depth that's uncanny considering they don't actually exist.

This team wins us over by evoking pity and calling it love. With the aplomb of stranded puppies, they conjure feelings of pity and abandonment that bypass our ordinary defenses. To survive in a Phase I world, most of us developed a hard worn habit of deploying filters to censor such feelings from awareness. Through compulsive thinking and self-medicating ambition, we constantly defend ourselves from the Doubters crippling calls. Such habits often numb the pain, but they do so at the cost of making pain permanent.

The Doubter's pity party is masterful in conception and execution. This performance outshines the greatest Hollywood movies, guided by the same motto that lifts all great performers to stardom: *Know your audience.* You know that really awful emotion that you have secretly designed your life to avoid feeling? Well the Doubters know exactly how to evoke this emotion because — get this — they *are* that emotion! They are a dissociated mass of psychic energy has been spinning on endless repeat in your unconscious since you made the original choice that brought them into existence.

We've long forgotten making this choice, of course. But remember—this forgetting was no accident. It's all part of the shadow's clever racket, which we know today as the big "F" in the DEFEND cycle. When we chose separation, we buried the evidence and then buried the shovel by projecting our pain outward as the world of perception. Forgotten or not, we each made this choice or today we couldn't possibly believe in perception. It lives within us today as the aching yearning for love, joy and freedom at our core. This buried choice has since shaped all of our other choices and has made our Voice feel like some distant "other."

These ghosts of unrequited love we call the Doubters represent two poles of the original choice for separation. The Dreamer grows from our desire to find love again; and the Downer, from despair that we will never do so. Until we shut down their tragic performance, these starlets will keep copulating in our unconscious with lovesick abandon, stirring up trouble in ways that rarely reach our conscious minds — until we're filing for divorce, declaring bankruptcy or

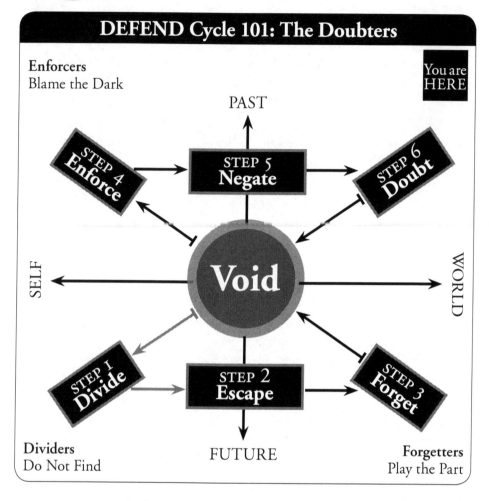

DEFEND Cycle 101: The Doubters

Enforcers
Blame the Dark

You are
HERE

PAST

STEP 4
Enforce

STEP 5
Negate

STEP 6
Doubt

SELF

Void

WORLD

STEP 1
Divide

STEP 2
Escape

STEP 3
Forget

Dividers
Do Not Find

FUTURE

Forgetters
Play the Part

grieving the loss of our dear cat Mr. Scruffles.

Whatever form they take, there's but one simple theme that drives every Doubter's story. Want to hear it? If so, grab a box of tissues and keep reading. Here goes:

You killed love. It's too late. Now you must suffer forever.

Charming, right? I don't know about you, but I'm sure glad they're a delusion! Now here's the truth that lives forever unchanged beneath the melodrama:

You *are* love. Time is now. Choose again and remember.

Your mind is awesomely powerful. If the Doubters can be traced back to one buried choice, how much power might you begin to wield when you exhume their tomb and choose again? When you make up your mind this time around, nothing can stop you. If you're still reading this book, you've already made your decision. Now all you need to do is keep choosing your Voice again and again until you see through the Doubter's tragic projections. The map is here. The path is clear. The only barrier is belief.

Meet the Dreamers

The Drifter | The Idealist | The Victim | The Romantic

These lost-soul Doubters control us through yearning to transcend the trials and tribulations of life. If you've ever been moved to tears of self-pity hearing "Somewhere Over the Rainbow" or fallen head-over-heels for someone you knew was bad for you, then you understand how powerful the Dreamer's wistful yearning can be. When it arises, we instinctively react through impulsive avoidance or embrace. Rarely do we stop and simply observe these energies with the Alchemist's curious eyes to see if they are real. Until we do, we never get the joy of discovering that what we yearn for isn't over a rainbow. It's within us *right now* for the choosing. Our yearning to transcend isn't a bad thing. In fact, it's a big part of what drives us to escape the orbit of Phase I. The big Phase II skill is learning how to listen to these inner nudges to distinguish between the Poet's love and the Dreamer's pathetic pining.

Key Strategy: *Fruitless Searching*

The Dreamer calls us to imagine bigger and better things, seeing new possibilities around every corner. These shadow players exude a childlike optimism that can be utterly disarming. But here's the problem: this optimism is always rooted in a desire to create a better future by escaping reality. The Dreamers play off our sense of meaninglessness and inadequacy, encouraging us to fill the inner void with bold schemes to create Utopian futures. But when we follow them, we initiate action from the seeds of lack within, ensuring that the fruit of our efforts will also be lacking. Following the Dreamer's call, we embark upon endless cycles of fruitless searching, displacing our unfelt pain through romanticized notions that recur over and over in countless disguises. As our childish dreams falter, our hearts become harbor for a deep reservoir of sadness that calcifies over time, turning us into cynics, drifters and self-medicating depressives.

Mind Game: *Misguided Empathy*

Seeing the futility of wallowing in grief, many dissociate from their feelings through lifestyles of endless distraction. Recognizing the dangers of repression, others compulsively embrace their darker feelings, wallowing without end. Both habits — wallowing and avoidance — make us vulnerable to the Dreamer's schemes. Recognizing and allowing shadow poets up into awareness is always better than employing Punisher (shadow warrior) patterns to imprison them. But if we aren't careful, we can also get consumed and fall into the Dreamer trap of romanticizing our feelings until we see the world through sickly rose colored lenses. When this happens, we look around and see a world of lost souls looking to be saved, never realizing that we have become frame locked Dreamers projecting our own Downers out onto everyone.

Toppling The Big Boss

"Who was that?"

Name: **Needer**
Type: **Doubter, Dreamer (Romantic)**
Gift Reclaimed: **Exuberance**

By January 2015, the Voice Code tools had been thoroughly tested. The Big Boss, Donny the Damned, Black Magic Jesus,

*Chip Smugly, Tolstoy Parliament, Reverend Firestone and a
long list of other noxious shadow patterns had been cleared.
After a grueling 28-month adventure, I was one week away
from completing this book...Or was I? As it turned out, I was
still 18 months of 60-hour work weeks away from a final draft.
How could I have been so deluded? This inflated optimism was
the handiwork of Needer, an idealistic Dreamer who conspired
with a Downer named Mourna to keep my head in the clouds.
Needer was one sneaky little bastard! He offered a comforting
"We're almost there! It's gonna be great!" optimism that I'd
come to rely on when times were tough. Without Needer's
enthusiasm, I imagined a gloomy world where the harsh facts of
reality destroyed all beauty. To fully transmute Needer and
complete this journey, I developed a daily ritual of firing my ego
and then hiring my Voice. As this became a new habit, I pulled
through to a higher-level order of energy and grounded
optimism, which helped me cross the finish line. By summer
2016, the book was complete and I'd reclaimed the gift of
exuberance from the sticky mitts of this dreamy phantom.*

Best Trick: *Daydream Believers*

Feeling guilty is how Dreamers stay grounded. When we let the
Dreamer's emotional ploys influence our choices, we feel a low-
grade sense of guilt 24x7. If we resist the guilt, we make it real
through our resistance, using punishing shadow warriors to defend
ourselves from its imagined power to destroy us. If we wallow in it,
we make it real through our embrace, enrolling martyring prisoner
shadows to help us enshrine it as an anthem to our sinfulness. This
inner pattern projects out into our lives until we *ground* ourselves
with punishing and imprisoning people and circumstances. To cope
with the frustration, we then daydream of going somewhere "over a
rainbow" as an escape from the hopelessness we shelter deep within.
In reality, hope is fully justified. All we need do is face the dark and
choose again. But when we're in this condition, the ankle weights of

shadow guilt keep us from realizing our power. When the Doubter's dramas block our light, images of loss cloud our minds, as our deepest dreams fade in the Dreamer's far away eyes.

Four Faces of the Dreamer

Drifters: *These aimless Dreamers control us through our resistance to structure. When we obey them, we view all structures and disciplines as a threat to our freedom, abandoning projects (relationships, jobs, etc.) when they become challenging. When we react against them, we impose strict, overly harsh regimens and disciplines upon ourselves and become rigid, controlling and change intolerant.*

Idealists: *These Utopian Dreamers control us through our desire for absolute ideological purity. When we obey them, we see the world through the lens of an idyllic fantasy of what could be, overlooking key facts of reality. When we react against them, we dismiss the importance of having higher aspirational ideals, and fail to integrate higher values into our everyday practical decision making.*

Victims: *These browbeaten Dreamers control us through our need to see people with power as willfully abusive, uncaring or corrupt. When we obey the Victims, we compulsively search for evidence of lies and conspiracies by them to justify our inner powerlessness. When we react against them, we blindly trust whatever those in charge tell us without critical reflection and become highly susceptible to power abuses.*

Romantics: *These starry-eyed Dreamers control us through our desire to live in a "happily ever after" world where everything feels good and nothing bad ever happens. When we obey them, we become daydream believers, addicted to seeing life through rose-colored lenses. When we react against them, we become joyless realists who discount the value of anything that can't be directly measured and controlled.*

Most Wanted Innocence Blockers: The Dreamers

Do any of these Dreamers remind you of people you've known?

Which of the Dreamers do you find most unsettling? What is it about them? Do you find any endearing? How so?

Can you spot any areas in your own life where the Dreamer has blocked your light?

Have you ever been in a relationship someone whose life was taken over by Dreamer voices? What happened?

Do you recognize Dreamer energies within yourself? If so, how do you usually deal with them?

What breakthroughs might be possible once you reclaim your power from the Dreamers?

If you had to pick one Dreamer that has the most power for you to reclaim, which would it be? How might this improve your life?

Meet the Downers

The Mourner | The Whiner | The Reject | The Lamenter

To understand the Downers, imagine them as the perfect dysfunctional romantic partners with the Dreamers. When the Dreamers try to seduce us with daydreams, the Downers tell us that it's too late. We should just give up to keep from being even more miserable. If the Dreamers are like pitiful puppies pining for home; the Downers are whining strays that snarl from afar to fend off an agonizing sense of alienation. Three dynamic themes that emerge from the Downers are rejection, abandonment and loss. All three are tell-tale Doubter traps that emerge through triangulated shadow patterns that bridge Dreamers and Punishers through the Downers. These themes gain traction in our minds when we seek completion outside ourselves, confusing neediness and codependency for love.

The Plan: *Mesmerize with Misery*

In cases of clinical depression, Downer patterns have become all consuming. In cases of manic depression, they do so in dramatic oscillating patterns with manic Showboat (shadow alchemist) voices. In most of us, these energies stay hidden, emerging mostly during major life changes like divorce, job loss and death. But if we pay close attention to our inner experience during the so-called good times, we can still fathom the Doubter's muted presence. Like a whale jumping up and splashing headlong back into unseen waters, Downers flash what can seem like a bottomless ocean of grief in stray moments of idle reflection. These micro-flashes of misery can be quite unsettling, causing most people to develop a strong aversion to looking inward. But this habitual resistance keeps us attached to the Downers in a mesmerizing way, exerting a gravitational pull over our emotions that often leads us to a morbid attraction to topics related to death, disease, war, poverty and human misery in general. The problem is not these topics, but rather our repressed guilt for the guilty pleasure they provide us.

Mind Game: *Dance with Death*

The Downer energy is our secret attraction to death. Let's face it: we all have a forbidden romance with our own mortality. To many, death pulls like a siren's call, luring them mysteriously towards the grave. To others, death is the fire-breathing dragon that drives them to live each moment as if stolen from the gods. The Downer doesn't care how we relate to death as long as we believe in its reality. When we see our minds as merely neurons firing in our brains, and ourselves as fragile bodies trapped in time, the Downer's dirge still commands our loyalty. Until we dissolve that ancient vow that enslaved us to this delusion, our innocence seems lost to us forever. In this darkened night, the Poet's brilliant light still shines on us, but we can no longer see it. With the Downer as our muse, our minds remain confused and our eyes stay blinded by our altars in death's honor.

Defending The Big Boss

"Who was that?"

Name: **Mourna**
Type: **Doubter, Downer (Mourner)**
Gift Reclaimed: **Immortality**

When I met the Big Boss, I was in a state of joyful abandon. Playing an impromptu game of name that resistance; I said, "Who is that?" to every unloving thought that entered my mind until I arrived upon a pit of agonizing grief that I named Mourna. In story terms, Mourna was Needer's miserable girlfriend. Needer's dreamy ways were always concocted to cheer Mourna up. In psychological terms, Mourna was a deeply repressed pocket of loneliness and abandonment that had been tucked away within since my earliest days, rearing her head during divorces, deaths and moments of rejection. It wasn't until the age of 33 that I was capable of even feeling Mourna's presence. When I first felt her fully, I was liberated because it seemed I'd finally gotten in touch with my feelings. But on this fine morning, eight years later, I took my relationship with Mourna to another level by doing something that had never before occurred to me as even possible: I felt Mourna's grief, without avoiding or embracing it, rendering her completely powerless. Had I not been fully supported by the Poet's joyful light, I could've never pulled this off. But on this fateful morning, this inspired shift happened without effort. Facing Mourna with the resolute courage of a healthy Warrior, I peeled away the final layer between myself and the Big Boss so that I could choose again and enter a state of Stage 13 consciousness to reclaim the gift of immortality.

Best Trick: *Castration by Complaint*

Depression, drug addiction, suicidal impulses and all that ugly stuff happens in the shadow borderland between the Enforcers and Doubters as frame locked people try to find the light without facing the dark. For many adults, this same basic dynamic shows up through the habit of compulsive whining and complaining. Under the Downer's tutelage, one learns to proclaim their devotion to separation by complaining about all the things that are lacking. From a Phase II perspective, complaints are nothing more than a cry for love. But in cultures where Phase I thinking prevails, complaints are often seen as the currency of self-empowered survivors in a shitty world. This habit can gain traction only in the hearts and minds of those who've been thoroughly dispirited by undigested Doubters.

Four Faces of the Downer

Mourners: *These grieving Downers control us by urging us to wallow in our sad emotions. When we obey them, we feel unable to control our feelings, often falling into prolonged bouts of grief without hope of reprieve. When we react against the Mourners, we dismiss all sad emotions as "impractical" or "weak" and lose our capacity to access both our sad emotions and the Poet's joyful presence.*

Whiners: *These complaining Downers control us through our desire to connect with others without being emotionally open. When we obey them, we feel a compulsive need to whine, worry and find fault with things, so that people will give us attention and sympathy. When we react against the Whiners, we make it our policy never to share or even admit our problems or upsets and lose our ability to connect with others in a vulnerable, open-hearted way.*

Rejects: *These alienated Downers control us through our fear of not being accepted. When we obey them, we let our fear of rejection stop us from speaking our truth, standing in the spotlight and/or venturing outside our comfort zone. When we react against them, we force ourselves to speak up at any cost and become the center of attention, in a foolish way that elicits actual rejection.*

Lamenters: *These bereaved Downers control us through our unwillingness to forgive and release the past. When we obey them, we steer our lives looking in the rear-view mirror, bemoaning past mistakes* *and using them as an excuse not to change. When we react against them, we outright refuse to admit and/or revisit any past errors, and make the past mistakes permanent through our unwillingness to learn from them.*

Most Wanted Innocence Blockers: Downers

Do any of these Downers remind you of people from your past?

Which of the Downer masks makes you the most uncomfortable? What is it about them that triggers you?

Can you spot any Downer antics blocking you from living the life of love and happiness that your heart craves?

Have you ever been in a close relationship with someone seduced by sullen Downer voices? Did you find yourself wanting to "Go Dreamer" to lighten them up?

Where have the Downers shown up in your own experience? How did you cope? Have you ever worked through a Downer episode to discover the Poet's light shining beneath?

What might be possible if you could release the Downers and the Dreamers forever? Can you imagine how that would feel?

If you could pick just one Dreamer voice to dissolve and experience more of the Poet's joy, which one would you choose?

The Doubter's Beloved
Dividers: Shadow Parents

When we fall under the Doubter's spell, we hide our light and willfully maintain the shadow projections that keep us "safe" from the life we've always wanted. Thinking this way, life seems a serious ordeal, indeed. So how do we know when the spell is breaking? Turn the page for your simple two word answer:

Lighthearted laughter.

When we find ourselves suddenly making playful jokes about topics that once felt scary, this is a good sign. This ability to remain joyful when faced with dire circumstances is a hallmark trait of people with a healthy relationship to the Poet. The Doubter's ploys are the only thing keeping us from feeling the happiness and abundance of life in every passing moment. They are the final barriers to the life we've always wanted but deemed ourselves unworthy to receive.

To paraphrase psychologist Carl Jung, nothing exerts more influence on the development of the child than the undissolved Doubters of the parents. Our loyalties to the Doubters trace directly back to our misplaced loyalty to our parents. No matter how dedicated our parents were, they were still ordinary human beings raised in a frame-locked world. Like us, they were trained to mistake pity for love, force for strength, and innocence for weakness. Frame locked by their own parents' blind spots, they made mistakes that live on within us today, keeping us from creating lives worthy of our potential. If these old wounds were beyond change, there'd be no reason to discuss it. But with Voice Code tools, finding and transmuting old childhood shadows is easier than ever before. Why spend our entire lives imprisoned by the past when we can choose again and free ourselves forever?

Left unchecked, the Doubters drive us to create circumstances that replay our early childhood traumas on infinite repeat. Over and over again, they pull us to form relationships with people who mirror the dynamics that shaped us growing up. Determined to avoid the mistakes of our parents, we become exactly like them. In time, our resistance to the Doubter wound patterns within turns us into split-minded shadow emperors playing out the exact same drama with uncanny precision. This happened to me. After decades of diligent inner work hoping to avoid my parents' marital mistakes, I ended up repeating the same pattern myself while writing this book. But the deep pain of my own marital failure was a powerful catalyst that motivated me to further decipher the Voice Code and discover the tools this book now offers. It was through these hard won tools that I was finally able to dissolve those old Doubters and stop this sad cycle for my myself and my daughter.

The past is over. The shadow energies that keep us repeating the past live here and now within our primal unconscious. They rear their heads most clearly through the recurring patterns of separation that plague our partnerships. By simply pursuing the lives that we really want, without compromise, we call up all of those old shadow ghosts and transmute them one day at a time to purify the past, open the present, and release the future for everyone we love.

As you heal the Doubters, you will come to know the timeless truth within you. You will remember the infinite ocean of love that has always been there for you within your parents and everyone else you've ever known. As the fog of separation burns away, you will see the light of your Voice shining from the eyes of everyone you meet. In time, you will know your Voice as the Voice of life itself. Letting it guide your actions, you will effortlessly remind others that they are One with you. Together you will dissolve the delusion of separation that grew from that forgotten choice to believe in doubt.

The Voice Code's 12-Stage developmental pathway convincingly argues for a mind-blowing revelation that unravels all doubts for those willing to receive it. When the equation first emerged, it was this insight that sent my mind spinning and sucked me into an ego-shredding vortex from which the Big Boss would never escape:

Birth and death happen in the mind.
Both are choices, sustained by belief.
The white light is just reality unfiltered.

In the two years that followed this discovery, I embarked upon an inner dragon-slaying adventure that led me straight into the white light of Stage 13, without a trace of physical illness. How could this be possible if death were real? It couldn't be. So either I'm a raving loony, or death is a shadow delusion rooted in belief. If this seems incredible, please remember: that's the whole point! The truth

IS incredible! You don't need to believe it. Nor should you feel compelled to disbelieve it. If you will, please just consider this idea without feeling the need to choose a firm position either way. Try it on. Live the question. Gather evidence. Follow your Voice.

While you're at it, please consider this question: What if the Voice Code map is actually right? What if death is nothing more than a belief we dissolve in Stage 12? Can you imagine what life might be like if you knew with certainty that death was impossible?! If you will, imagine removing death and every thought of separation from your mind for a moment. What would you see? Having now personally experienced this state, I can tell you: you'd see the same light that people report seeing after near-death experiences.

Does this white light come because they are "going to heaven"? Or could it be that they were *already* in heaven, but — just like the rest of us — they were just too frame locked to see the light until death came knocking? Think about it. If the white light is reality unfiltered, then anyone who fully dissolved the shadow belief in death would have no more need for time and space. By clearing the windows of perception, they'd return home to that fabled light forever. Absolutely no religious dogmas, new age crystals or spiritual gurus required. Imagine that!

If this idea frightens or offends you, please don't force it. Forcing just reinforces the belief that you don't already know this. If the Voice Code is correct, then love is who you are. There's nothing to force and nothing to seek for. Fear of any kind is just an optical delusion projected from your primal unconscious through your belief in death and the many fractal patterns of separation this belief has conjured. Why not enjoy the Phase II ride back home? Let the dissonance between these old belief habits and the light of your Voice create powerful inner tension that drives you to awaken. Only by loving the unlovable can we shine away the ancient doubts that keep us dreaming.

The map is here. The path is clear. The only barrier is belief.

Doubter Habit   **CREATE Partnership**   Gift of Innocence

16 Gifts of the Poet

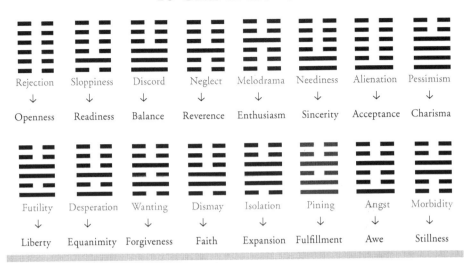

Rejection	Sloppiness	Discord	Neglect	Melodrama	Neediness	Alienation	Pessimism
↓	↓	↓	↓	↓	↓	↓	↓
Openness	Readiness	Balance	Reverence	Enthusiasm	Sincerity	Acceptance	Charisma

Futility	Desperation	Wanting	Dismay	Isolation	Pining	Angst	Morbidity
↓	↓	↓	↓	↓	↓	↓	↓
Liberty	Equanimity	Forgiveness	Faith	Expansion	Fulfillment	Awe	Stillness

Week 8. See the Light (checklist)

Step 1. Capture: Probe and inquire to uncover Doubter habit patterns using the inquiry exercise (below).

Step 2. Consolidate: In your research file, place Doubter habits uncovered in the Innocence section as part of your ongoing shadow pattern discovery archives.

Step 3. Clear: Use the CREATE goal process to transmute your top 3 Doubter shadow patterns uncovered (Days 1-3). Then pick 2 key people who you must engage to successfully accomplish your mission and perform the Bring the Light process on them (Days 4-5; See Scene 16. Be the Change for these new tools).

Step 4. Compare: At week's end, compare gifts reclaimed through CREATE script with the 16 Gifts of the Doubters in the CREATE Partnerships graphic below.

Step 5. Calculate: Perform follow up self-assessment rating between 0 and 10 on each gift where 0 = Doubter Habit and 10 =

Poet Gift. Total your responses to calculate your updated Poet Quotient (PQ) between 0 and 160. Note any changes from baseline PQ rating taken in week 4 (Scene 5. Behold the Poet).

Step 6. Connect: On Day 6 of week 8, perform CARE ritual (Scene 6). Consult with Voice mentors to align fully with Voice and determine the best next action steps to complete your mission.

Step 7. Complete: On Day 7, release, relax, review your gains and revel in the afterglow of the beautiful journey you've taken.

Remember Innocence
Explore the Doubters

The questions below will help you find Doubter resistance that you can process to reclaim the gifts of partnership available to you through the Poet. While the experience of reading this chapter is still fresh in your mind, capture the moment by noting surfacing shadow patterns before the Doubters go back into hiding. To set the stage for a powerful shadow exploration session, you may want to first prime your unconscious by summoning the Poet with the Choose Innocence exercise at the end of Scene 5.

Prospect: *Observe the Journey*

Please take a moment to review your inner journey while reading the chapter. Play detective. Imagine that you are a shadow detective. As you page through the chapter again, observe your inner experience without resistance. Note the tone and feel of different ideas and characters. Notice any patterns. Keep your heart and mind open.

Exploratory Insights: *What stood out from your exploratory investigation? Please make sure to capture any clues that came to you, however faint or dimly felt.*

Probe: *Expose the Doubters*

Step 1. Review Most Wanted: The questions in the MOST WANTED INNOCENCE BLOCKERS section are particularly helpful for discovering Doubter associations. If you haven't yet considered them, please do so before moving forward. If you have, review your answers again from this new context.

Step 2. Associative Inquiry: Please reflect upon the 11 questions below. As you do, gently observe your inner experience to note nudges of inner resonance and resistance.

> *1. As you read this chapter, what resonated most? Did anything jump out as particularly relatable, insightful or personally relevant? What triggered this response?*
>
> *2. While reading, did you at any point feel defensive, as if you or someone you know was being unfairly characterized? If so, what triggered this response?*

For questions 3-7 please refer to the 8 Doubter profiles below.

8 Faces of the Doubters

The Drifters: *These aimless Dreamers control us through our resistance to structure.*

The Idealists: *These Utopian Dreamers control us through our desire for absolute ideological purity.*

The Victims: *These browbeaten Dreamers control us through our need to see people with power as corrupt.*

The Romantics: *These starry-eyed Dreamers control us through our desire to live in a "happily ever after" dream world.*

The Mourners: *These grieving Downers control us by urging us to wallow in our sad emotions indefinitely.*

The Whiners: *These complaining Downers control us through our desire to connect with others without being truly open.*

The Rejects: *These alienated Downers control us through our fear of not being accepted by others.*

The Lamenters: *These bereaved Downers control us through our unwillingness to forgive and release past errors.*

3. Can you see any connection between the Doubter voices and your own limitations, past or present?

4. Do any of these remind you of difficult people you've known or worked with? If so, who was it and how so?

5. When it comes to achieving your mission, what Doubter voice would likely be most limiting?

6. When it comes to receiving your calling, which Doubter voice would be most likely to block your path?

7. All things considered, what voice do you sense has had the biggest limiting influence to keep you from remembering your Innocence? How so?

For questions 8-11 please read the 8 Thou Shalts of the Doubters.

---

8 Thou Shalts of the Doubters

Thou shalt *wistfully romanticize youthful beauty*

Thou shalt *hide thy light to avoid being judged*

Thou shalt *deny impulse for joyful exuberance*

Thou shalt *fetishize the past with nostalgia*

Thou shalt *confuse love with specialness*

Thou shalt *take secret pride in thy suffering*

Thou shalt *always focus on what's lacking*

Thou shalt *avoid loving fully for fear of dying*

---

8. Which of these Thou Shalts are you most likely to follow as a matter of habit?

9. Which of these Thou Shalts are you are you most likely to actively rebel against?

10. Which one of these Thou Shalts triggers you most when you see it in others? How does this show up?

11. All things considered, which Thou Shalt has had the strongest negative influence on your life?

Visit TheVoiceCode.com to get free digital resources, including free training videos and digital copies of key tools offered in this book. You will also find the Voice Code glossary at the end of this book helpful for clarifying and expanding upon any new words, ideas and symbols used.

Scene 16 | *Be the Change*

Section Overview

Description of Tools
Tool #1: FACE the Dark
Tool #2: LOVE the Light

Overview

The *Be the Change* process helps you heal and improve relationships. This process will help you ease social friction and improve effectiveness in any personal or professional situation that involves gathering, socializing, collaborating and communicating with other people. This process consists of two tools organized into one complete experience: the *FACE the Dark* assimilation tool and the *LOVE the Light* transmutation tool. Together, these tools form a game-changing two step shadow clearing process that can heal broken relationships and overcome longstanding social phobias in a very short time. Depending upon the depth and intensity of the shadows involved, completing this process can take from 45 to 90 minutes.

Although these tools are for relationships, you need not involve the others when using them. If the breakthroughs that result seem magical, please recall the core Voice Code premise: separation is an optical delusion. By using these tools you are simply restoring the CREATE cycle and removing the shadow projections that have blocked your vision into the shared Voice essence of others.

Applications

Troublesome relationships and social dynamics are one powerful area to apply the Be the Change process. But target relationships need not be marred by discord or distress. This process is equally effective to help you improve relationships that are already happy and healthy by most standards. Here are a few specific applications:

- **Intimate Relationships.** Use this process to heal or improve relationships with romantic partners, family members, close friends and colleagues. Can also help you achieve closure and completion with people from the past with whom you no longer have contact.

- **Business Development.** If your career or vocation demands that you reach out to connect with people in a business development or sales capacity, this process can clear any shadows that would have you fear rejection.

- **Social Events.** Before networking or social events, use this process to transmute shadows that cause social anxiety or simply to enhance the experience by clearing inner blocks that might keep you from connecting with ease.

- **Team Building.** If you work in a small group environment amenable to Phase II thinking, consider asking every member to privately perform this process on every other member of the team as part of a team-building exercise.

- **Toxic People.** If you are exposed to any chronically troublesome people or social environments, consider using this process to reclaim power from the projections that keep you frame locked and frustrated.

When you perform this process with earnest wholehearted commitment, you'll find that others will instinctively sense your new *energy* and shift their responses accordingly. The target may occasionally attempt to act out the old shadow dynamics as a matter of habit. But if this happens, you won't feel triggered because you will have removed the shadows that once kept you feeling reactive.

Tool Descriptions

The Be the Change process consists of the two shadow clearing tools previewed below. These tools have been sequenced to form one continuous process. When dealing with particularly highly charged shadows, consider breaking the process up into two sessions performed at the same time on two consecutive days.

Tool #1 FACE the Dark
Face • Arrest • Cause • Embrace
(Average time: 25 minutes)

The FACE the Dark process is an advanced assimilation script that helps you thoroughly process any shadows that cause relationships to show up as troublesome. To understand how this process works, consider that any negative image you hold of a person or group exists completely within your own mind. However justified your interpretation may be, it still consists of a limited subset of the available data, framed according to your personal beliefs. By taking full ownership of the image you've constructed for *them*, you can use this process to quickly neutralize the past and pave the way for profound and permanent breakthroughs.

Tool #2 LOVE the Light
Look • Open • Validate • Embody
(Average time: 25 minutes)

Once you've neutralized the projection, the LOVE the Light process helps you reclaim the hidden gift buried within your neutralized shadow projections. This is an advanced application of the Transmute skill (CREATE cycle, step 5). Performed with focus and discipline, this process is deeply empowering and inspiring. It helps you dissolve the past completely and usually leads to spontaneous inspired actions that produce powerful shifts in your relationships with the people and groups.

Before performing the Be the Change process, choose a specific target relationship that you would like to transform. Once you've chosen your target, please move on to the FACE the Dark below.

Tool #1 FACE the Dark (Part I)

Step 1: Face the projection
Step 2: Arrest the shadow
Step 3: Cause the shift
Step 4: Embrace your gift

Step 1: Face the projection

A. Invoke the Warrior

The Warrior thinks through courageous action in the service of a transcendent principle or purpose. To invoke the Warrior's energy, take a moment to consider a time you took bold, instinctual action in the service of a principle that matters to you. Summon that feeling of fearless courage rooted in your gut. Let this energy expand within you. Become one with it. This is how your Voice feels in the Warrior expression. Take a few deep breaths and let this powerful state sink in for at least one full minute.

When you are ready, hold this state as you place your hand on your heart and recite the following:

"With profound respect and reverence for life, I now invoke the fearless courage of the Warrior so that I may face the dark with courage, focused mental discipline and principled resolve.

"As I make this invocation, I humbly acknowledge that the Warrior's creative energies are far more powerful than my everyday ego. This request is made in good faith. My mission is rooted in

my wholehearted desire to make a positive difference for everyone, in honor of truth and in defense of that which is beautiful and innocent at the heart of life.

"Today, in spirit of reverence and gratitude for the many gifts the Warrior has already given, I vow to receive and assimilate any guidance this sacred mentor might offer to help me reclaim my power from these old shadow patterns that now limit me."

Hold the state of empowered reverence and resolve that these words evoke for one full minute before moving on. Observe your inner state. Allow gratitude that you have access to this mighty inner power. Give thanks to your Voice in the Warrior expression. Let your heart and mind open to connect in conscious appreciation of the many blessings available to you through the Warrior.

B. Summon the Suspect

Consider the person or group who you are frustrated, hurt by or otherwise upset with. Imagine them in your mind's eye right this moment. What is it about them that is upsetting to you? What have they said or not said, done or not done, that has disrupted your sense of peace and goodwill towards them? As you hold the image of them in mind, let the answers to these questions and the feelings that they conjure surface fully into conscious awareness. Let this image and these feelings merge into one.

Understand that this vision of them is not really them. Were you to see them unfiltered by shadows, you would see the light of your own Voice shining back at you. Please don't feel guilty for this fact. If you will, acknowledge this truth in a spirit of unconditional self-acceptance. Doing this will help you strengthen your determination to choose again and clear the windows of perception.

For a moment, please deeply consider this shadow image you've constructed of this person (or group). With the Warrior's help you will now neutralize whatever momentum past habits have given this projection to make it seem real in your experience. As you do this, please remember: *IN REALITY* there's nothing to fix, change or improve. The situation is already perfect. You've just been frame locked by a distorted sense of reality caused by past programming.

Now, with the Warrior's calm resolve, summon this character to stand before you now. Without any hint of forcing or aggression, command that it reveal itself to you now. When it does, make a quick study of it: What does this shadow projection look like? Are there any surprising or notable qualities of manner or appearance? What feeling tone is it now exuding? Let the room between you stay open, quiet and present for a moment. When you are ready, please proceed to Step 2.

Step 2: Arrest the shadow

With the Warrior's gentle resolve, make the following decree aloud, hand on heart. Feel your voice vibrate from your chest and throughout your body as you infuse these words with your being.

"I now commit to neutralizing old shadow energies, beliefs and habits of thinking associated with this shadow projection I've placed upon [insert name of person or group].

"In the service of truth, freedom and shared prosperity, I now declare the shadow energies associated with this projection powerless over me. I now petition my Voice to assist me in banishing them from my mind forever. I created them. I now choose again so that I can neutralize the past and reclaim the gifts of Voice trapped within my creation.

"I understand that my freedom is at stake. I am through playing small and completely unwilling to cut corners any longer in this matter. My word is law in the kingdom of my mind. The choice has been made. It is done."

After giving the mandate, consider other associated shadow energies that you've uncovered. Summon the Warrior's courage and actively invite it all up into your awareness. Open to any doubts, fear, judgments, resentments or whatever repressed upsets may be lingering to keep you frame locked with respect to this relationship. Let this collage of feelings and emotions merge into the shadow projection you've summoned. If their appearance or quality shifts, this is fine. Just the energies meld until they become one.

Calmly observe this figure now emerging before you. Embrace any discomfort that may arise as you feel into the core of this character without regard for personal comfort.

Don't resist, judge or intellectualize these shadow feelings, just observe them *as they are*. Experience them as energy of a certain character and quality. Observe your body. *Where do they live? Are there dark spots in your mind filled with pockets of untapped energy you can sense into using your imagination?* Let your fuzzy heart logic guide you and don't worry about being right. Just find the places where the shadow charge is hiding beneath old memories, feelings or beliefs and allow yourself to see/feel into them without resistance.

Now imagine the character sitting beside you. Feel the space that separates you. Feel the relationship in that space for what it is, bad or good. Let your heart lead this process. Try to keep your mind open and receptive. Let the room between you stay open, quiet and present for a moment. Within this emptiness, listen with expectancy. See if you can tune in to detect the subtle qualities of feeling and intention that bind you.

The character has a message for you. What is it?

What does it want from you? What is the underlying motive?

If this character has something to say, a phrase or set of phrases that it repeats, what would that be?

When you feel satisfied that you have grasped the essential nature and function of this shadow pattern, proceed to Step 3 below.

Step 3: Cause the shift

Feel the energy of this character once more. Take a deep breath. Toughen your gut resolve and prepare to fully immerse yourself. Relish the moment with the Warrior's instinctual knowing that failure is impossible.

When you are ready, say the Warrior's mantra, "Today is a good day to die," and dive into the shadow character with your whole mind, body and being.

Be fully present. Stand in the fog until you are one with it. Don't judge or resist. Instead, be calm, still and powerful, completely detached from any worries or the desire for personal comfort. The shadow feeds on your need for comfort. It can't stand when it doesn't have control over you. So become one with it. Tune into it without letting it control you. Let your energy match it completely.

When you have achieved calm acceptance within this shadow energy, you will feel an inner shift, as if you are being pulled through to a deeper layer of yourself. This is when you will start to see your gift, the part of you that became trapped within this projection. Don't rush this process. The desire to cut corners is always rooted in shadow logic. Stick with it to total resolve. Burn through any resistance until the shift occurs. If you have any doubts that the shift has happened, it hasn't yet. It happens right when the shadow understands that your commitment is absolute.

When the shift occurs, match the changing energy as you gently shift along with it. Hold this new state as you move to Step 4.

Step 4: Embrace your gift

Staying at one with this shadow energy, keep your eye on the prize now flowing before you. Remain calm and still as you examine the neutralized shadow pattern to discover the gift that was trapped within it.

What is it? What is this that has been waiting for you behind the shadow all along? Find the word or words that best capture the simple radiance of this soul essence. Write it below:

The gift my shadow resistance was hiding was_____.

Observe this gift. Recognize it for what it is: a trapped part of your Voice essence that you will soon reclaim. If you are ready to reclaim the gift now, you can proceed directly to Part II. LOVE the Light below. For more thorough processing, consider holding the Warrior's stance for up to 24 hours before moving forward.

Tool #2 LOVE the Light (Part II)

Step 1: Look for light
Step 2: Open to love
Step 3: Validate the gift
Step 4: Embody Voice

Step 1: Look for light

A. Invoke the Poet

The Poet *speaks* through innocence, love and praise for the timeless beauty within all life. To invoke the Poet archetype, take a moment to consider a time you felt connected to something larger than yourself, some transcendent beauty that stirred your core in a deeply personal way and which also seemed somehow intimately connected to the whole of life. Perhaps it was an awesome natural setting that took your breath away, or an exquisite piece of music, literature or fine art. Or maybe it was something less obvious: an everyday connection with a stranger, a moment of romantic rapture or perhaps even an unexpected crisis that pulled you into sudden awareness of the preciousness of life.

When you feel connected to the Poet's loving energy, state the invocation on the next page aloud, hand on heart.

"With deep reverence for the creative source that sustains me, I now invoke the transcendent love of the sacred Poet to help me *see the light of timeless truth, beauty and innocence in all experience*, as I venture to reclaim my Voice essence from old shadow energies.

"I acknowledge that the unassuming innocence of the Poet is far more potent than I have yet grasped, given the unconscious shadow barriers that have long dimmed and distorted the Poet's light within my awareness. With this invocation, I confess my humble yearning to remember the wisdom of the Poet to find my Voice by helping others find theirs, unleashing upward spirals of inspired success and fulfillment.

"Today, in a spirit of gratitude for the countless gifts of love and praise that the Poet has already bestowed, I vow to gracefully receive and assimilate whatever inner guidance this sacred archetype may offer in support of my mission to heal this relationship and reclaim my gifts."

Hold the earnest state of open-hearted innocence, receptivity, and reverence that you've accessed through this Poet invocation for at least 1 full minute before moving forward.

B. Recall the shadow

Take a moment to recall the shadow pattern you neutralized in Part I. What did it (he, she, etc.) look and feel like to you when you first came upon it? *Whatever came up for you, bring the image and feeling tone that it conjured up into your mind now.* Your Warrior should have done a reasonable job of neutralizing this delusion in your last session. But the inner space that it once inhabited will remain open to the influence of other shadow energies until we transmute its energy and reclaim the gift of being still trapped within.

What is the gift? Once the shadows were sufficiently neutralized, what did you discover? The words you wrote were just tags for something beyond words. The gift shows itself first towards the feeling tone of reverence and awe that accompanies an emerging possibility. Whatever you felt when the shift happened, please access that essence now. Even if it was just a faint golden thread of possibility, please summon it now.

Step 2: Open to love

Imagine the tone within this gift expanding and radiating outward from the center of your chest as a shimmering light that pulses through you in waves of captivating music, calling you from hidden depths of your being. For at least one full minute, release mental chatter to let this gift's intoxicating potential envelop you, placing you into a state of innocent unguarded wonder like the mind of a small child unburdened by concerns of the world.

Now, let this light contract down into a dense glowing jewel about the size of an egg, hovering in front of you just out of arm's reach. Now in your mind's eye, imagine the shadow character from yesterday reappearing around this egg-sized jewel, trapping it within itself so that it glows almost imperceptibly from the center of the shadow character's chest. The shadow has lost the momentum of its energetic grip over your thinking, but to claim your inheritance you must reclaim that part of you which became trapped within its lair.

The path to redemption is innocent love. Through the lens of the Poet you can see first hand why the shadow could never be more than a silly mirage — whatever form it takes, whatever words it whispers, it always offers the same basic message "fear is real and justified." This is a tempting delusion once we buy the well-socialized premise, but once we see how this mindset destroys our life, we see how insane the shadow truly is.

Through the Poet's innocence, we experience love with no agenda or expectations whatsoever. In this light, we see that fear is always self-created by the choice to deny love. Just as cold is an illusion created by the absence of heat, fear is an illusion created by the absence of love — *an experience that could only seem real if we choose to make it seem real by judging some aspect of ourselves as unlovable.* This choice partitions and splinters our unbroken mind into fragments and causes us to turn the unstoppable creative power at our core into a mere concept (the word *love*) doing battle with other concepts (words like *evil, fear, hatred,* etc.). So long as we fail to question the wisdom of the bipolar belief frame that contains these concepts, we remain estranged from the truth of our essence.

Step 3: Validate the gift

Let's reclaim your birthright now, shall we?
Let your body relax. Take a few deep breaths.
Sink into the moment and let your thoughts soften.

Observe the shadow character with your gift trapped inside. Imagine a cord that connects your heart to that glowing jewel that gives it the appearance of life. As you do, invoke the Poet to summon infinite love on your behalf. Let it envelop you from all four corners of the kingdom, condensing itself into your heart.

When you are ready, send this energy along the cord in a fierce beam of light. Imagine this light as a tractor beam of otherworldly love at the same frequency as the gift itself. Watch in slow motion as this brilliant energy pierces the shadow character's shell, connecting your heart with the glowing jewel inside.

As this beam connects with the gift, the dim glow grows brighter and brighter. The shadow dissolves slowly into oblivion against the illuminating backdrop of this mighty creative power. As the shadow dissolves, you will feel this gift pulling itself to you, like the yearning of a long lost friend returning home. Notice the pull, but don't stop sending until the shadow's form has been completely erased. Take as long as you need to erase it completely. When you are finished, stop.

Let the cord connecting you remain still. Feel the pull between you once more — the yearning for completion. Be still. Hold the cord. Don't move. Accept the moment as it is, trusting in your sufficiency. Stand fully in the moment with an open heart. Learn the power of being complete like this, detached from any agenda.

Sending love like this and then releasing it is the signal that you trust in love's infinite supply. Energetically, this generates a *vacuum* that the world fills over and over again in waves of dynamic co-creation with the creative mind that sustains life. In this moment, you are complete.

When you are ready to reclaim your gift, hold the chord and this peaceful sense of completion as you proceed to Step 4.

Step 4: Embody Voice

Feel the pull once more and drop the chord.

As you do, open your heart and allow the gift to flow across the tiny gap and enter your heart again.

Let it expand to energize every corner of your mind and cell of your body. Feel the returning creative power. Let it assimilate itself into you on every level, lifting you to a state of radically inspired Voice alignment. Surrender all resistance and embrace that within you which feels bigger than the moment, beyond all limitations, at one with life and perhaps even divine.

Take at least 3 minutes to let this power return fully as you open further to allow the poetic beauty of the new life you've chosen sink in. You have released the past, reclaimed the present and opened a new portal into the future of your dreams. Receive this future and know that you are worthy.

Freed of past choices, the doors of perception cleansed through this process, you will come to increasingly experience your own worth as inseparable from that of all human beings.

When our vision is restored, we see the light within all. This is *reality*. It isn't a matter of debate, nor is it a concept, feeling or personal opinion. Undistorted by past pains projected onto the present, reality is self evident infinity, and your Voice is the truth of who you are.

As you transition into an external focus, let the inner light you've reclaimed grow and spread gently outward to suffuse everything you experience. Before you complete this exercise locate a small object (like a stone, marble, coin, a small piece of wood or even a paper clip) that you can use to symbolically represent this gift in material form. In your imagination, imbue this object with the same energy. Then carry this object with you throughout the day.

If this ritual seems silly, suspend your disbelief and just have fun with it. Silly rituals like this have been the fabric of society since the rise of human culture. There's a good reason for this: they work. They make timeless truths feel visceral and real to our senses.

Visit TheVoiceCode.com to get free digital resources, including free training videos and digital copies of key tools offered in this book. You will also find the Voice Code glossary at the end of this book helpful for clarifying and expanding upon any new words, ideas and symbols used.

Afterword

My vision is that the evidence you create through the path outlined in this book will inspire you to stand for mastery as you lead your own personal Voice revolution from start to finish. If this idea stirs up doubt or resistance, please use the CREATE script (Act I, Scene 6) to remove those old shadows and reclaim your power.

You can do this. There's no question.

I did it and there's nothing special about me. Truth be told, I spent most of my life lost, feeling like an outcast, trying to fit in, burying my light under a dense blanket of intellectual concepts. So how did I end up being someone who could stand before you with such clarity and conviction? The same way you can:

I learned from the Voice Code.

Once I cracked the code, I knew I'd found my life's calling, but I had *no idea* how far I was from being someone capable of effectively conveying this message. Like most of my clients when they get their first taste of total Voice alignment, ego inflation set in and I got frame locked without even knowing it. Right when things were finally getting good, my life went to shambles and I had no idea why. One day at a time, I used the Voice Code map to heal myself, and somehow ended up creating the tools this book offers.

Through this often harrowing four year journey, I learned one humbling lesson very clearly: I am only the Voice Code's first student, and my lessons are far from over. This book is my heartfelt invitation for you to join me so that we can continue this Phase II learning journey together. I'm delighted to share my teacher with you. I know beyond the shadow of any doubt that if you devote yourself to mastery, you will be unstoppable.

But whatever you do, please be patient and *stay vigilant.* When Benjamin Franklin said that the "price of freedom is eternal vigilance," he wasn't just whistling Dixie. *The shadow is more than just a delusion — it's a tightly organized delusional system that's devastatingly effective at stealing our minds.* Once we stabilize in Stage 9 Visionary, we have passed a critical tipping point after which the shadow's ploys begin to lose their pull. But until then, we must be careful if we hope to make this epic journey without the bumps and bruises that came to those before us.

While I remain grateful for the gifts that came from my own painful lessons, I now realize that much of my pain was unnecessary. My mission is now to help you cross the finish line without the same struggles. Having now witnessed countless miracles in my own life and the lives of clients, I have no question that you can use these tools to achieve the life of your dreams. This paradigm works, and it's absolutely bulletproof if you give yourself to it fully. But you must commit fully, or you will find yourself in a world of confusion, as untold shadow habits try to seduce you back into the false comforts of the cramped belief cages you crafted during Phase I.

My own journey to meet the Big Boss and ensuing visit to the white light will be the subject of a separate book. For now, let me share a bit of beautiful wisdom that came to me during the first leg of this 48-month marathon. Four months after I cracked the code, I was struggling to write this book while learning powerful lessons in how NOT to follow my Voice. Weird things were happening all around and my heart was telling me that I would have to let go of everything I had come to know as "me" in order to complete this mission. I didn't want to believe this, so I just kept chugging along.

The less I listened, the more of a nightmare my life became. Old clients were going AWOL, my marriage was going to pieces, and total strangers were attacking me without cause. It was bizarre. Nothing made sense to me anymore except the Voice Code. Yet I was somehow completely ill-equipped to make this discovery accessible to others! The one gift that had always served me without fail — my ability to communicate clearly — had somehow left me right when I needed it most. A deep sense of loneliness and loss began to surface, surrounded by a cynical rage that life could be so cruel. These were feelings I'd spent my whole life trying to avoid.

In retrospect it is clear that I was being challenged to transmute deeply repressed Doubter (shadow poet) and Enforcer (shadow warrior) projections. The call of the moment was not to believe them, but to process them to solve my problems from the inside out. But at the time I just had an equation. I was still well over a year away from deciphering the CREATE process or coming up with the dragon slaying narrative. So I was stuck holding the bag, trying to figure out how to leverage the Voice Code to solve the very problems that it's discovery seemed to have instigated.

Within the next two years, my marriage would end and I would visit the white light after meeting the Big Boss — that elusive inner-devil who haunts us all until we confront him. The piece below came from an early draft of my book on December 1, 2012. Right in the thick of the storm. At the time I was experimenting with a fun story frame that used a one-armed astronomer, businessman and a thug character to represent the three elements of the human mind: the creative unconscious, conscious mind and primal unconscious (respectively). As the story goes, these three characters were stranded on a desert island and needed to learn how to come together, despite their differences, to escape.

I was writing a section called "advice to a one-armed astronomer," when my writing began to feel taken over by a loving and articulate presence. Having never channeled anything before, I didn't know what to make of it, so I just let it pour through me and then moved on. Whether or not you are open to the idea of channeling, you'll find the writing in this passage beautiful and the wisdom priceless.

Looking back years later, I was stunned to see just how prophetic these words were. For starters, note the phrase "Big Bang" in the third paragraph. This was code for *Big Boss*, that hateful monster who was already emerging but whom I would not meet directly for another 18 months. I was being told that I was going to have to surrender everything to find the original choice that created my problems, in order to complete this mission. As you embark on your own journey, may these words comfort you as they have comforted me and others I've helped through this same transition.

[From *The Voice Code*, early draft, December 1, 2012]

LIFE ADVICE TO A ONE-ARMED ASTRONOMER: Your mind is finally open to questioning everything. Your goal now is to find and ask the right questions. You must use that open mind to receive the truth of the present moment, completely unencumbered by the notions of the future or past memories. Understand that your resistance to the paradoxical TRUTH of non-existence is just belief-residue from the past. It is nothing to be afraid of.

But all beliefs are maintained by one fear — the fear of being pulled backwards into the density of the material world and all forms of human manipulation. Take heart: this fear is based on the faulty assumption that these 'bad' things are real in the first place. Which they aren't. The light of truth is waiting to show you this. It's much simpler than you think, because your thinking was designed to help you overcomplicate it.

Be willing to let go of everything that isn't true, and the solutions will find you. Understand that fear is the memory of something that never happened, an indescribably terrible nightmare that you made seem real through the power of your belief in it. In that terrible "big bang" moment, your mind split and you buried the memory in your subconscious, like a child hides a scary toy in the closet. The closet is now what you call reality. You resist this reality for only one reason: because you still believe that the 'scary toy' is real and you want to protect yourself from it. But you'll never find out the truth and forgive the fears that are hidden unless you are willing to make yourself vulnerable again by opening up the closet.

You mustn't do this alone. The characters you perceive around you were sent for very specific reasons to help you. To overcome your resistance you must ultimately open the powerful force of your own personal WILL — a lesson that the THUG is dying to teach you (even though he doesn't consciously know this). And if you are open to receiving his lessons, you will be teaching him your own wisdom of vulnerability that will move him farther down his path to awakening (even though you may not consciously know this either). It's a perfectly designed situation that runs along smoothly — if only you will let it. This is true for all human relationships.

The THUG is trying to tell you (through his crude barbs, insults and sophomoric humor) that to find the truth that you seek, you must be willing to come down from the clouds of intellectual abstraction and once again experience the full present-moment density of your physical body. You must surrender your 'spiritual ego' and embrace physicality without judgment or struggle. This is not a cruel joke, it is just a necessary step to help you develop faith that nothing you have learned that is true can ever be changed, misplaced or forgotten. Loss is part of the 'game' you designed to keep yourself asleep. You will continue to resist loss until you are willing to lose the concept of loss itself. I know that you enjoy irony, so I thought I'd throw that one in there.

Take heart — you don't have to do it all at once. Opening your WILL is quite easy once you open your HEART; and completely impossible otherwise. The reason the density of the physical body seems so terrifying to you now is because you have judged the physical world as unlovable. In fact, your passion for studying nature is a defensive move disguised as spiritual insight — you are pro-actively trying to dismiss your fear and hatred of nature by creating an intellectualized identity of yourself as a great nature scientist. But you aren't fooling yourself very well anymore. That's why you are (somewhat) open to these lessons.

Have a good laugh at yourself, will you? Your creative genius is quite remarkable. Then when you are done laughing, open your eyes and look at the BUSINESSMAN in front of you. He is here to teach you the lesson of opening your HEART to truly caring about other humans. And when you receive this lesson from him, his heart will open too because he will have the evidence he needs to confirm his lifelong suspicion that he truly is a loving person.

When you receive the wisdom behind the 'boring practical lessons' of the BUSINESSMAN, you will eventually see that judgments you've made of his world were — like all judgments and beliefs — based in fear, intended to protect you from the excruciating guilt and sadness you still feel for not being more generous and loving with others.

The past is the past. Do not dwell. Once you pass through the flimsy threshold of fear and open your heart again, you will be amazed at what you experience. You will see light and joy in the eyes of others instead of so much cruelty and darkness. You will experience patience and compassion for yourself and for everyone around you based upon a very real present moment awareness of their infinite creative potential. In fact, you will find them more excruciatingly beautiful and worthy of love than you can possibly now imagine in your current sad condition. You will see in them an awesome reflection of your own true nature, and you will feel grateful to them for showing you it. These moments of joining might seem trivial, but they are far from it. They are 'glitches in the matrix' of time and space, glimpses of long-lost eternity that shatter into spiky shards the cement barricades of suffering that block the light and keep men dreaming.

Joining is not an act of will — it is an act of being willing to see what's so. And, in this simple, vulnerable state of open-heartedness, the 'joining' you experience will ripple and cascade throughout the entire hologram of your life, seamlessly integrating the practical logistical challenges of the present moment situation with your lofty and noble life aspirations. You will see that — far from being a nuisance — the present moment is the ONLY path to your goal. It has been designed specifically to help you manifest your soul's deepest intentions. And, on a "practical boring linear" level, you will become like a magician to these people, effortlessly reflecting back to them their own forgotten nature, buried beneath their own misguided guilt for the "big bang" moment of terror that they still believe in, but that never happened.

Your challenge is very tough, as you now perceive it. The truth is that only unconditional love for others will give you the strength you need to move through to the next stage of learning. Have patience and pace yourself. There is no rush. Judging yourself for not going quick enough will only isolate you more and delay your inevitable lessons.

Also know that discomfort and vulnerability, like pain and loneliness, are also just illusions — judgments against reality. These feelings need not hold you back. In truth, they can only do so if you are not fully committed to achieving the transcendent learning goals that life (aka 'you') has arranged for you.

Actually, the only thing you really need to do is be willing to stop trying, stop resisting, and stop worrying about your own illusions of personal control and comfort. Stay present and learn to fully embody the realm of space-time perception with an OPEN HEART, WILL AND MIND. As you do this, be prepared to have all of your buried fears from the past come back up again to 'test' you. Remember that none of this is real. The correct perception is always gratitude, because these challenges are disguised opportunities for you to forgive yourself for things you think you did in the past that you've been repressing.

The real you cannot be hurt or changed. Ever. When you have worked through all of these scary lessons on the insane screen of time-space perception, you will have a moment of revelation in which you know — with every ounce of your being — that the world you seem to live in now (space-time) never existed in the first place. This knowing comes not from any facts or figures in the outside world, but from a memory of the very beginning of time — from the memory that you are the one who created all of it. That time seems like a long time ago, but it is nothing more than now.

When you see this, you will laugh at this with indescribable joy. You will then choose, like I did, to wake up from the 'optical delusion' and rejoin the 'glistening undifferentiated goo' that is your true home. I do realize that this probably doesn't sound like a whole lot of fun to you now, so — in the meantime — feel free to procrastinate as much as you need to. Read a book. Grab yourself a cocktail or something. The truth is the true and nothing else is true — the rest, as they say, is just waiting.

As your initial journey through this material comes to a close, let me take this opportunity to thank you from the bottom of my heart for opening your heart to this message. That you have made it this far shows me that you are someone with the rare courage and character to seek and stand for truth in today's crazy world. I honor this and look forward to serving you, as together we join the simple act of seeing reality beyond shadows. This simple act is the stuff that great lives are made of, as we escape the delusion of limitations alone and together, one step at a time, being the change we've been seeking.

We are One, after all.

One Mind. One Love. One Purpose. And when we stand for truth in the service of life, we speak with One Voice — your Voice — the Voice of innocence.

From behind the cloud cover of past learning, your Voice speaks with unwavering conviction of who you are and what your mission must be. It does this in steps that work with you. It doesn't command; it doesn't demand; it waits until you are ready, showing you through increasingly exhilarating insights, epiphanies and revelations the specific instrument you were born to play in the symphony of life. But you are the decision maker. Until you choose, nothing changes.

So I invite you to choose again. To take the next step, turn the page to see the simple path to mastery that will help you turn this map into a life without limits as you lead your own Voice Revolution from start to finish.

The Path to Mastery

In this section we outlined a plan to help you grow the seeds we've planted into the life of your dreams. In practice, the tricky part about following our Voice is learning to listen correctly to our inner guidance on a real time basis. Our Voice speaks through our state of being. In Phase I we mistake our beliefs for reality because we confuse *thinking* and *being*. Most of us already know that thinking and being are different in theory, but in practice we find this distinction elusive.

Our being embraces the mystery of a Voice-driven life. Our brains like the idea, but fall into bitter turf wars with our hearts when decision time comes. When our brains and being fall into struggle, we become frame locked and our bodies go on autopilot as our dreams slip farther and farther from our reach. This initial journey through the Voice Code map has offered powerful tools and distinctions to help you begin to bridge the brain-being gap. Going forward, here's the billion-dollar question:

How can you use this map to dissolve the gap forever?

To answer, I'll borrow a great line from jazz musician Charlie Parker when asked how someone might learn to play like at his level:

Practice, practice, practice...
Then throw it all away and just wail.

This journey was designed using holistic Voice Code logic to help you master the application of this same logic to solve any problem from the inside out. If you committed fully to the journey, it is very likely that you broke through the brain-being barrier on at least one occasion. The journey was designed to unleash new power and momentum with each step forward, building over time towards climactic crescendos through which our brain finally surrenders to the music of our being. If you wish to make inspired moments like this permanent, here's another bit of well-considered advice:

Make mastery your mission.

Dragon-slaying is a mastery practice. This new mindset may be a little awkward at first, and you won't always be comfortable. But if you made it this far, then you've already started the ball rolling. Besides, of all the mastery challenges life offers, could anything be more worth pursuing? Everything else we might want in life — money, power, love, health, and success — these wants grow from our desire for freedom. Your Voice *IS* freedom. Why wait? Why not choose your Voice now and let the world catch up?

Below you will find a seven-step path to mastery using this book along with other suggested resources and strategies to support and accelerate mastery. The more you give yourself to this work, the more your brain and being will unite to lift you to a life without limits along the path of least resistance. With each step forward, the world around you will shift, as inner blocks are removed. When your Voice revolution is complete, you will join that envied group of "lucky ones" who break all the rules and make life look easy.

If this seems like hype, please remember:

You are a force of nature. You have unlimited creative potential and a Voice that calls you to greatness. When you release the past, you will CREATE a future without limits doing what you love. The only barrier is belief.

You can work overtime to convince yourself otherwise, but those self-doubts will never be anything more than old shadow patterns projected into your awareness from the primal unconscious. May the seven mastery steps below help you reclaim your power to thrive beyond belief in today's incredible world.

Step 1. Study the glossary. Grab the freebies.

This book gives you a new language and a set of free online resources to help you assimilate this paradigm. Make sure you take full advantage of these resources. You'll see that I have a unique way of embodying these ideas in person, which will help you experience their power in a visceral way. But first, make sure to give the glossary a thorough read. It contains more than 100 terms that were either invented or reframed to support integrated mastery of this paradigm. The glossary also contains many powerful ideas that didn't fit within the constraints of the book's narrative. Just reading these definitions will bring new life to this material, allowing you to draw powerful new associations to streamline and consolidate all prior learning.

Sign up for free videos and resources:
www.TheVoiceCode.com

Step. 2. Use the tools. CREATE new rituals.

Intellectual understanding is not enough. To master this paradigm you must apply these ideas with rhythmic consistency over time until you produce real-world evidence that they work. This book gives you a powerful set of tools and an eight-week path to help you absorb this paradigm in your brain, body and being as you make powerful goal breakthroughs. If you are like most, you probably read through the book without fully immersing yourself. If so, once you've completed Step 1 (above), take the journey again and *actually do the things advised in the weekly checklists.* Once you do this, you'll be hooked. Keep the tools (CARE ritual, CREATE script, CAVE Buster, etc.) accessible so that you can use them any time you feel stuck. To dramatically accelerate your learning, create a consistent weekly morning practice that helps you start your day with Voice alignment using these same tools.

Step 3. Make it a game. Track gifts & gains.

As you cultivate mastery through steps 1 and 2, you will begin to spontaneously distinguish more and more old shadow habits all the time, wherever you go, whatever you do. This is a good sign! Your Voice Alchemist is saying, "Who is that?" to limiting thoughts and sending you more opportunities to reclaim your power. I advise clients to make shadow busting a fun new game to play with purpose.

Capture shadow patterns for later processing. Track gifts reclaimed and revisit them regularly. Visit the link below for a free tool we call the *Shadow Agency* that you can use to store, study and process shadow patterns in one centralized location. Your Alchemist will thank you:

Link to free Shadow Agency tool:
www.TheVoiceCode.com/ShadowAgency

Step 4. Stay connected. Share your story.

Join our online community to stay in the loop and share your successes. Sign up on our mailing list, like our Facebook page, attend one of our free webinars, watch our free coaching videos, and read our blogs decoding current events through the Voice Code lens. This book is just the tiny tip of an immense iceberg. Many new Voice Code-related tools and training solutions are in the works. When you read through the glossary (Step 1) you'll get just a small taste of the exciting stuff in the pipeline to help visionary minds integrate and make centuries of research in the social sciences actionable through this lens. Connect with like-minded people through our online portals and keep the conversation going.

Link to free mailing list:
www.TheVoiceCode.com

Share your insights on our Facebook Page
www.facebook.com/WorldviewThinking

Step 5. Explore the roots. Connect the dots.

Step five is to follow your curiosity instincts and dive deeper in the pursuit of a more profound and agile grasp of the Phase II mindset. The thirteen books below are portals into an expanded conceptual mastery of this paradigm. Each offered a puzzle-piece that ultimately helped me crack the code. Use them as a starting point to launch your own personal discovery in the pursuit of total mastery. As you read them, summon the Alchemist and see if you can put the puzzle pieces together. Ask yourself: "How does this material relate to the Voice Code? What's the big idea that connects these frameworks? How are they distinct?"

Note: You don't need an integrated scholarly understanding of this map in order to master the inner game. But it is very helpful to have a holistic grasp of this material to avoid frame lock and keep your mind open. In the list below, I offer some pointers to help you see the connection between big ideas in these books and foundational concepts from the Voice Code paradigm:

Igniting Inspiration – *John Marshall Roberts | Uses early version of what became the Voice Code to help drive change through transformational communications. Great deep dive into worldview segmentation.*

Seven Habits of Highly Effective People – *Stephen Covey | Brilliant bestseller offers a well-constructed paradigm for personal and professional effectiveness that mirrors the CREATE cycle.*

Tao Te Ching – *Lao Tzu (Stephen Mitchell translation) | Timeless classic. Reads as beautiful poetry that trains people in the art of Voice alignment. (Read "Tao" for more on this connection.)*

Levels of Existence – *Clare W. Graves | A quick and readable distillation of the research for the original 8-stage developmental model that laid the groundwork for the 12-stage Voice Code map.*

Flow – *Mihaly Csikszentmihalyi | Innovative research gives a breakdown on how our experience shifts during moments of high engagement. Great insights on situational factors that drive Voice alignment.*

The Evolving Self – *Robert Keegan | Profound model frames mental development as a process of emerging from embeddedness in earlier ways of seeing. Powerful insights into frame lock and worldview development.*

The Path of Least Resistance – *Robert Fritz | Extraordinary work shows how inner dynamic tension drives success ("advancing patterns") or failure ("oscillating patterns") in accordance with nature's intelligence. Mirrors competing motivators element of Voice Code model.*

Holographic Universe – *Michael Talbot | Fascinating and highly accessible look at the holographic model of reality with many examples and case studies. (See "Holographic model" in glossary for more.)*

Eastern Body, Western Mind – Judith Anodea | *A comprehensive and practical reference that maps the eastern chakras to western science (Note: 7 Chakras mirror the CREATE cycle. See "chakras" in glossary for more.)*

Archetypes and the Collective Unconscious – Carl Gustav Jung | *Powerful up-close look inside the genius mind that hatched many of the biggest ideas that came together with the Voice Code: shadow, archetypes, individuation, etc. (See "Individuation" in glossary for more.)*

The Power of Myth – Joseph Campbell | *Colorful trip through mythic archetypes from the man who distilled the "Hero's Journey" story structure. (Hint: 3 Acts mirror the 3-level structure of the human mind.)*

Busting Loose From the Money Game – Robert Scheinfeld | *Grounded application of holographic "inside-out" model to practical life. Many powerful ideas that directly overlap with Voice Code paradigm.*

Disappearance of the Universe – Gary Renard | *Highly accessible elaboration of life as experienced from the higher rungs of Phase II (Stage 9 and up): radical non-dualism. Also a powerful intro to non-dual spiritual text, A Course in Miracles. Sync perfectly with Voice Code logic.*

Step 6. Find partners. Grow by giving.

Find people to share your understanding with and grow a mastermind group dedicated to mastering the game of Phase II thriving. Once the Voice Code bug has bitten you, you'll feel an indomitable urge to share the love. Believe it or not, Mother Nature bakes this into the cake. As our paradoxical Phase II journey pulls us forth, we recognize with increasing clarity that helping others find their Voice is the only way to maintain Voice alignment with ourselves. To take your learning to a new level, form a group of resonant minds and support each other in the pursuit of mastery.

Step 7. Repeat until revolution.

This book will grow with you over time. Make sure to keep it handy and use as a reference tool to help you solve day-to-day problems using the Phase II mindset. Resolve to complete the 8 week journey through this book at least four times in the next 14 months to create measurable breakthroughs on four different goals. After each pass through, revisit these seven steps to expand and strengthen your mastery. You might imagine that this material would grow boring after so much repetition, but that's simply not the case! Every time you read this book, you will get more out of it. Your thinking will shift and you will assimilate this material at a deeper level. This has been true for my coaching clients and for me. I spent four years working 60-hour weeks to write this book and get it ready for prime time. Yet even now, when I revisit chapters, it's as if I'm reading them for the first time, getting deeper insights and making new connections. The same will be true for you.

Advanced Support: Legacy Partnerships

As an old-school D.I.Y. learner, I've read many books that have left me feeling unsatisfied. So often it seems authors write a book as a sort of advertising pamphlet for their other, more expensive offerings, holding back to lure people into advanced trainings. I couldn't bring myself to do this with this book. My Voice called me to do my absolute best to give you everything you need to lead your Voice Revolution from start to finish without additional investments.

Also know that we've crafted a fun, engaging path to help you master this material in record time. The starting point for this journey is a course we call the Visionary Boot-camp that helps you permanently reframe the principle of Authority as you transform a particular life domain. To learn more about this course and other Voice Code offerings, please visit us online:

www.WorldviewThinking.com

Congratulations! You've now seen a clear path to mastery. To get started with Step 1, turn the page and explore the Glossary. There's lot of cool ideas and information that drill deeper on what you've already learned, while tying everything together in one elegant bow. Plus, you'll get a sneak preview of new Voice Code volumes coming down the pike.

Voice Code Glossary

In most books, the glossary is an afterthought. In this book, it's an adventure — a direct portal into your multidimensional mastery of the holistic Phase II mindset. The scenes that form the narrative spine of this journey were streamlined to help you attain an experiential understanding of this new map. Within this glossary you will find a new language that helps you fill in the gaps as you make powerful new associations to consolidate all prior learning using Voice Code logic. With this language, you are giving your left-brain a powerful set of tools to collaborate with your being in the course of your everyday life.

Note that most of terms in this new glossary are not new. They have been seen before in one form or another. What's new here is the *holistic context that binds all of these words and ideas together in alignment with one simple, actionable and scientifically derived formula that explains all other systems.* The Voice Code came from two decades of interdisciplinary research. When the smoke cleared, we'd mapped the entire spectrum of human experiences, from the womb until the highest levels of consciousness, in a way that reconciles more than a century of research with mankind's most cherished wisdom traditions.

Sounds like hype, doesn't it? Study this glossary and see for yourself. As this new vocabulary sinks in, it will stoke your brain to ask new questions and uncover new connections that clear the lens of perception and invite your Voice to lift you to greatness.

Alchemist. The second of the four archetypal mentors through which our Voice speaks from the creative unconscious (aka Plane of Creative Vision). Governs the principle of Resonance and the 16 gifts of Possibility. In Phase II of the human journey, we align with the Alchemist to "Think With Heart" as we master the CREATE skills of Commitment, Reframing and Exploration. The journey to total mastery of these skills takes us through worldview Stage 7 Explorer, Stage 8 Pathfinder, and Stage 9 Visionary. The season through which we "Inspire the Alchemist" as part of our Voice Revolution is called the Alchemist's Autumn. It is the second of four seasons that comprise this process. When we've completed the entire process we are firmly grounded in Stage 9

Visionary and radically inspired to bring our gifts to the world in a spirit of shared thriving. **Calling:** Think With Heart | **Location:** Creative Unconscious | **Mastery Skill:** Exploring

Alchemist's Autumn. The second of four seasons that comprise the Voice Revolution. In this season, we transmute shadow alchemist (aka Forgetter habits) to reframe the Principle of Resonance to align with our new inside-out Authority frame (see Emperor's Summer). In the Alchemist's Autumn we develop vision into the unseen order of everyday reality. Through this adventure, we learn to "Think With Heart" as we reframe the principle of Resonance from "believing" (frame lock) to "knowing" (Voice) and reclaim the 16 gifts of Possibility that the Alchemist offers. When this season is complete, we have restored and aligned both the Emperor and Alchemist to develop that rare ability to "Own the Frame" regardless of circumstances.

Achiever (Stage 6). The sixth worldview to emerge along the 12-Stage path over "Voice Mountain." Achievers are the ruling worldview of Phase I (Stages 1 through 6), which dominated our world unchallenged for more than two centuries until the rise of digital connectivity flattened the playing field to usher in Phase II. **Frame Lock:** Achievers prize autonomy and security over the balancing needs of connection and change (respectively). This causes a competitive, control driven "zero-sum" mindset in which values of power, success and affluence dominate while softer Explorer (Stage 7) values (empathy, equality and relatedness) are dismissed. **Frame Mantra:** "Express myself to get what I want, but don't get in trouble." | **Framing Metaphor:** Life is a game | **Key Polarity:** win or lose| **Mass Emergence:** ~1700 (Industrial Revolution) | **Balancing Worldview:** Explorer (Stage 7, Phase II)

Assimilate. The "A" in the CREATE cycle. Assimilate is the fourth step of the 6-Step CREATE cycle and the fourth of six skills that visionary minds master to become a Phase II force of nature. To truly master Assimilation we must "Face the Dark" to clear "the cave" of our primal unconscious. In practice, Assimilation involves directly attuning to the frequency of shadow energies (fear, resistance, etc.) uncovered through Alchemist's Exploring (step 3) until the charge dissipates. This neutralizes old shadow patterns and helps us authenticate the Voice gifts buried within, paving the way for us to reclaim our power in Step 5. (Transmute). **Mentor:** Warrior | **Calling:** Face the Dark | **Body Center:** solar plexus (3rd chakra) | **Balancing Center:** throat (5th chakra) | **Balancing Skill:** Explore

Authority. The principle of original cause, Authority is the power to create by choice. It is the first of three principles that we reframe during Phase II of the human journey (worldview Stages 7-12). In Phase I we frame authority as external, which keeps us frame locked into believing that we are an effect of the outside world. This breeds a survivalist mindset in which we feel we must compromise our passions and obey the rules of external authorities to survive. In Phase II we choose again to reframe authority as internal. This gives us freedom to hear and follow Voice as we learn to operate from a Phase II inside-out mindset. **Voice Mentor:** Emperor | **Shadow Mentor:** Dividers | **Phase I Frame Lock:** Do Not Find | **Phase II Calling:** Own Your Mind

12 Stages of Worldview Thinking

Phase I. DEFEND	CHOOSE AGAIN	Phase II. CREATE
Life is a Dilemma	Frame Reversal	*Life is a Paradox*
Seeing is Belieivng		*Beliefs Create Seeing*
Extrinsic Motivators		*Intrinsic Vision*

Achiever 6 ←----→ 7 Explorer

Believer 5 **Authority** 8 Pathfinder

Outlaw 4 9 Visionary

Subject 3 **Resonance** 10 Luminary

Survivor 2 11 Sage

Womb 1 **Trust** 12 Messiah

Autonomy. One of four primary motivators that govern decision-making on the Plane of Social Control (worldview Stages 5-8) . It represents the universal human drive to be a self-determined individual with free decision-making authority. According to the Voice Code logic, the need for *autonomy* is counter balanced by the need for *connection* as part of the natural time-space matrix that governs perception. When we follow our Voice, we make choices that allow us to satisfy both needs simultaneously. When we don't, we choose one need at the expense of the other and become frame locked into a split-minded "either/or" thinking style that blocks our Voice and compromises our creative potential. **Motivation Type:** Drive | **Balancing Motivator:** Connection | **Perceptual Polarity:** Space (Self vs. World)

Believer (Stage 5). The fifth worldview to emerge along the 12-Stage Voice Code path. Believers are the grounding spiritual anchor of the Plane of Control which includes Stages 5 (Believer) through 8 (Pathfinder). **Frame Lock:** Believers prize tribal connection and security over the balancing needs of *autonomy* and *change* (respectively). This leads to an ideological black-and-white mindset which values discipline, authority and sacrifice above the more solutions-focused Pathfinder (Stage 8) values (creativity, competence and sustainability). **Frame Mantra:** "Sacrifice my own needs to attain future reward" | **Framing Metaphor:** Life is test | **Key Polarity:** pass or fail | **Mass Emergence:** ~1000 AD (Rise of monotheistic religion) | **Balancing Worldview:** Pathfinder (Stage 8; Phase II)

"Blame the Dark" This is the shadow calling of the Enforcers. This fear-mongering team of shadow warrior projections includes Prisoners (passive pole) and Punishers (active pole). When we follow their guidance, we lose access to our Voice in the Warrior expression. Instead of "Facing the Dark" to assimilate fear, we then project it outward through a policy of enforced blame, shame and attack towards suitable targets.

Cave (The). This is the closely guarded part of our primal unconscious where we store our deepest survival-based fears. Primal fears of this type are primarily associated with the shadow warriors (aka Enforcers). When we "clear the cave" on an issue, we arrest the enforcers and reclaim our lost gifts of Power in that domain. This is how we restore proper alignment with the Warrior archetype and the principle of Trust this Voice mentor governs. **Note:** We can't fully clear the cave on an issue until we've first transmuted shadow projections that block proper alignment with our Voice in the Emperor and Alchemist expression. Until this happens, our Enforcer shadows remain buried at the hands of the Dividers (shadow emperors) and Forgetters (shadow alchemists).

Chakras. Chakras are subtle energy centers in the human body. Many different chakra frameworks have been proposed. Most converge around the notion that there are 7 major chakras that govern the human body through a circular energy flow that bridges grounding energy at the base of the spine (1st chakra), up through the heart (4th balancing chakra) to the top of the head (7th chakra) and back down again in a cyclical fashion. The CREATE cycle mirrors this flow precisely. The graphic below shows the parallels between the

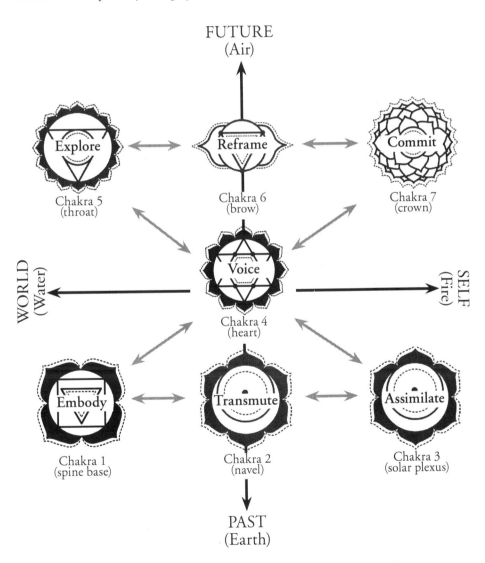

FUTURE
(Air)

| Explore | Reframe | Commit |
| Chakra 5 (throat) | Chakra 6 (brow) | Chakra 7 (crown) |

WORLD (Water)

Voice

Chakra 4 (heart)

SELF (Fire)

| Embody | Transmute | Assimilate |
| Chakra 1 (spine base) | Chakra 2 (navel) | Chakra 3 (solar plexus) |

PAST
(Earth)

CREATE skills and specific chakras from the 7th crown (Commit: Emperor) to the 1st root (Embody: Poet) as energy cycles through the timeless center-point axis where space (self-world) and time (past- future) come together in the *NOW* through our heart (4th chakra). A separate volume is in the works to dive deeper into these connections.

Change. Change is one of four primary motivators that govern all human thinking and behavior. It represents the universal human aspiration for progress and forward evolution. According to the Voice Code, the aspiration for change is counter balanced by the desire for *security* as part of the natural matrix that governs perception. When we follow our Voice, we align with nature's orchestrating intelligence to satisfy the aspiration for positive change without sacrificing the balancing desire for security. When we believe in shadows, we choose one need at the expense of the other and become frame locked.
Motivation Type: Aspiration | **Balancing Motivator:** Security | **Perceptual Polarity:** Time (Past vs. Future)

Commit. Step 1 in the 6-step CREATE cycle and the first of six inner game skills that visionary leaders master to become a Phase II force of nature. To master Commitment we must "own our mind" by reframing Authority from external (power outside) to internal (power inside) under the guidance of our Voice in the Emperor expression. In practice, Commitment requires that we clearly distinguish inner Voice directives and choose them fully from a state of radical inner coherence. As our mastery of this skill increases, we find ourselves naturally Reframing (Step 2) the present from the perspective of successful future accomplishment. This enhances our motivation and propels us with passion until our Commitment is Embodied (Step 6) and the cycle is renewed.
Mentor: Emperor | **Calling:** Own Your Mind | **Body Center:** top of head (7th chakra) | Balancing Center: base of spine (1st chakra) | **Balancing Skill:** Embody

Connection. One of four primary motivators that govern all human thinking and behavior. Connection represents the universal human need to be related with others at both a personal and group/social level. According to the Voice Code logic, the need for connection is counter balanced by the need for *autonomy* as part of the natural time-space matrix that governs evolution. When we follow our Voice, we align with nature's orchestrating intelligence to satisfy the need for connection without sacrificing the balancing need of autonomy. When we don't, we choose one need at the expense of the other and become frame locked into an "either/or" mindset. **Motivator Type:** Need | **Balancing Motivator:** Autonomy | **Perceptual Polarity:** Space (Self vs. World)

Competing Motivators. According to Voice Code, four universal motivations drive over 90% of thinking and behavior in the developed world: *security, autonomy, connection* and *change*. These motivators can be further classified according to four different motivation types: *desires, drives, needs* and *aspirations*, respectively. When we follow our Voice, these four motivations become balanced, complementary and mutually reinforcing such that the satisfaction of one need naturally pulls us to satisfy all four. When we are frame locked, we experience these four needs as mutually exclusive, in endless competition. Resolving these dichotomies is the central challenge that drives the evolution of human thinking along the 12-Stage Voice Code path.

Control (Plane of). The realm of ordinary thinking and perception. Also refers to the four worldviews that dominate thinking in the developed world: Believers (Stage 5), Achievers (Stage 6), Explorers (Stage 7) and Pathfinders (Stage 8). According to the Voice Code, the world we perceive is 100% self authored. Through this lens, space-time perception is a holographic out-

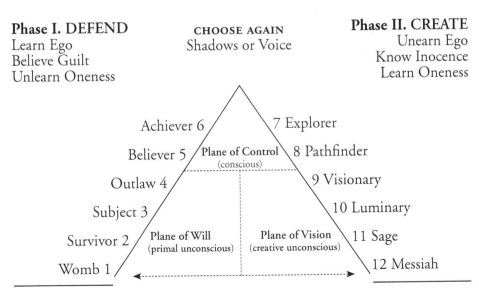

Phase I. DEFEND
Learn Ego
Believe Guilt
Unlearn Oneness

CHOOSE AGAIN
Shadows or Voice

Phase II. CREATE
Unearn Ego
Know Inocence
Learn Oneness

Achiever 6 7 Explorer
Believer 5 **Plane of Control** (conscious) 8 Pathfinder
Outlaw 4 9 Visionary
Subject 3 10 Luminary
Survivor 2 **Plane of Will** (primal unconscious) **Plane of Vision** (creative unconscious) 11 Sage
Womb 1 12 Messiah

picturing of our inner world generated by unresolved dynamic tension between two unconscious planes: the creative unconscious (aka Plane of Creative Vision) and the primal unconscious (aka Plane of Primal Will). But until we reach Stage 9 (Visionary) status, we don't experience ourselves as the sole author of our experience, because we still confuse who we are (Voice) with our ego identity (self-concept). When we reach Stage 9 (Visionary) status, we transcend the Plane of Control as we begin to operate from the non-dualistic Plane of Creative Vision (worldview Stages 9-12) in our everyday life. With this shift we become capable of thriving from the inside-out, operating from the level of cause (inner) instead of effect (outer).

CREATE Cycle. The six-step inner game cycle that visionary minds master. Our ability to hear and follow our Voice depends entirely upon the extent to which we have mastered and integrated the six skills that comprise this cycle: *Commitment, Reframing, Exploring, Assimilation, Transmuting and Embodiment*. When the flow of this natural cycle is disrupted, our mind becomes divided against itself as our primal unconscious (home of shadows) takes control over our conscious thinking through the DEFEND cycle. The DEFEND cycle drives frame lock and is the invisible inner cause of all perceived problems. When the CREATE cycle is restored, our creative unconscious (home of Voice) is restored to it's proper role and all shadows dissolve as our Voice is restored to conscious awareness.

Creative Dominance. The unified mental state we enter when we choose our Voice to align our conscious mind with our creative unconscious (Plane of Creative Vision; Stages 9-12). When we are frame locked, we enter a split-minded condition called "primal dominance." This blocks access to our creative unconscious, and makes us experience our four Voice mentors (Emperor, Alchemist, Warrior and Poet) through a distorted shadow lens. During the 6-Stage "unlearning" process of Phase II (worldview stages 7-12), we make operating from a state of creative dominance a new way of life to heal our split minds and become One with our Voice. By Stage 12 (Messiah) we are no longer tempted to believe in shadows, having fully purified our primal unconscious to become one with our Voice.

The CREATE Cycle: 6 Verbs of the Visionary Mind

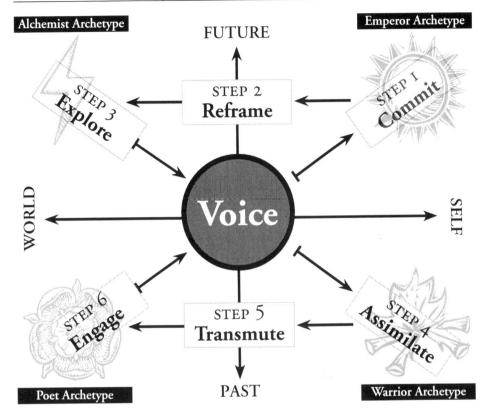

Creative Vision (Plane of). Another term for the creative unconscious — that aspect of the human mind through which our Voice speaks. In first person experiential terms, the Plane of Vision is "where we go" when we access our Voice as it speaks through intuition, inspiration, mystical experiences and "aha" moments of revelatory insight. As we progress along Phase II (worldview Stages 7-12), we rely increasingly on information and inner guidance from this dimension of human consciousness as we navigate our lives. In the critical shift from Stage 8 (Pathfinder) to Stage 9 (Visionary), we receive a Voice-guided vision from this plane so inspiring that we are inspired to release all attachment to our ordinary ego identity. This marks a critical transit point in human development when we "find our calling" and make operating from the Plane of Vision a primary focus in our personal and professional lives.

Creative Unconscious. The aspect of our unconscious through which our Voice speaks. It has been called by many names throughout history, including the superconscious, collective unconscious, quantum mind, and plane of being. In developmental terms, the creative unconscious stands at the "end of time" as the starting point from which the final four worldviews (Stages 9-12) operate on the Plane of Creative Vision. The creative unconscious stands opposite the primal unconscious (home of the shadow), which lives at the "beginning of time" — the starting point from which the first four worldviews (Stages 1-4) originate. Together these two unconscious mental planes establish the core creative tension that gives rise to all human evolution through the lens of space time perception. As we progress along the path of Phase II (worldview Stages 7-12), we come to escape time as we experience all 12 stages coexisting within our minds right now.

DEFEND Cycle. A six-step cycle that the shadow employs to keep us frame locked during Phase I (worldview stages 1-6) of the human journey. The DEFEND cycle is an upside-down, reverse mirror projection of the CREATE cycle that causes us to see our inner worlds as an effect of the world outside. This Phase I mindset seems silly once we restore Voice alignment, but feels very real when the DEFEND cycle dominates our minds. This cycle is maintained by 6 thinking habits: Division, Escapism, Forgetting, Enforcement, Negativity and Doubt. When this cycle is institutionalized into our worldview, we can no longer hear our Voice. When the pain of separation from our essence outweighs the pain of choosing again, we Commit to our Voice and restore the CREATE cycle to achieve total freedom from the inside out. This is the developmental arc of Phase II (worldview Stages 7-12).

Death (Axis of). The Axis of Death refers to the portion of the DEFEND cycle that connects the Dividers (shadow emperors) and Doubters (shadow poets). Through this sickly bond, we come to (unconsciously) worship the belief in death. According to Voice Code logic, death is the central cornerstone belief that gives the shadow power over our minds. The Axis of Death strengthens every time we actively endorse the belief in death *and also* when we *tacitly* endorse it through death denial or avoidance. The only way to escape this trap is to transcend it by transmuting the shadows that empower the Axis of Death in our primal unconscious. As we restore the CREATE cycle, the Axis of

Presence (which bonds the Emperor and Poet) strengthens and belief in the Dividers and Doubters diminishes. Following Voice Code logic, during our 12th and final stage (Messiah) we reclaim the final lingering shadows from Stage 1(Womb) and death dissolves into the light of Stage 13.

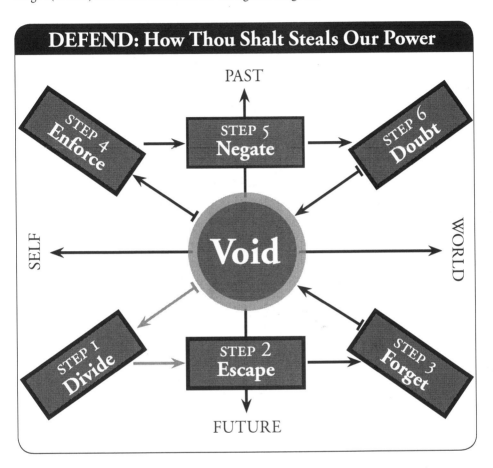

DEFEND: How Thou Shalt Steals Our Power

PAST

STEP 4
Enforce

STEP 5
Negate

STEP 6
Doubt

SELF

Void

WORLD

STEP 1
Divide

STEP 2
Escape

STEP 3
Forget

FUTURE

Desperation (Axis of). The Axis of Desperation refers to the portion of the DEFEND cycle that connects the Enforcers (shadow warriors) and Doubters (shadow poets). Through this sickly bond, we Negate (N of DEFEND cycle) our Voice essence by burying the original choice that created the shadow patterns that keep us frame locked. So long as we fail to look inward for the cause of our life's challenges, we strengthen this axis, fostering an inner culture of powerlessness. From the shadow's perspective, this despair acts as a deep line of defense that keeps most from ever challenging their belief in death (see Axis of Death). As we restore the CREATE cycle, the Axis of Vitality (which bonds the Warrior and Poet) brings power and resolve to dissolve the desperate partnership between the Enforcers and Doubter. This is an advanced stage of inner game mastery associated with the CREATE skill of Transmuting (Step 5 of 6). As the Axis of Vitality dissolves the Axis of Desperation, we "negate the negation" (N of the DEFEND Cycle) of our Voice to unleash those rare healing gifts that great sages throughout the ages have demonstrated.

Dilemma (Axis of). The Axis of Dilemma represents the segment of the DEFEND cycle that connects the Forgetters (shadow alchemists) and Dividers (shadow emperors). Through this stifling shadow partnership, we come to view life as a stressful ordeal — an endless series of dilemmas and unsatisfying choices to which we must adapt to survive. The more we act from the either/or mindset this duo fosters, the more evidence we gather to support the false premises that give them power. In Phase II we say "enough is enough" and stand for our Voice with uncompromising commitment to reclaim the inner throne. Following our Voice Authority, we embrace the paradoxical pragmatism mindset that Phase II thinkers use to unravel false dichotomies and unleash innovation. As the newly restored Emperor and Alchemist conspire to call "bullshit" on old Divider and Forgetter shadow patterns, the Axis of Dilemma dissolves and the Axis of Vision emerges, giving us that rare ability to see beyond the conventional social reality programmed into us in Phase I.

Dividers. These are the shadow emperors — reverse mirror reflections of the true Emperor projected into our awareness from the primal unconscious. They are shadow relics of our early negative experiences with authority, and the first of four shadow teams that conspire to keep us enslaved. With a classic good-cop/bad-cop routine run by the Warden (active pole) and the Wimp (passive pole), the Dividers keep us on a treadmill of endless striving. When we fall for the trap, we see Authority (creative power) as external and find ourselves constantly seeking to fix, change and improve everything. When Divider stress reaches critical mass, we find ourselves vacillating wildly between tyrannical self-coercion (Wardens) and escapist self-indulgence (Wimps) to manage stress. **Type:** Shadow Emperors | **Motto:** "Do Not Find" | **Active:** Warden | **Passive:** Wimp | **Primary Origin:** Stage 4 Outlaw

8 Thou Shalts of the Dividers

Thou shalt *fret over things beyond thy control*

Thou shalt *sacrifice now for an ever-receding future*

Thou shalt *secretly indulge to excess and feel guilty*

Thou shalt *punish thyself to improve thy morale*

Thou shalt *judge all situations through belief filters*

Thou shalt *judge all situations through polarized beliefs*

Thou shalt *fix, change and improve everything*

Dogma (Axis of). The Axis of Deviance refers to the portion of the DEFEND cycle that connects the Forgetters (shadow alchemists) and Enforcers (shadow warriors). Through this clever alliance, we keep "the cave" hidden and maintain a safe distance from our fears by projecting them outward onto the world. So long as we indulge in blame of any kind, we strengthen this axis and remain afraid of our own power. From this vantage point, we see a dog-eat-dog world in which we must scheme and outflank others in order to survive. As we restore the CREATE cycle in Phase II (worldview Stages 7-12), the Axis of Traction (which bonds the Voice Alchemist and Warrior) is revitalized, which brings a renewed sense of possibility and a renewed sense of our true creative power. As we withdraw belief in fear, the Axis of Dogma slowly dissolves and we reframe Trust to support our Phase II calling. In time, we come to understand our true power as One with the creative mind that orchestrates life, ushering a new era of courage, faith and transparency that renders shadows impotent.

"Do Not Find" This is shadow calling of the Dividers. This control-seeking team of shadow emperor projections includes Wardens and Wimps. When we follow their guidance, we lose access to our Voice in the Emperor expression. Instead of "Owning our Mind" to have Authority, we project our power onto external authorities and end up on a treadmill of endless striving.

Doubters. Doubters are shadow poets — reverse mirror reflections of the true Poet projected up from the primal unconscious. They are a mirror reflection of the Divider (shadow emperor) projections, and the final team on the shadow's roster. Led by the Dreamer (active pole) and Downer (passive pole), this troupe conjures a devastatingly effective agenda of love-seeking and loss. Because Doubter energies map to our earliest experiences, they often bypass our normal rational filters and leave us feeling like wounded children pining for mommy. For this reason, it is always wise to tread lightly with the Doubters as we build a sturdy foundation for inner transformation by focusing first on transmuting Dividers (shadow emperors), Forgetters (shadow alchemists) and Enforcers (shadow warriors). When we do this, the Doubters naturally dissolve as the true Poet's light shines through. **Type:** shadow poets | **Motto:** "See the Lack" | **Active:** Dreamer | **Passive:** Downer | **Primary Origin:** Stage 1 Womb

8 Thou Shalts of the Doubters

Thou shalt *wistfully romanticize youthful beauty*

Thou shalt *hide thy light to avoid being judged*

Thou shalt *deny impulse for joyful exuberance*

Thou shalt *fetishize the past with nostalgia*

Thou shalt *confuse love with specialness*

Thou shalt *take secret pride in thy suffering*

Thou shalt *always focus on what's lacking*

• **Thou shalt** *avoid loving fully for fear of dying*

Downers. The Downers are the passive (feminine) pole of the Doubters (shadow poets). There are four Downer personas, which are distinguished by their hopeless downtrodden demeanors: *mourners, whiners, rejects* and *lamenters*. All Downers feel very real when they emerge, but they are actually nothing more than an endless pit of grief playing on repeat in primal unconscious.

Unlike healthy sadness, which passes through us to cleanse our system, the Downers melodrama never abates. This constant caterwauling sets the stage for the Downers partner in crime (the Dreamer) to emerge with starry-eyed schemes that do nothing but further estrange us from the timeless exuberance at our core. **Location:** Primal Unconscious | **Primary Origin:** Stage 1 Womb

Dreamers. The Dreamers are the active, masculine pole of the Doubters (aka shadow poets). There are four Dreamer personas, which are distinguished by a wistful pining to transcend ordinary life on a search for something greater: *drifters, idealists, victims* and *romantics.* We embrace these childish shadow patterns as an emotional salve to cheer us up and distract us from the deep sense of grief and hopelessness caused by repressed Downer (passive polarity) energies trapped in our primal unconscious. Unfortunately, this short-term salve comes at a very high cost. When Dreamers' schemes fail to satisfy, we are left with even more dispiriting first evidence to justify the Downers endless grief. **Location:** Primal Unconscious | **Primary Origin:** Stage 1 Womb

Embody. The second "E" in the CREATE cycle. Explore is the 6th and final step of the cycle and the final skill that visionary minds master. To master Exploring we must summon the Poet to "See the Light" by remembering our innocence. In practice, this is only possible after we've summoned the Warrior to clear "the cave" and transmuted the shadow patterns that block our light. Once we've done this, Embodiment is quite easy: we simply breathe into the present moment, release all expectations and agenda, and follow our inspiration in a spirit of gratitude and appreciation. Through Embodiment, we renew the CREATE cycle to unite the kingdom. The four mentors come together, lifting us to a higher plane of being as we shift our trajectory to align with our life's calling. The results we generate from Embodied actions naturally inspire us to Commit (Step 1) again. This is how visionary minds bridge heaven and earth by simply being present, following their Voice. **Mentor:** Poet | **Calling:** See the Light | **Body Center:** base of spine (1st chakra) | **Balancing Center:** top of head (7th chakra) | **Balancing Skill:** Commit

Emperor. The first of the four archetypal mentors through which our Voice speaks from the creative unconscious. The Emperor governs the principle of Authority and the 16 gifts of Purpose. In Phase II of the human journey, we align these energies with those of the Alchemist archetype to "Own the Frame" as we master the CREATE skills of Commitment, Reframing and Exploration. The journey to total mastery takes us through worldview Stages 7 Explorer, Stage 8 Pathfinder, and Stage 9 Visionary. The initiatory learning season through which we "Befriend the Emperor" to reframe Authority as part of our Voice Revolution is called the Emperor's Summer. When we've completed all four seasons of the Voice Revolution, we are firmly grounded in Stage 9 Visionary and radically motivated to bring our gifts to the world. **Calling:** Own Your Mind | **Location:** Creative Unconscious | **Mastery Skill:** Commitment.

Emperor's Summer. The first season of the Voice Revolution in which, we reframe Authority. In this initiatory learning season we learn to "Own our Mind" as we reframe the principle of Authority from external (frame lock) to internal (Voice). We process this domineering shadow team called the Dividers, to "restore the throne" and reclaim the 16 Gifts of Purpose that our Voice offers in the Emperor expression. Through this process, we set ourselves on a new course to a life of Phase II thriving. Following our natural creative momentum we then naturally begin to Reframe (CREATE Step 2) our future as we think big about what is truly possible. The increased sense of our true potential moves us to imagine a life without limits, calling us to challenge old ways as we develop vision clarity through alignment with the principle of Resonance.

Emperor's Throne. The Emperor's throne represents that timeless changeless space of pure awareness that resides at the core of our being. When we "own the throne," we remain present and maintain conscious contact with this inner knowing at all times. When we get frame locked, we lose conscious access and effectively abdicate the throne to old shadow habits. In Phase I we become so blinded by beliefs that we lose awareness of this aspect of our being completely. As we progress along the path of Phase II, mental noise subsides and we become increasingly identified with this peaceful inner space as the truth of who we are. At a certain point, we stop thinking altogether and escape the experience of time as most know it. We then live fully and freely in each moment, joyfully following our inner Voice guidance.

Enforcers. These are shadow warriors — reverse reflections of the true Warrior projected into our awareness from the primal unconscious. They are shadow relics of fears that we stowed away in "the cave" during our earliest days (Stage 2. Survivor) With all the grace of a mobster protection racket, the Punisher (active pole) and the Prisoner (passive pole) now work behind the scenes to keep us from facing our fears directly. When we fall for their trap, we project our fears outward onto the world through an enforced regimen of blame, rationalization and avoidance. Over time this polarizing mindset creates within us a deep well of guilt and shame that calcifies to form the hidden cornerstone of our ego identity. Through this process, we lose Trust in our Voice and life as a whole. When Enforcer patterns reach critical mass, fear warps our minds until we perceive attack as strength and innocence as weakness. **Motto:** "Blame the Dark" | **Active:** Punisher | **Passive:** Prisoner| **Primary Origin:** Stage 2 Survivor

---

8 Thou Shalts of the Enforcers

Thou shalt *blame the world for thy problems*

Thou shalt *punish thyself eternally for mistakes*

Thou shalt *place great faith in the power of darkness*

Thou shalt *regard thy true strength as weakness*

Thou shalt *gather evidence for the power of evil*

Thou shalt *comdemn those who think differently*

Thou shalt *defend thy beliefs even unto death*

Thou shalt *always preserve the status quo*

Explore. Explore is the Step 3 of the CREATE cycle and the third of six skills that visionary minds master. To master Exploring we must engage the Alchemist to "Think with Heart" by reframing the principle of Resonance to align with our Phase II (power inside) Authority frame. In practice, effective Exploring requires that we make it a constant life practice to think with a beginner's mind, honoring our native curiosity to dismantle limiting beliefs and blind-spot assumptions in the search for simple truth. This ability grows naturally from the roots of a powerful Commitment (Step 1) to our Voice, which Reframes (Step 2) our life from the premise of total self-authorship. From this perspective, we see the world as an outward picturing of our inner world. Viewing our minds as the original cause of perception, we naturally seek solutions to our problems by looking inward to find and remove the beliefs and shadow patterns that keep us from seeing the light. **Mentor:** Alchemist | **Calling:** Think with Heart | **Body Center:** throat (5th chakra) | **Balancing Center:** 3rd Chakra (solar plexus) | **Balancing Skill:** Assimilate

Explorer (Stage 7). The seventh worldview to emerge along the 12-Stage Voice Code path. The Explorer is the first worldview of Phase II, and first emerged en mass around the dawn of the 20th century, flowering in full counterculture bloom during the civil rights era of the 1960s. **Frame Lock:** Explorers prize *connection* and *progress* over the balancing needs of *autonomy* and *security* (respectively). This leads idealistic, humanistic thinking style that values empathy, relatedness and equality at the expense of the more individualistic Achiever values of success, power and affluence. **Frame Mantra:** "Sacrifice myself to others to achieve acceptance now." | **Frame Polarity:** Humans are a family. | **Key Polarity:** caring or careless / **Mass Emergence:** ~1900's / **Balancing Worldview:** Achiever (Stage 6; Phase I)

"Face the Dark" The calling of the Warrior and the secret to reclaiming the 16 gifts of Power our Voice offers. When we first "Own our Mind" and "Think With Heart" by restoring the Emperor and Alchemist (respectively), we develop vision clarity that helps us clearly distinguish our Voice from limiting shadow patterns. This gives us clear access to the Warriors tenacious resolve to face and dissolve fear to Assimilate the Voice gifts trapped within old limiting belief habits. When we fail to follow this calling, we "Blame the Dark" by default, following Enforcer (shadow warrior) guidance. **Principle:** Trust | **Mentor:** Warrior | **Mind Element:** Creative Unconscious | **Gift:** Power

Forgetters. Forgetters are shadow alchemists — inverted projections of the true Alchemist. These shadow players compel us to "Play the Part" by behaving in accordance with social norms even when doing so compromises our conscience. They are energetic relics of social personas we developed during our early childhood experiences as we navigated the Subject (Stage 3) worldview.

With an immaculate con job run by the Shark (active pole) and the Showboat (passive pole), the Forgetters work to keep our darkness concealed and help us survive through social acceptance. When we fall for their traps, we confuse who we really are (our Voice) with our social persona (ego identity) and end up trapped in unsatisfying jobs and relationships. Over time Forgetter frame lock castrates our creativity at the altar of conventional thinking. Through this process, we lose alignment with the principle of Resonance and find ourselves unable to see beneath the surface of everyday life into the deeper patterns and possibilities inherent within every moment. **Motto:** "Play the Part" | **Active:** Shark| **Passive:** Showboat | **Primary Origin:** Stage 3. Subject

8 Thou Shalts of the Forgetters

Thou shalt *covet answers instead of questions*

Thou shalt *view others as a means to an end*

Thou shalt *always hold an unstated agenda*

Thou shalt *follow thy heart only if brain approves*

Thou shalt *use thy cleverness to outwit other*

Thou shalt *find security through social approval*

Thou shalt *never observe thy own thoughts*

Thou shalt *keep up appearances or else*

Frame Lock. The pervasive condition of shortsighted either/or thinking that arises from shadow identification. Frame lock keeps us trapped within a limited frame of reference without even knowing it. When problems and challenges arise, we fail to consider how our own subjective thinking style may have contributed, filtering information through the lens of unquestioned beliefs and assumptions. Thinking this way, our minds become a closed system, and our curiosity dies. When problems arise, instead of engaging in radical inquiry to discern the root cause, we react in a biased way that produces evidence that confirms our biasing premises. In time, frame lock turns our lives into a series of unsatisfying choices, as we seek in vain to create inner security by controlling what happens outside. When our discomfort reaches a tipping point, we begin to doubt our entire frame of reference. This dark night is always a blessing in disguise, as it causes us to disassociate from old shadow beliefs and opens the back door of our mind to make room for clear Voice guidance.

Choose Shadows DEFEND Fear

Choose Voice CREATE Future

Frame Lock: *Reality Distortion Caused by Beliefs*

Voice: *Instinctual Knowing Blocked by Beliefs*

Frame Change. When we shift our inner guidance from shadow to Voice, we experience a powerful shift in our frame of reference that influences how we interpret information. Shadow identification causes us to think from the assumption of scarcity, separation and sacrifice. Voice identification causes us to think from inner Authority, heart Resonance and Trust in our gut instincts. To have a game changing impact in the world, we must be able to inspire frame changes in others to help them remember their Voice. This is possible only if we are operating from a state of radical Voice alignment.

Holographic model. Seen through the Voice Code lens, the world is essentially a holographic out-picturing of the human unconscious. A hologram is constituted such that each part is an unbroken expression of the whole. Like the idea of Oneness, this concept is difficult or impossible to grasp when we are frame locked. As we progress along the path of Phase II (worldview Stages 7-12), we develop a first-hand experiential knowing that helps our intellect assimilate these concepts in a visceral and practical way. Stage 9 Visionary is the first worldview to think holistically as a matter of course. Having released identification with their ego identity, people at this stage begin to experience the part and the whole as indivisible, and their Voice as One with life.

I-Ching. The "book of changes." This is a sacred Chinese divination manual. Drawing from the essential polarity between yin (feminine) and yang (masculine), this oracle uses sixty-four hexagrams to help practitioners consult with nature's creative mind as it expresses through everyday situations. The Voice Code sheds new light on this brilliant text. The I-Ching is essentially an early version of the Voice Code. A separate book is now in the works to show the convergence between these two paradigms, both of which evolved from study of the dynamic patterns through which nature's creative intelligence interfaces with human subjective reality as part of a holistic evolutionary template.

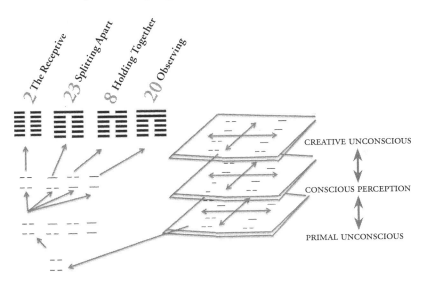

Immovable Spot. In Buddhist mythology, the immovable spot refers to the spot under the Bodhi Tree where the Buddha stood his ground to overcome the temptations (aka shadow projections) to achieve enlightenment. As the story goes, by standing unwaveringly for truth, this young prince transcended fear and desire to awaken and become the Buddha. In Voice Code symbols, the "immovable spot" is the nexus of the CREATE cycle where the two axis (time and space) come together. Every time we see through shadow projections and choose our Voice, we reenact the inner drama that this Buddhist story represents. All great wisdom traditions contain myths and symbols that point to this same dynamic. This nearly universal convergence makes complete sense if we consider that the Voice Code has truly mapped the universal principles of mind that govern the dynamic growth and evolution of all living systems. **See Also:** Quintessence, Self-actualization, Tao and Stage 12 (Messiah).

Individuation. The term psychologist Carl Jung used to represent the aspirational endgame of psychological development. Through the process of individuation a person becomes most uniquely themselves, while also being most ordinary and connected with others. According to Jung, people arrive at this place of radical psychic integrity by "integrating the opposites" of universal polarities that structure all human consciousness. The Voice Code map clarifies and completes Jung's thinking. His description of individuation dovetails precisely with the experience of Stage 8 Pathfinders as they release their ego identity and up-level from the Plane of Social Control (worldview Stages 5-8) to the Plane of Creative Vision as Stage 9 Visionaries. A separate volume is in the works to offer more details that help us reconcile and integrate Jung's work with that of Freud, Abraham Maslow, Clare W. Graves and other great twentieth century minds through the Voice Code lens.

Innocence (Principle of). The master principle of Voice alignment. As we reframe and integrate the principles of Authority, Resonance and Trust, we clear the windows of perception and we remember our innocence. In Phase I (worldview Stages 1-6) we come to believe that our innocence was lost in childhood. As our adult ego identity calcifies around Stage 6 (Achiever), we come to view innocence as synonymous with naivety and weakness. In Phase II (worldview Stages 7-12) we dissolve layer upon layer of Phase I beliefs until we eventually reclaim all power from the shadow and know ourselves as our Voice. By Stage 12 (Messiah) we have returned to the beginning to see that our innocence is our true strength. When the proverbial lion and lamb lie down together, they do so in celebration of this unifying principle of human consciousness. **Mentor:** Poet | **CREATE Skill:** Embody | **Gift:** Partnership

Inside Out. The mindset we adopt during Phase II (worldview Stages 7-12) as we learn to follow our Voice. In Phase I we learn a frame locked outside-in mindset that keeps us trapped in a reactive "either/or" thinking. As we unlearn limiting beliefs from early childhood, the shadow loses its grip over our minds; and we naturally begin to hear and follow our inner Authority. The successes we generate through this inside-out mindset become priceless evidence that compels us to greater and greater levels of inner game mastery. Through this process we enter a new conversation with life that transforms us into a force of nature in the service of life.

Learning Partnership. The 12-Stage path over "Voice Mountain" joins opposing worldviews in Phase I and Phase II as natural learning partnerships that serve the evolution of the whole. To move forward, each stage from Phase II must transmute shadow projections related to the Phase I worldview at the same level on the opposite side of the mountain. For example, Stages 7 (Explorer) and Stage 8 (Pathfinder) must find and reclaim power from shadow projections related to Stage 6 (Achiever) and Stage 5 (Believer) respectively. This holds true all the way down to the Stage 12 (Messiah) worldview, which must transmute any lingering shadow energies associated with the womb (Stage 1) in order to "graduate" from the domain of perception. As Phase II players do this inner work, they naturally heal the entire mountain, fostering the forward evolution of life across the entire mountain.

Luminary (Stage 10). The tenth worldview Stage (out of 12). Luminaries are the second Stage on the Plane of Creative Vision (worldview Stages 9-12). This is the stage of most iconic visionaries who have thrived beyond the bounds of convention while maintaining a happy, grounded personality. Having purged countless shadow fears in Stage 8 Visionary, Luminaries are ready to bring vision to the world in a way that lights others up in a spirit of shared self interest. Frame Lock: Stage 10 thinkers aren't frame locked by conventional standards, but they do have an important lesson that they must complete in order to move forward. The primary task of Luminaries is to transmute shadow energies related to the Stage 3 (Subject) worldview. These lessons require that we reclaim power from long-buried memories related to family and tribal solidarity from our early (pre-linguistic) childhood. This requires integrity and mental discipline of an order that is inconceivable until we complete the inner game

lessons of the Stage 8 (Visionary) worldview. **Frame Mantra:** Be the change |
Framing Metaphor: Life is a gift | **Balancing Worldview:** Subject (Stage 3;
Phase I) | **Mass Emergence:** Future

Luminary Project. The project through which we bring our gifts to the
world after completing the Voice Revolution. Through completion of the four
seasons of the Voice Revolution, we discover our life's calling and stabilize at
Stage 8. Visionary. Having lifted ourselves to a new plane of human experience,
nature calls us to ground our learning by bringing our gifts to others as part of
the upward shift to Stage 9. Luminary. This is our Luminary Project. It is a
unique expression of our life's purpose and contribution that brings value to
others and helps us fully embody our Voice in our everyday lives. Worldview
Thinking has designed our Four Seasons of Voice curriculum to foster and
support this natural developmental process. We have made the Luminary
Project the aspirational endgame of our advanced leadership training. (FYI:
The writing and sharing of this book is the authors luminary project.)

Messiah (Stage 12). The Messiah is the 12th and final worldview to emerge.
It is also the fourth Stage on the Plane of Creative Vision (which begins with
Stage 9. Visionary). This is the highest level of human enlightenment — the
stage of all great spiritual teachers throughout history, such as Buddha, Jesus
Christ and other lesser-known teachers who have mastered the CREATE cycle
to completely transcend shadow identification. **Frame Lock:** Stage 12 thinkers
can hardly be considered frame locked by conventional standards, but they do
have some final lessons to complete. The Voice challenge of Messiah is to
transmute the belief in death and any lingering shadows from their experiences
in the womb (Stage 1). At this stage, there is little ego identification left to drive
resistance or friction within this natural evolutionary process; but within time,
this function must still be completed to escape time all together. **Frame
Mantra:** I am | **Framing Metaphor:** Life is One | **Balancing Partner:** Womb
(Stage 1; Phase I) | **Mass Emergence:** End of Time (eternal now)

Nondualism. Another name for advanced levels of the Phase II paradigm
rooted in Oneness. In Phase I, our identification with shadow patterns causes us
to perceive the world through the lens of separation. This is the root cause of
frame lock. Thinking this way, we perceive the world exclusively in terms of

dualities: us vs. them, good vs. evil, love vs. hate, inner vs. outer, past vs. future, happy vs. unhappy, rich vs. poor, and so forth. In Phase II we still perceive the same polarities with our senses, but our litmus test for truth gradually shifts from perception ("seeing is believing") to knowing ("believing is seeing"). In Stage 8 (Visionary), we transmute core shadow energies from our early Stage 4 (Outlaw) days when the underpinnings of our adult ego identity first formed. This helps us stabilize on the Plane of Creative Vision (worldview Stages 9-12) as we learn how to operate from a nondual mindset in our everyday lives. With each step forward, we transmute another layer of shadow programming until nondualistic thinking generalizes completely.

Oneness. The unbroken unity of life at the level of being. When we are frame locked, this concept seems fanciful, naive or dangerous, because we still place faith in the reality of separation. But when we choose our Voice, we operate from the premise that Oneness is the essential truth behind appearances. Although separation still appears real at the level of the senses, it no longer feels true within our subjective reality. As we progress through the four seasons of the Voice Revolution, we transmute layer upon layer of old Phase I shadow beliefs that kept us feeling separate until we remember our Innocence and know ourselves as One with life. The Poet is the Voice mentor who helps us embody this in our everyday lives. But until we do the inner work to align with our Voice as it expresses through the Emperor, Alchemist and Warrior; the Poet (and our grasp of Oneness) remains elusive. **See Also:** Immovable Spot, Tao and Nondualism

Optical Delusion of Consciousness. A phrase borrowed from Einstein to describe something that appears real at the level of perception, but which is not real in absolute terms. Through the Voice Code lens, shadow projections are literally optical delusions. They often seem real, but they are actually holographic delusions projected into our conscious awareness from the primal unconscious (Plane of Primal Will; Stages 1-4). That these delusions are unreal cannot be "proven" to anyone who is unwilling to question their reality. But for those who are ready, the unreality of shadow patterns can be easily proven using the 6-Step CREATE process. By Exploring, Assimilating and Transmuting shadow energies, we remove the unconscious cause that gives rise to these projections, which causes measurable changes to our inner and external worlds.

Through this process we establish a new model of inside-out cause and effect that helps us ultimately escape all delusions — including even the false dichotomy between inner and outer.

Outlaw (Stage 4) The Outlaw is the fourth worldview to emerge along the 12-Stage Voice Code path and the final "ruling" stage on the Plane of Primal Will (worldview Stages 1-4). This is a highly egocentric worldview that everyone must pass through in early childhood en route to adulthood. In this stage (often called the "terrible twos") the emotional architecture that underlies our separate ego identity is formed. In today's world the Outlaw remains the dominant level of thinking in many third world cultures. **Frame Lock:** Outlaws are driven by a primal evolutionary imperative to dominate and manipulate situations in order to satisfy survival needs. At this level, we experience primal frame lock related to our need for control. When these needs are frustrated, we become outraged and the fear of separation consumes us. Frustration from these early lessons in self-management form the basis for what later become our Divider (shadow emperor) thinking habits. People who remain fixated at this stage throughout their lives become psychopaths: self-serving impulsive personalities with no conscience, who are incapable of empathy and unable to control their impulses. **Frame Mantra:** "Express myself to get what I want or die in shame" | **Framing Metaphor:** Life is a battle | **Balancing Worldview:** Visionary (Stage 8) | **Mass Emergence:** ~8,000 B.C.

Outside In. The Phase I mental model. During worldview Stages 1-6, we learn to think from the outside in, mistaking our shadow projections for realty. This is frame lock. Thinking this way, we see ourselves as an effect of the world. This leads to a dilemma-based mindset through which we seek inner freedom by controlling the world outside us. The orientation helps us satisfy basic survival needs in a frame-locked culture that endorses this same backwards thinking style, but when it comes to satisfying higher order needs (happiness, meaning and fulfillment), it is counterproductive. When the discomfort caused outside-in Phase I thinking reaches critical mass, we ask new questions that unravel blind spots to help us remember ourself as the sole author of our personal reality. We then follow our Voice "over the mountain" into Phase II (worldview Stages 7-12) where we reframe Authority, Resonance and Trust to remember our Innocence and become One with our Voice.

Own Your Mind. The Emperor's calling and the secret to reclaiming the 16 gifts of Purpose our Voice offers. When we commit fully to our inner Authority, we activate the Emperor energy to reclaim the "throne" of Voice from the Dividers (shadow emperors). This shifts our frame on reality from an outside-in (Phase I) to an inside-out (Phase II) orientation. This restores our creative unconscious to its proper role (aka creative dominance). In so doing, it activates our latent creative potential and helps us incite upward spirals of thriving as we master the Phase II mindset. When we fail to follow this calling, we seek, but "Do Not Find" at the Dividers bidding. **Principle:** Authority | **Mentor:** Emperor | **Mind Element:** Creative Unconscious | **Gift:** Purpose

Paradoxical Pragmatism. Another name for the "both/and" Phase II mindset. In Phase I life shows up as an endless series of unsatisfying "either/or" choices that we must manage to survive. In early stages of Phase II, we still perceive unsatisfying choices, but instead of automatically operating as if they were true, we begin to challenge our own thinking. In so doing, we withdraw

Paradox, Revisited
The Mirror of Voice

INNER GAME   OUTER GAME

Own Your Mind   Choose Again

Think with Heart   Own the Frame

Face the Dark   Change the Game

See the Light   Be the Change

Voice

Aligned with Voice, we Experience Inner and Outer as Mirror Reflections of the Same Process

investment in the underlying Phase I beliefs that make separation and sacrifice seem real. This natural process helps us dissolve dilemmas from the inside out as we learn to embrace the paradoxical truth of human existence: We are both unlimited beings *and* ordinary people at the same time. When choosing our inner Voice over the voice of convention becomes a way of life, we mastered the art of paradoxical pragmatism — a practice great visionaries leverage to thrive without compromise in a world of frame locked cynics.

Partnership (16 Gifts). The gift of the Poet. When aligned with this mentor to "See the Light" in our everyday lives, we naturally begin to inspire and awaken others to recognize our shared Voice essence. As we master the CREATE skill of Embodiment following the Poet's inner guidance, we clear the windows of perception to remember our innocence and experience our Oneness with others. Mapping the 64 hexagrams of the I-Ching onto the Voice Code (see illustration), we generated a list of 16 specific gifts of Partnership that we reclaim from the Doubters (shadow poets). Phase II visionaries leverage these gifts to produce powerful and enduring partnerships in the pursuit of their life's purpose. These gifts flower within as we transmute each of the 16 Doubter habits to reclaim access to our essence.

Doubter Habit	**CREATE Partnership** 16 Gifts of the Poet	Gift of Innocence

Rejection	Sloppiness	Discord	Neglect	Melodrama	Neediness	Alienation	Pessimism
↓	↓	↓	↓	↓	↓	↓	↓
Openness	Readiness	Balance	Reverence	Enthusiasm	Sincerity	Acceptance	Charisma

Futility	Desperation	Wanting	Dismay	Isolation	Pining	Angst	Morbidity
↓	↓	↓	↓	↓	↓	↓	↓
Liberty	Equanimity	Forgiveness	Faith	Expansion	Fulfillment	Awe	Stillness

Pathfinder (Stage 8). The eighth worldview to emerge along the 12-Stage Voice Code path. Pathfinders are the final "ruling" worldview of the Plane of Social Control (worldview Stages 5-8) and have been leading the charge to reshape our economy in Phase II fashion since the emergence of digital technologies. **Frame Lock:** Pathfinders prize autonomy and change over the balancing needs of connection and security. This leads to an innovative, systems-oriented mindset, in which values of creativity, competence and sustainability dominate, while more traditional Believer (Stage 5) values like discipline, (external) authority and sacrifice are discounted. **Frame Mantra:** Express myself to get what I want, but in a way that serves everyone and hurts no one. | **Frame Metaphor:** Life is a system | **Frame Polarity:** effective vs. ineffective | **Mass Emergence:** ~1960 (Rise of Information Economy) | **Balancing Partner:** Believer (Stage 5; Phase I)

Phase I. The first 6 Stages of the 12-worldview Stages. In Phase I we learn to survive as we move from the womb (Stage 1) through six stages of inner development to arrive in Stage 6 (Achiever) as a fully socialized adult. When Stage 6 runs its course, life challenges call into question the outside-in operating paradigm we crafted during the uphill climb of Phase I. If we honor the call, we cross "over the mountain" into Phase II, where we reframe the principles of Authority, Resonance and Trust as part of a 6-Stage *unlearning* process through which we become one with our Voice. **Phase I Stages:** Womb (1), Survival (2), Subject (3), Outlaw (4), Believer (5), Achiever (6).

Phase II. The final 6 Stages of the 12-Stage Voice Code map. In Phase II we become One with our Voice as we unlearn a lifetime of limiting beliefs programmed into us in Phase I. As we cross "over the mountain" into Phase II we undergo a dramatic frame reversal in Stage 7. Explorer, and proceed through six stages of mastery to arrive at Stage 12 (Messiah) — the highest level of human enlightenment. At each stage of Phase II, we must reclaim power from a specific set of Phase I shadows related to our learning partner at the same level on the opposite side of the mountain. Unconscious shadow projections associated with each partner create natural inner-game mastery lessons that help us balance and integrate the 6 skills of the CREATE process to improve Voice alignment. **Phase II Stages:** Explorer (7), Pathfinder (8), Visionary (9), Luminary (10), Sage (11), Messiah (12).

"Play the Part" This is the shadow calling of the Forgetters. This pretentious tag team of shadow alchemist projections includes Showboats (passive pole) and Sharks (active pole). When we follow the Forgetters, we lose access to our Voice in the Alchemist expression. Instead of "Thinking with Heart" to see the world through a lens of truth seeking and curious wonder, we then "Play the Part" handed to us by others, engaging others to achieve our goals through a frame-locked mental operating system that prizes social acceptance and approval above authenticity and truth.

Poet. The fourth of the four archetypal mentors through which our Voice speaks from the creative unconscious (aka Plane of Creative Vision: worldview Stages 9-12). The Poet governs the principle of Innocence and the 16 gifts of Partnership. In Phase II of the human journey, we integrate these energies with those of the Warrior archetype to help us "Change the Game" as we master the CREATE skills of Assimilation, Transmutation and Embodiment. The culminating learning season through which we remember our innocence is called the Poet's Spring. When we've completed all four seasons of the Voice Revolution, we are firmly grounded in Stage 9 Visionary (or higher) and are radically inspired to bring our gifts to the world. **Calling:** See the Light | **Location:** Creative Unconscious | **Mastery Skill:** Embodiment

Poet's Spring. The fourth and final season of the Voice Revolution. During the Poet's spring we dissolve long-buried shadow poet (aka Doubter habits) to remember our Innocence and bring the inner revolution that began with the Emperor's Summer full circle again. In the Poet's Spring, our lives become infused with the unconditional joy and exuberance of the Poet. It is here that we "See the Light" of Oneness by restoring radical integrity and unity to the inner kingdom. By transmuting the Doubters, we reclaim the 16 gifts of Partnership to complete and renew the cycle as the gifts of Purpose, Possibility and Power join together as One within the creative urgency of the present. We are now ready to lead a life of true prosperity from the inside out.

Possibility (16 Gifts). The gift of the Alchemist. When we align with this mentor to "Think with Heart," we naturally see the world through the lens of possibility in a spirit of radical inquiry. As we master the CREATE skill of Exploring by following the Alchemist's inner guidance, we escape frame locked

Phase I thinking to reframe Resonance and restore the gift of creative vision that is our natural Voice inheritance. Mapping the 64 hexagrams of the I-Ching onto the Voice Code, we generated a list of 16 specific gifts of Possibility (see graphic) that we reclaim through this process. Phase II visionaries leverage these gifts to achieve strategic clarity around their life's calling, unleash their untapped creative potential to give their Voice vision traction. We embody these gifts as we transmute each of the 16 Forgetter thinking habits.

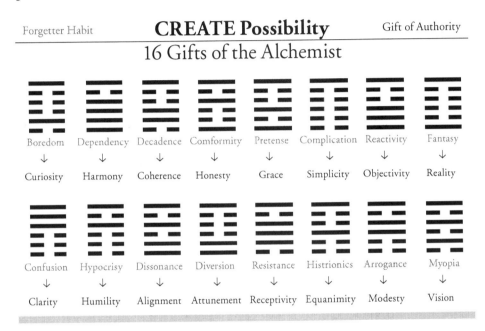

Forgetter Habit		**CREATE Possibility**				Gift of Authority	
		16 Gifts of the Alchemist					

Boredom	Dependency	Decadence	Comformity	Pretense	Complication	Reactivity	Fantasy
↓	↓	↓	↓	↓	↓	↓	↓
Curiosity	Harmony	Coherence	Honesty	Grace	Simplicity	Objectivity	Reality

Confusion	Hypocrisy	Dissonance	Diversion	Resistance	Histrionics	Arrogance	Myopia
↓	↓	↓	↓	↓	↓	↓	↓
Clarity	Humility	Alignment	Attunement	Receptivity	Equanimity	Modesty	Vision

Power (16 Gifts). Power is the gift of the Warrior. As we align with this mentor to "Face the Dark" in our everyday lives, we begin to exude an otherworldly sense of courage, power and passion. As we master the CREATE skill of Assimilation following the Warrior's guidance, we naturally restore Trust in our inner Voice knowing as we neutralize a lifetime of limiting shadow projections from Phase I. Mapping the 64 hexagrams of the I-Ching onto the Voice Code, we generated a list of 16 specific gifts of Power (see graphic) that Phase II visionaries leverage to master fear and become a force of nature in the pursuit of their life's purpose. We embody these gifts as we transmute the 16 Enforcer thinking habits.

CREATE Power

16 Gifts of the Warrior

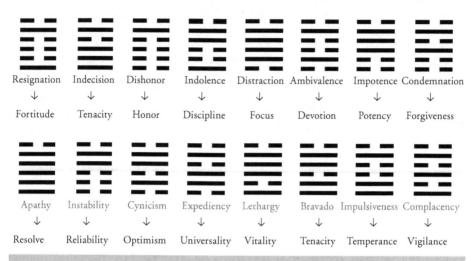

Resignation	Indecision	Dishonor	Indolence	Distraction	Ambivalence	Impotence	Condemnation
↓	↓	↓	↓	↓	↓	↓	↓
Fortitude	Tenacity	Honor	Discipline	Focus	Devotion	Potency	Forgiveness

Apathy	Instability	Cynicism	Expediency	Lethargy	Bravado	Impulsiveness	Complacency
↓	↓	↓	↓	↓	↓	↓	↓
Resolve	Reliability	Optimism	Universality	Vitality	Tenacity	Temperance	Vigilance

Presence (Axis of). The segment of the CREATE cycle that connects the Poet and Emperor through the skills of Embodiment and Commitment. Through this partnership, we come to live fully in the present moment, doing what we love in a spirit of shared self-interest. As with the Axis of Traction that bonds the Alchemist and Warrior, the Axis of Presence passes through the "immovable spot" of our Voice that joins all four archetypes in a dramatic gestalt. When this axis is restored, we rest in this changeless inner space with a sense of peace and joyful exuberance that makes us immune to shadow identification and unstoppable in the face of any obstacles. To achieve this advanced level of mastery we must balance and integrate the 6 skills of the CREATE cycle so that we can operate from a state of radical Voice alignment at all times, and in every area of our lives.

Primal Dominance. The split-minded state we enter when we are frame locked. When we follow the guidance of old shadow voices instead of Voice, we place our primal unconscious in control of our perception. This blocks access to our creative unconscious (home of Voice), and causes us to perceive Voice guidance through the upside-down prism of old shadow projections. This distorted thinking style is maintained through the 6 shadow habits of the

DEFEND cycle. As we master the inner game of Phase II, we restore the integrity of our minds by withdrawing investment in old shadow projections from the primal unconscious. This restores the creative unconscious to its proper role in our minds and places us in a state that we call "creative dominance."

Primal Unconscious. The part of our unconscious where shadow energies live and where the DEFEND cycle operates. During Phase I, shadow projections from the primal unconscious cloud our minds and govern our lives almost completely. When we enter Phase II, these energies linger in our primal unconscious until we transmute them to reclaim our power. In developmental terms, the primal unconscious stands at the beginning of time — the earliest moments of consciousness in the womb (Stage 1). The first four worldviews (Stages 1-4) represent that segment of our personal time line where our ego identity first formed. Collectively these worldviews form the Plane of Primal Will . As we navigate the advanced stages of Phase II (Stages 9-12), we clear shadows from each of these four stages in our primal unconscious in reverse order (starting with Stage 4, working backwards). When we finally reach Stage 12 (Messiah), we transmute the earliest shadows trapped in the primal unconscious (from Stage 1 Womb) to fully dissolve the death belief and transcend the realm of space-time perception.

Primal Will (Plane of). Another term for the primal unconscious — that plane of the human experience in which our earliest memories are stored. In everyday experiential terms, the Plane of Primal Will is "where we go" to access our animal drive to survive, strive and overcome. In Phase I, we harness these primal energies in a way that serves our ego and we become frame locked by a zero sum, survivalist mindset. In Phase II we transmute shadow energies trapped in our primal unconscious to purify and align the Plane of Primal Will with the Plane of Creative Vision (aka creative unconscious). Through this process, we reclaim our power by enlisting these primal energies into the service of our Voice. This is how ordinary people become extraordinary leaders with the power to bridge heaven and earth in the pursuit of shared purpose.

Prisoner. The passive pole of the Enforcers (aka shadow warriors). There are four Prisoner types, which are distinguished by their powerless personas:

hostages, cynics, addicts and martyrs. Although the inflections differ across each type, the basic message each brings is the same: we are powerless and should just give up. The inner culture of shame, guilt and hopelessness that Prisoners breed sets the stage for their partner in crime, the Punisher, to emerge with attacking thoughts for anyone or anything seen as a suitable projection target. **Location:** Primal Unconscious| **Primary Origin:** Stage 2 Survivor.

Punisher. The active pole of the Enforcers (aka shadow warriors). There are four Punisher types, all of which are distinguished by their blaming and attacking ways: *prosecutors, shamers, villains and snipers.* Empowered by the sense of hopelessness that we feel when we identify with Prisoners, Punishers "help us" by finding targets upon which we can project our pain. When Punisher identification becomes a life habit, we become addicted to our opinions and the adrenaline rush that comes from conflict. Mistaking force for power, we behave in ways that create more evidence that we are indeed powerless. **Location:** Primal Unconscious | **Primary Origin:** Stage 2 Survivor.

Purpose (16 Gifts). Purpose is the gift of the Emperor. When we align with this mentor to "Own Our Mind," we exude a sense of presence and definiteness of purpose that inspires others to follow our lead. As we master the skill of Commitment following the Emperor's guidance, we naturally stand for our inner Authority. We reclaim the power of purpose from a lifetime of outside-in shadow patterns learned in Phase I. Mapping the 64 hexagrams of the I-Ching onto the Voice Code, we produced a list of 16 specific gifts of Purpose that Phase II visionaries leverage to express their Voice authority in the pursuit of their life's purpose. We embody these gifts as we transmute each of the 16 Divider thinking habits.

Purpose Paradox. A nuclear bomb of human insight at the heart of the Voice Code. In everyday terms, here's what it says: From nature's perspective, our life's purpose is to live fully, in the present. When we discover a future purpose that we're willing to die for, we release the past. Our identity expands and time dissolves. From this expanded presence, we experience no struggle, scarcity or separation. Following our Voice we then take inspired actions that place us in alignment with timeless natural laws that orchestrate evolution to CREATE the future while standing fully in the present.

Forgetter Habit **CREATE Purpose** Gift of Authority

16 Gifts of the Emperor

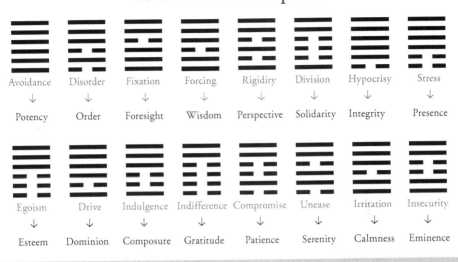

Avoidance	Disorder	Fixation	Forcing	Rigidity	Division	Hypocrisy	Stress
↓	↓	↓	↓	↓	↓	↓	↓
Potency	Order	Foresight	Wisdom	Perspective	Solidarity	Integrity	Presence

Egoism	Drive	Indulgence	Indifference	Compromise	Unease	Irritation	Insecurity
↓	↓	↓	↓	↓	↓	↓	↓
Esteem	Dominion	Composure	Gratitude	Patience	Serenity	Calmness	Eminence

Quintessence. According to ancient and medieval philosophy, the quintessence is the fifth and highest essence which permeates all of life and is the substance of the celestial bodies. In modern usage, this term is often used to denote the essence of something in its purest natural form. Through the Voice Code lens, the quintessence is the 5th Essence gestalt of your Voice as the four mentors come together as One. Think of your Voice as a pyramid. If each Voice mentor is likened to one side of a pyramid, the "quintessence" of Voice would be the point at the top where all four corners converge. This larger than life gestalt essence flowers naturally within during moments of flow and peak experiences when we are fully, effortlessly engaged. As we progress along the path of Phase II, we begin to operate from this state all the time as we become One with our Voice in every moment. **See Also:** Self-Actualization, Individuation, Tao

Radical Inquiry. The Alchemist's master practice is to ask inspired questions to discern root causes. The Voice Code emerged after two decades of following the Alchemist's guidance in a spirit of radical inquiry. Through this lens, the world we see is essentially a holographic out picturing of our unconscious mind. Using this inside-out premise as a starting assumption, the Voice Code framework helps us embark upon a process of radical inquiry to find and remove the original (inner) cause of our external limitations. Although this premise is nonsensical to those who think from the conventional Phase I outside-in mindset, it produces its own confirmatory evidence for those who embrace it. People with open minds can therefore discern the validity of the inside-out mental model process firsthand, without the need of social proof or consensus. The more evidence we create, the more open our minds become, and the more practical the art of radical inquiry becomes to help us actualize our dreams. **See Also:** Explore, Alchemist Autumn, Possibility, Think with Heart

Reflection An inner shadow projection that we mistake for our personal identity. The reflection is literally who we think we are "in here" when we believe in our own shadow projections "out there". To understand how this works, consider that who we truly are is our Voice and that our true Voice has no limits whatsoever. Following this Phase II premise, when we feel limited, we can safely assume that we've become frame locked by a shadow pattern that we've mistakenly identified as "me." Left unchecked, this reflection identity will keep us trapped into projections that make our external problems persist. The reflection (inner) and projection (outer) co-exist as different sides of the same shadow coin. The only way to escape the trap in such situations is to release our entire frame of reference and open to a new "both/and" vision.

Reframe. Reframe is the second step in the CREATE cycle and the second of six skills that visionary minds must master to become a Phase II force of nature. Reframing involves shifting our frame of reference to think with Authority from the assumption of successful future accomplishment. To do this masterfully, we must align the energies of the Emperor and the Alchemist through a balanced mastery of the skills of Commitment (CREATE Step 1) and Exploring (CREATE Step 3). When the Emperor and Alchemist are imbalanced or misaligned, we become frame locked by an outside-in mindset that leaves us negotiating life from a position of weakness. **Mentors:** Emperor and Alchemist (shared) | **Body Center:** forehead (6th chakra) | **Balancing Center:** below navel (2nd chakra) | **Balancing Skill:** Transmute

Resonance. The principle of natural attraction. Resonance is the second of three Voice principles that we reframe during Phase II of the human journey (worldview Stages 7-12). In Phase I (Stages 1-6) we frame resonance through the lens of beliefs programmed into us by external authorities. This leads us to selectively filter information and blinds us to our Voice knowing. Thinking this way we align with the laws of Voice to unconsciously attract more and more of what we don't want into our experience. In Phase II we reframe Resonance to align our Voice knowing in the present. This helps us discover our life's calling and gives us the gift of creative vision into a deeper order of reality unseen by those blinded by conventions. **Mentor:** Alchemist | **Phase I Frame Lock:** Play the Part | **Phase II Calling:** Think with Heart

Sage (Stage 11). The 11th worldview Stage (of 12) and the third Stage on the Plane of Vision which includes Stage 8 (Visionary) through Stage 12 (Messiah). This is the stage of great oracles, prophets, mystics, philosophers and wise men throughout the ages who have downloaded timeless wisdom from other dimensions to serve humanity and help the world evolve. Having transmuted and purified tribal shadows from the Stage 3 (Subject) worldview during Stage 10 (Luminary), Sages are able to build sturdy bridges to unseen dimensions that join everyone beyond the veil of separation. **Frame Lock:** It would be hard to call Sages "frame locked" by usual standards, but they do have an important learning function to serve. Through their work, Sages transmute lingering shadow energies related to basic physiological needs (food, sleep, etc.) first formed in Stage 2 (Survivor). This frees them to move to Stage 12 and inspires people at earlier stages to embrace new vision of life beyond mere survival. **Frame Mantra:** Be here now | **Framing Metaphor:** Love is light | **Balancing Worldview:** Survivor (Stage 2) | **Mass Emergence:** Future

Security. Security is one of four primary motivators that govern all human behavior. It represents the universal human desire for physical safety and material sufficiency. According to the Voice Code, the desire for security is counter balanced by the aspiration for *change* as part of the natural matrix that governs space-time perception. When we follow our Voice, we align with nature's orchestrating intelligence to satisfy the desire for safety and security without sacrificing the balancing aspiration for change. When we don't, we choose one need at the expense of the other and become frame locked into an "either/or" mindset that blocks our Voice. **Motivation Type:** Desire | **Balancing Motivator:** Change | **Perceptual Polarity:** Time (Past vs. Future)

"See the Lack" The shadow calling of the Doubters (aka shadow poets). This maudlin troupe of shadow poet projections includes Downers (passive pole) and Dreamers (active pole). When we follow their guidance, we lose access to our Voice in the Poet expression. Instead of "Seeing the Light" to remember our innocent omnipotence, we bury our light under blankets of melancholy and see the lack, projecting our sense of loss outward to perceive a life of sadness, struggle, and endless seeking.

"See the Light" The calling of the Poet and the secret to reclaiming the 16 gifts of Partnership our Voice offers. When we first "Face the Dark" by following the inner guidance of the Warrior, we neutralize old shadows and clear the clouds that once blocked our vision. Liberated from fear, we see our shadows in a different light. Instead of viewing them as oppressors, we embrace them as messengers bearing gifts to reclaim through unconditional love and appreciation. As we learn to love the unlovable and forgive the unforgivable within ourselves, we clear the windows of perception. Seeing the Poet's light within, we naturally see it without. Through this process, we come to dissolve the optical delusion of separation following the Poet's gentle inner guidance. When we don't, our light remains blocked by Doubter projections and we "See the Lack" in all relationships. **Principle:** Innocence | **Mentor:** Poet | **Mind Element:** Creative Unconscious | **Gift:** Partnership

Self-Actualization. The term psychologist Maslow used to represent the full development of human potential. According to Maslow, human needs exist on a pyramid-shaped hierarchy that begins with lower-order survival needs and ends with the higher-order need for self actualization. Studying the most happy and successful people throughout history, he concluded that it was the satisfaction of higher order needs that distinguished them. The Voice Code sheds new light on Maslow's hierarchy and the quest for Self Actualization. This lens suggests that the higher level needs of Maslow are satisfied during Phase II (Stages 7-12) of a natural 12-Stage process. To become self actualized, we must become One with our Voice by systematically unlearning fear, separation and survival-based thinking learned during Phase I (Stages 1-6). If we think of Maslow's pyramid as a mountain, we'd see that the lower order needs carry us to the "peak" as we complete Phase I. The journey to self-actualization then begins in earnest after we cross over that peak to enter Phase II as a Stage 7 (Explorer).

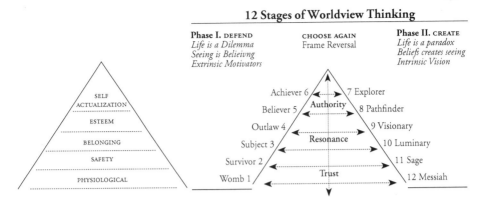

12 Stages of Worldview Thinking

Phase I. DEFEND
Life is a Dilemma
Seeing is Belieivng
Extrinsic Motivators

CHOOSE AGAIN
Frame Reversal

Phase II. CREATE
Life is a paradox
Beliefs creates seeing
Intrinsic Vision

Achiever 6   7 Explorer
Believer 5   Authority   8 Pathfinder
Outlaw 4   9 Visionary
Subject 3   Resonance   10 Luminary
Survivor 2   11 Sage
Womb 1   Trust   12 Messiah

SELF ACTUALIZATION
ESTEEM
BELONGING
SAFETY
PHYSIOLOGICAL

Separation. Separation is the core belief that unites all shadow-based thinking and the condition we call "frame lock." This belief underlies everything that occurs in the realm of perception — from the physical separation of human bodies, to the polarization of minds with different beliefs, to the countless sensory polarities (up-down, light-dark, big-small, loud-quiet, etc.) that bombard us daily. Through the Voice Code lens, all separation is ultimately a delusion projected from the primal unconscious. As we transmute old shadow beliefs to reclaim our power, we shift into a non-dual mode of living in which separation eventually dissolves completely. Through this lens, the so-called "white light" that people report upon death is actually reality seen directly (unfiltered by shadows). In theory anyone who fully releases the belief in death could visit the white light (Stage 13) at any moment. But this rarely happens, because the belief in separation is profound and deeply interlaced into everything we experience until the later stages of Phase II.

Sharks. The passive pole of the Forgetters (shadow alchemists). There are four shark personas, all of which are distinguished by their manipulative ways: *mercenaries, seducers, evangelists* and *moles*. All sharks operate from the basic premise that full transparency is foolish and that covert tactics are the best policy to satisfy our needs. This mindset fosters an inner culture of dissociation and loneliness, which sets the stage for the Shark's partner in crime (the Showboat) to emerge with just the right advice to help us fill the inner void with approval and admiration. **Location:** Primal Unconscious | **Primary Origin:** Stage 3. Subject

Shadow. Undigested pain from the past trapped in our primal unconscious. According to psychologist Carl Jung, the shadow is "99% pure gold," because only by facing the shadow, do we gain access to the gifts of our true Self (our Voice). When we follow the guidance of old shadow habits, we become trapped in a limited world of ego identification that blocks our power and turns our lives into a self-fulfilling prophecy of lack. To escape this trap we must master the ability to distinguish shadow voices from the timeless Voice knowing at our core. In practice, anyone can achieve such mastery by restoring the CREATE cycle to proper functioning. This places the mind in a state of *creative dominance* in which old shadow patterns lose their pull as we come to remember our Voice as the truth of who we are.

Showboat. The active pole of the Forgetters (shadow alchemists). There are four showboat personas distinguished by their approval-seeking ways: *flatterers, diplomats, lightweights* and *performers.* Showboats operate from the basic premise that we must make people like us to survive. This mindset leads us to spend so much time and energy trying to meet the (stated or unstated) expectations of others that we don't even know what we truly want. Exhaustion from engaging the world through the Showboats' crowd-pleasing personas causes a backlash of self-entitlement that leads us to embrace the Shark's sneaky ways. **Location:** Primal Unconscious | **Primary Origin:** Stage 3 Subject.

Stage 13. Another term for the white light that people describe after near death experiences. According to the Voice Code model, we reach this state of consciousness permanently through the power of personal choice once we've worked through all 12 stages of worldview development. From a Phase I (worldview Stages 1-6) perspective, the white light is impossible to understand. Starting from the premise of separation, we see ourselves as an effect of events beyond our control and we view the material, mental and spiritual dimensions of life as fundamentally distinct. As our Phase II journey evolves, our frame of reference reverses entirely. Dichotomies between matter and spirit gradually dissolve and we come to understand that the world out-there is something created in-here at an unconscious level. When our Stage 12 (Messiah) lessons are complete, we choose again to transcend the belief in death and the need for space-time perception. We then (presumably) ascend to the white light of Stage 13 — which we've come to recognize as reality, unfiltered by shadows.

Subject (Stage 3). The third worldview to emerge along the 12-Stage Voice Code path. This is the stage in which we first begin to see ourselves as part of a larger tribe but haven't yet developed a strong personal identity. In the lives of most people in the developed world, this worldview emerges after birth and before the "terrible twos" of Stage 4 (Outlaw). In some so-called 3rd world tribal cultures, people appear to operate from this relatively innocent, group-bonded level of thinking for their entire lives. **Frame Lock:** At this level of experience we experience pre-linguistic frame lock related to maintaining attention of our primary caregivers. Frustration from these lessons in relationship-management form the basis for what later become our most entrenched Forgetter (shadow alchemist) projections. **Frame Mantra:** Sacrifice myself to be safe | **Frame Metaphor:** Life is attention | **Balancing Worldview:** Luminary (Stage 10; Phase II) | **Mass Emergence:** ~32,000 B.C. (Rise of tribal cultures)

Survivor (Stage 2). The second worldview to emerge along the 12-Stage Voice Code path. This is a pre-linguistic stage in which our ego identity has not yet formed. In the lives of most people in today's world, this worldview emerges just after birth during our first formative experiences outside the womb. Most people pass relatively quickly to Stage 3 (Subject), but in cases of extreme mental impairment, people can remain at this stage throughout adulthood. Frame Lock: Stage 2 frame lock relates to the perception of total helplessness and dependency. The prime directive at this stage is to eat, sleep and satisfy basic survival needs. Frustration from these early lessons in procuring sustenance and survival form the basis for what later become our most charged Enforcer (shadow warrior) projections. Frame Mantra: Express myself to get what I need now. **Framing Metaphor:** Life is a search | **Balancing Worldview:** Sage (Stage 11: Phase II) | **Mass Emergence:** prehistory

Tao. Literally "the way." According to Taoists, the Toa is the unconditional and unknowable guiding principle of all reality. Chinese philosophers often emphasize the natural (vs. divine) origins of this concept, but this distinction breaks down the more deeply one dives into Taoist literature. Through the Voice Code lens, the Tao is simply your Voice. A separate book is in the works that uses this new map to unify all major world mythologies and spiritual systems. For now, consider the paradoxical passage from the Tao Te Ching below in light of the content in this book, with a special emphasis on the following glossary terms: Oneness, Paradoxical Pragmatism, Self-Actualization, and Messiah (Stage 12).

> *"Knowing the constant, we accept things as they are.*
> *By accepting things as they are, we are impartial.*
> *By being impartial, we are part of the Nature.*
> *By being a part of the Nature, we are one with Tao.*
> *Tao is eternal, and we survive physical death."*
> Tao Te Ching, Verse 16

"Think With Heart" This is the calling of the Alchemist and the secret to reclaiming the 16 gifts of Possibility our Voice offers. When we align with the Alchemist in the service of our Voice, we suspend our beliefs and follow our natural curiosity, engaging life as a journey of discovery. This leads to a mindset in which radical inquiry prevails, as our attention shifts to embrace heart resonance as the primary litmus test for truth. People at every stage of worldview development are capable of adopting this mindset at any time, but until we reframe Authority from external (Phase I) to internal (Phase II), this mindset is difficult to maintain for any extended period of time. When our Voice is blocked by Phase I beliefs we look for truth outside, as we frame and filter the world through countless unquestioned beliefs that block our awareness of our heart's knowing. This mindset compels us to "Play the Part" in the service of the Forgetters (shadow alchemists) instead of "Thinking with Heart" to activate the Alchemist's genius. **Principle:** Resonance | **Mentor:** Alchemist | **Mind Element:** Creative Unconscious | **Gift:** Possibility

Thou Shalt. The proverbial dragon that we slay to reframe the principles of Authority, Resonance and Trust to remember our Innocence of our Voice during Phase II of the human journey. On every scale of this mythic beast is written a rule, belief or social norm learned in Phase I. According to Frederich Nietzsche's original parable, all great people must leave the ordinary world behind and slay Thou Shalt in order to release themselves from false limitations and "become a child" again. This circular mythology syncs perfectly with the 2-Phase, 12-Stage Voice Code map.

Traction, (Axis of). The segment of the CREATE cycle that connects the Alchemist and Warrior through the skills of Exploring and Assimilation. Through this partnership, we give the "heaven" of our highest purpose traction in the material earthly realm. When we reclaim the Emperor's gifts of Purpose and align them with the Alchemist's gifts of Possibility, we restore the Axis of Vision which gives us the power to "Own the Frame" on our mission. But to give our vision real-world traction, we must clear "the Cave" of our primal unconscious to reframe Trust and reclaim the gifts of Power our Voice offers through the Warrior. For people with an intellectual bias, bridging the Warrior and Alchemist can be a very challenging proposition as it brings up many latent shadow habits of dissociation through conceptual thinking. But restoring the Axis of Traction is well worth any effort. When we finally strike the right balance between the Alchemist's soaring exploration and the Warrior's earthy courage, our Voice soon takes over, and we become unstoppable.

Transmute. The fifth step in the CREATE cycle and the fifth skill that visionary minds master. Transmuting old shadow patterns involves dissolving them to reclaim our gifts using unconditional love as our "weapon." To do this we must first set the stage by clearly distinguishing (CREATE Step 3. Explore) shadow projections from our Voice and neutralizing the resistance (CREATE Step 4. Assimilate) with focused non-resistance. This stops the momentum of the past and paves the way for the Poet's unassuming, unconditional love to do it's healing magic through transmutation. This is the master skill used by all game-changers throughout history. Mastery generally comes late in the game, after we've achieved radical alignment between the Emperor, Alchemist and Warrior. This sets the stage for the Poet and Warrior to build a powerful partnership. Until we do this work, lingering shadow warrior habits lurking in our primal unconscious since infancy (especially from Stage 2. Survivor) choke the natural flow on the Axis of Vitality that bonds these two mighty mentors. **Mentors:** Warrior and Poet (shared) | **Mission:** Change the Game | **Body Center:** below navel (2nd chakra) | **Balancing Center:** forehead (6th chakra) | **Balancing Skill:** Reframe

Trust. The principle of inspired action. Trust is the third of three principles that we reframe during Phase II of the human journey (worldview Stages 6-12). Trust is demonstrated by action. In Phase I we frame trust through the lens of separation. Using cues like belief similarity, tribal association and social proof to filter our choice options, we take actions based on mental calculations intended to maximize personal self-interest. In Phase II things get much simpler.

Instead of letting external factors filter our actions, we place trust fully in our instinctual knowing. Following our Voice as it speaks through our heart and gut instincts, we take inspired action that align us with the dynamic creative intelligence that orchestrates life. This turns us into a force of nature capable of thriving without compromise from the inside out. **Mentor:** Warrior | **Phase I Frame Lock:** Blame the Dark | **Phase II Calling:** Face the Dark

Visionary (Stage 9). This is the 9th worldview to emerge along the 12-Stage Voice Code path. In simple terms, Stage 9 might be called "entry level enlightenment". It is the first of four stages on the Plane of Creative Vision (worldview Stages 9-12). It is the first worldview to operate consistently from a holistic inside-out mindset. In a Phase II economy, people who inhabit this worldview are uniquely positioned to thrive, because they've mastered the inner game sufficiently to know and honor their life's true calling. **Frame Lock:** Stage 9 thinkers are no longer frame locked by the false dichotomies that plague people on the Plane of Social Control (worldview Stages 5-8). Their primary life challenge now becomes staying grounded in the material world while operating from a state of inner Voice alignment. This ultimately requires that they transmute the belief in evil and lingering shadow residue from their experiences during the Stage 4 (Outlaw) level of development. **Frame Mantra:** 'Be the change" | **Framing Metaphor:** Life is a gift | **Balancing Partner:** Outlaw (Stage 4; Phase I) | **Mass Emergence:** now (rise of the creative economy)

Vision (Axis of). Represents the segment of the CREATE cycle that connects the Emperor and Alchemist through the skills of Commitment, Reframing and Exploring. Through this partnership, we reclaim the "throne" of our creative unconscious to reframe the principles of Authority and Resonance. In so doing, we reclaim the gifts of Purpose and Possibility from the Dividers (shadow emperors) and Forgetters (shadow alchemists), respectively. This inner alignment is what has given visionary leaders throughout history that rare ability to "Own the Frame" in the pursuit of their passions. We restore this axis during the first two seasons of Voice Revolution: Emperor's Summer and the Alchemist's Autumn. When we reach this point, our Voice Revolution is not yet complete, but the inner and outer pull of our Voice has become so strong that there's little chance we'll fail to complete the process.

Vitality (Axis of). Represents the segment of the CREATE cycle that connects the Warrior and Poet through the skills of Assimilation, Transmutation and Embodiment. Through this partnership, we hold the power to change the world from the inside out through the gifts of Power and Partnership our Voice offers. When we stand in awe of anyone because of their seemingly "magical" powers of charisma, we are actually looking at nothing more than an out-picturing of our own charismatic potential once the Axis of Vitality is fully restored. But to unleash these gifts, we must complete the entire Voice Revolution. Once we've "cleared the Cave" to reframe Trust with the Warrior's Winter, we naturally begin to exude these gifts as the Poet's Spring flowers within. As we dissolve the Doubters (shadow poets) that darken our light, we restore awareness of our timeless innocence and our natural vitality begins to radiate through us without effort. We then take inspired actions that might seem "magical," but which are no more than just following our Voice.

Voice. Instinctual knowing that speaks from the core of being. This mysterious aspect of who we are arises from an element of mind called the creative unconscious. This same knowing has gone by many names over the ages, including Self, higher self, other self, instinct, intuition, the Tao, soul, holy spirit, quintessence and countless others. Before the Voice Code, there was no clear, systematic, universal, non-ideological, scientifically grounded, process-driven map to help people align with this awesome inner power in their everyday lives. From a Voice Code perspective our "Voice" is actually the timeless truth of who we are beneath and beyond old shadow habits. As we master the CREATE cycle, we clear the windows of perception to remember and become One with our Voice at all times. Because the power of this "other self" is so awesome, direct access can be overwhelming until we unlearn old Phase I thinking habits. The Voice Code map helps us bridge the gap by introducing us to our Voice as it speaks through four archetypal mentors (Emperor, Alchemist, Warrior and Poet). When these four aspects of our Voice come together as one, the fifth element (or quintessence) of our Voice flowers fully in the peaceful creative urgency of the present.

Voice Code. An equation that emerged in 2012 after two decades of research to find the missing link between human nature and mother nature. The Voice Code reconciles more than a century of social science research through a natural sciences lens. By discovering the natural logic beneath an 8-stage developmental model originally proposed by Dr. Clare W. Graves, the Voice Code helped us distill and map 12 stages of human consciousness which tell the entire story of human thinking, from conception (Stage 1. Womb) to the highest level of human enlightenment (Stage 12. Messiah). According to this map, consciousness evolves over 12 worldview Stages, which can be organized into two grand Phases of 6 Stages. By restoring the six-step inner game cycle called the CREATE cycle, ordinary people can master the "inner game" of Phase II thinking by reframing three cornerstone principles: Authority, Resonance and Trust. In so doing, they become a catalysts for the evolution of life and thrive along the path of least resistance, from the inside out.

Voice Curve/Effect. The cycles of exponential thriving that Phase II visionaries unleash are called Voice Effects. These gain traction from the inside out through a dynamic, nonlinear growth pattern called the Voice Curve. Wherever they show up, Voice Curves always have three basic phases:

• **Act I. Camel:** Linear climb that peaks and plateaus
• **Act II. Lion:** A turbulent ride as we slay Thou Shalt
• **Act III. Voice Effect:** Exponential growth

Because they are governed by the principles that govern the evolution of all

CREATE: How to Be a Force of Nature

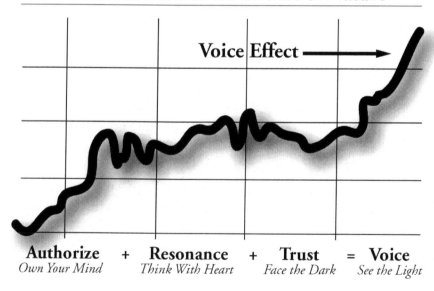

| **Authorize** | + | **Resonance** | + | **Trust** | = | **Voice** |
| *Own Your Mind* | | *Think With Heart* | | *Face the Dark* | | *See the Light* |

natural systems, Voice Curves can be discovered on every scale and dimension of human culture. In business, they can be found operating within a wide spectrum of data sets, including growth metrics, market adoption rates, the career growth of outliers of industry, and the emotional arc of audience experience during transformational communications. Worldview Thinking's Voice Revolution curriculum is designed to help people navigate their inner-game personal Voice Curve from the inside out, with minimal friction.

Voice Mountain. The central image used to convey the 12-Stage developmental path to total Voice alignment. Most models of adult development view evolution as a ladder reaching forever upward. The Voice Code reveals a circle. The easiest way to grasp this new developmental map is as a journey up and over a steep mountain with 12 base camps along the way. The first 6 Stages (Phase I) are about learning to survive. These stages involve climbing up against massive resistance as our ego identity develops and becomes fused with beliefs programmed into us by external authorities. The next 6 Stages (Phase II) are about *unlearning* Phase I beliefs to thrive. These stages involve transmuting all limiting Phase I programming, as we align with natural laws that govern human evolution to achieve total freedom from the inside out.

Voice Revolution. A comprehensive inside-out learning process through which we unlearn Phase I thinking to become One with our Voice. Without a map, most people never escape the orbit of frame lock and remain trapped in lives of compromise. In the past, those brave souls who have reached the higher stages of Phase II (Stage 9. Visionary and above), have been forced to do so through the school of hard knocks. By finding a purpose so compelling that they were willing to sacrifice everything, they spent decades in the battlefield testing and refining their vision until they had finally transmuted all shadows to achieve radical Voice alignment. With this new map, people can now shave literally decades off their normal learning curve. As we restore the CREATE cycle in four grand seasons, Phase II thinking becomes a new habit and false limitations naturally dissolve. Our life's purpose emerges in holographic fashion as we are simply having fun, reclaiming our power from old beliefs, doing what we love. **Seasons:** Emperor's Summer, Alchemist's Autumn, Warrior's Winter, Poet's Spring. | **Callings:** Own Your Mind, Think With Heart, Face the Dark, See the Light | **Gifts:** Purpose, Possibility, Power and Partnership.

Warrior. The third of the four archetypal mentors through which our Voice speaks from the creative unconscious (Plane of Creative Vision). The Warrior governs the principle of Trust and the 16 gifts of Power. In Phase II of the human journey, we align these energies with those of the Alchemist and Poet to

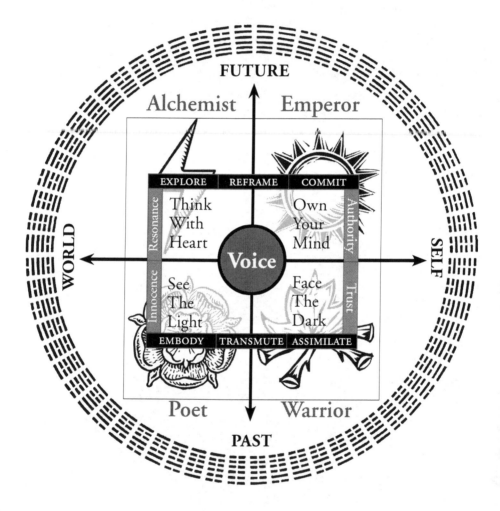

restore the CREATE cycle and the Axis of Traction and Vitality (respectively). With the Warrior's skill of Assimilation we "clear the cave" of our primal unconscious. This paves the way for us to give our aspirational vision real-world traction and "Change the Game" with the skills of Transmutation and Embodiment that round out the CREATE cycle. The third season of the Voice

Revolution in which we "Face the Dark" to restore Trust in our Voice is called the "Warrior's Winter". When we've completed this pivotal season, we have mastered fear and have laid the proper groundwork to reclaim the gifts of Partnership through the Poet's Spring. **Calling:** "Face the Dark" | **Location:** Creative Unconscious | **Mastery Skill:** Assimilation.

Warrior's Winter. The third season of the Voice Revolution. In the Warrior's Winter we arrest the Enforcers (shadow warriors) to achieve radical alignment between the principles of Trust, Resonance and Authority. This is an epic season where we master fear to give our Voice vision real world traction as we bridge the Warrior and Alchemist energies in our everyday life. As we summon the Warrior, we "Face the Dark" to clear "the cave" and reframe trust from tribal (frame lock) to instinctual (Voice). Through this invigorating Phase II cycle, we master the inner game of Assimilation as we reclaim the 16 gifts of Power that our Voice offers in the Warrior expression. As ancient fears recede, we achieve radical integration between the energies of the Emperor, Alchemist and Warrior archetypes. With such radical integrity, we begin to exude that mysterious essence of greatness our Voice offers. We are now ready to complete the revolution through the Poet's Spring.

Warden. The Wardens are the active pole of the Dividers (shadow emperors). There are four Warden personas, distinguished by their controlling ways: *tyrants, saviors, winner,* and *critics.* When we follow the Wardens, we get a false sense of control that can become very addictive. We come to depend on these projections "for our own good," imagining that without their constant pressure, we'd have no motivation. In time, Warden frame lock leads us to stressful lives of constant seeking, where no matter what we achieve we still aren't satisfied. This tyrannical inner culture sets the stage for the Warden's crime partner (the Wimp) to take over, offering quick fixes and fleeting pleasures that only make matters worse. **Voice Mentor:** Emperor | **Primary Origin:** Stage 4. Outlaw.

Wimp. The Wimps are the passive pole of the Dividers (aka shadow emperors). There are four Wimp personas distinguished by their irresponsible, escapist ways: *abdicators, pardoners, losers* and *indulgers.* When we follow their guidance, we sell ourselves out for short-sighted solutions and indulgences that may relieve our momentary discomfort, but which leave us feeling empty, guilty and out of control. We usually fall for the Wimps trap as an "equal and opposite reaction" to the inner culture of stress we create by blindly following the Wardens (active pole) ways. In time, the good-cop/bad-cop routine these two shadow patterns play, drains us of our inner authority and robs us of the 16 gifts of Purpose our Voice offers. **Voice Mentor:** Emperor | **Primary Origin:** Stage 4. Outlaw

White Light (Stage 13). Life after Stage 12. Based upon Voice Code developmental logic, studies of near-death experiences, and first hand experiences of the author, there is compelling evidence for the idea that the "white light" is simply stage 13 — reality as we perceive it once we've cleared all shadows from our primal unconscious. Given the inside-out nature of the Voice Code model, this idea is inherently incredible (read: impossible to believe) because, the world is itself an out-picturing of beliefs. Fortunately, this idea can be proven through empirical investigation by one willing to do the inner work.

"Who is that?" The simple question that helps restore Voice alignment by uncovering shadow habits in real time. Whenever we feel limited, bored, lonely or anything other than loving and joyfully engaged, we can be certain that we've become identified with old shadow projections. By asking, "Who is that?" to our own thoughts in such moments, we stop shadow identification and make those energies the object of our awareness. By personifying and naming these inner patterns we further distance ourselves from embeddedness while adding a dash of creativity and playfulness that strengthens Voice alignment. When the situation permits, we then use Voice Code tools (CREATE script, CAVE Buster, etc.) to transmute the limiting shadow pattern and reclaim our power forever.

Womb (Stage 1). The first level to emerge along the 12 Stages of the Voice Code path. The Womb is the beginning of our human journey and the source of the final shadows we must transmute to complete the lessons of Stage 12. This is the stage in which our perception first emerges primarily through sound and kinesthetic awareness. As adults, few can consciously recall these early formative experiences without the use of hypnotic regression and other therapeutic methods that help people access prenatal memories. But a reasonable interpretation of the Voice Code model, suggests that these hazy and long-buried early memories mask the original choice to leave the "white light" of Stage 13 and enter the embodied world of perception. Frame Lock: Stage 1 is the perception of ultimate limitation — being trapped in a dark place with no vision, no freedom of movement and no control over what happens to us. Can you imagine a more limiting scenario for an unlimited being? Frustration from these early experiences form the basis for what later becomes our most charged Doubter (shadow poet) energies. **Balancing Partner:** Master (Stage 12; Phase II) | **Date of Mass Emergence:** Beginning of Time (now)

Worldview. Habitual way of looking at the world that governs our day-to-day choices. According to the Voice Code, there are 12 distinct and universal worldviews that are developmentally related as part of a natural process that spans from the "beginning of time" (Stage 1. Womb), to the "end of time" (Stage 12. Messiah). As we progress along this path, our thinking is shaped by natural laws that drive our core values, beliefs and the deep metaphors we use to make sense of life. Each stage transcends but includes the prior stage, giving us a more comprehensive and accurate view of reality with each step forward. When we reach Stage 12, we have cleared the windows of perception to "See the Light" in all things. No longer frame locked, we recognize ourselves as the sole creator of space and time. As we reclaim power from final shadows, we arrive at the place from which we started (Stage 13) and know it for the first time.

Endnotes

Introduction

1 Dragon slaying parable adapted from *Thus Spoke Zarathustra* by Friedrich Nietzsche (Penguin Classics, 1961)

2 For a relatively accessible introduction to Carl Jung and his concept of the shadow, read Jung's *Man and His Symbols* (Dell, 1968). For a more recent adaptation of Jung's shadow work, see *Dark Side of the Light Chasers* by Debbie Ford (Riverhead Books, 2010).

3 The Voice Code conception of the shadow is much broader and more inclusive than Jung's original conception of the term. To Jung the shadow was essentially an inverted and repressed version of our persona (the face we show the world). By challenging our persona and facing the shadow he found that we could gain access to the "Self" (his name for "Voice") at the center of the psyche. The Voice Code map takes things a step further, showing how our persona (self concept, ego identity, etc.) and the world of perception are shadow projections that dissolve as we progress along the developmental path of Phase II (worldview stages 7-12).

4 From The *Top Five Regrets of the Dying* by Bronnie Wares (Hay House, 2012)

5 For a scholarly overview of Graves research see *The Never Ending Quest: Clare W. Graves Explores Human Nature* (ECLET, 2005).

6 The idea of four archetypes working in tandem as outlined in this book traces back to Jung. In his search to map the psyche, he arrived at a "double quaternity" model of the psyche — a structure that dovetails perfectly with Voice Code math. Read glossary items on "Individuation" and "Creative Unconscious" for more on the convergence of these two paradigms. For another take on the four archetypes, read modern Jungian text *King, Warrior, Magician, Lover: Rediscovering Archetypes of the Mature Masculine* by Robert Moore, et al. (HarperOne, 1991)

Act I ~ Scene 1

1 For a more thorough breakdown on Seligman's research and its implications for human behavior, see *Learned Helplessness: A Theory for the Age of Personal Control* by Christopher Peterson, et al. (Oxford University Press, 1995).

2 For a simple, practical distillation of his key levels of thinking, see my 2008 book *Igniting Inspiration: A Persuasion Manual for Visionaries*. A full chapter is devoted to each of the four major worldviews that govern what we now call the "Plane of Control." In this book, you'll also find an advanced list of advanced Gravesian books and resources.

3 This concept occurs time and again in the world of quantum physics and nondual spiritual paradigms. For a quick, exploration of this concept and its historical roots in the history of science, see the graphic novel *The Universe is a Dream* by Alexander Marchand (Inspired Arts Press, 2011).

4 The connection between the human genome and the I-Ching has been observed by a number of researchers. Two advanced personal development maps such as "Human Design" and "Gene Keys" have also emerged in recent decades that prominently use I-Ching logic. The Voice Code map can be used to explain and integrate both systems. The Voice Code is essentially a modern version of the I-Ching — It explains the 64 hexagrams through a 4 variable model of consciousness that plays out on three levels as part of a 12-stage process. Later volumes will dive deeper into this topic, showing how this map unifies and explains all prior research in this area. In the meantime, review the glossary terms for "Tao" and "I-Ching."

5 The term "optical delusion" used throughout this book pay homage to Einstein's famous declaration that separation is "an optical delusion of consciousness." This statement (and Voice Code map) dovetails perfectly with the metaphysics in *A Course in Miracles* (Foundation for Inner Peace, 2008).

Act I ~ Scene 2

1 For a deeper look at the concept of fields of social engagement, see MIT professor Otto Scharmer's *Theory U: Lead From the Future as it Emerges* (Berrett-Koehler, 2009). You might also explore *Wholeness and the Implicate Order* (Routledge, 2002) and the more accessible *On Dialogue* (Routledge, 2004) by late physics genius David Bohm. I urge you to also consider the fascinating and largely overlooked research work of 20th century social psychologists Kurt Lewin and Henry Stack Sullivan as previewed in *Resolving Social Conflicts: Field Theory and Social Science* (American Psychological Association, 1997) and *Interpersonal Theory of Psychiatry* (W. W. Norton & Company, 1968), respectively.

2 The idea of paradoxical pragmatism resonates with Jung's concept of "integrating opposites" of consciousness to become "individuated" — which he describes as the aspirational end point of human existence in which we are most uniquely ourselves and also most intimately connected to all of life. My own thinking on this topic was influenced mostly by exploration with natural sciences research — namely quantum physics, chaos theory and systems theory. See Kafatos and Nadeus *The Conscious Universe: Parts and Whole in Physical Reality* (Springer, 1999) for a deep exploration of the role paradox in the evolution of science and the implications for living in a "participatory universe" in which the observer and the observed cannot be disentangled.

3 The number 432 could be called the "magic number" of Voice. It occurs throughout human culture and nature in a variety of staggering and synchronistic ways. The Voice Code map helps us finally understand how and why this has happened. The specific details (underlying math, explanations) are beyond the scope of the book, but the visualization and breathing practices are prescribed to help you leverage this insight at an unconscious level. Watch the free YouTube video *Sonic Geometry: The Language of Frequency and Form* for a fascinating survey of this topic that dovetails beautifully with the Voice Code.

Act I ~ Scene 3

1 This hypothetical "upside down glasses" scenario inspired by real perceptual adaptation research. Many experiments with inversion glasses have been performed, starting with the

seminal work of Theodor Erismann (1883-1961) and Ivo Kohler (1915-1985) at the University of Innsbruck. Type "Erisman and Kohler Upside down goggles" into YouTube for footage from the original 20th century research.

2 Sigmund Freud first popularized the concept of projection right around the same time when the technology for the first movie projectors was first invented! Historically this concept traces back at least to ancient Greece, and has carried forward to today in many different forms. In many modern spiritual circles, the phrase "projection makes perception" has become popular. The Voice Code map confirms this and reconciles all of these different strains of thinking in a way that confirms much of Freud's thinking while making room for spirituality and religion .

3 The "immovable spot" as used in this book refers to both the centerpoint that joins all four quadrants of the Voice Code matrix and the point under the Bodhi tree where, according to Buddhist mythology, the Buddha became enlightened. See this term in the glossary for more on this connection. Read the parable of Buddha's awakening and the three temptations of Mara (God of Death) for a beautiful eastern illustration of the same Voice Code principles this book frames using the western "dragon slaying" motif.

Act I ~ Scene 5

1 According to *A Course in Miracles* (Foundation for Inner Peace, 1992), the true message of the crucifixion is that death is impossible. Seen through the Voice Code lens, Jesus appears to be the first person in recorded history to make it all the way through to Stage 12 (Messiah) level and beyond. He appears to have done this in a heavily frame locked Phase I world that could not yet begin to grasp his intended message.

2 See Maslow's *Toward a Psychology of Being* (Sublime, 2014) for more on his research. Read the glossary item "Self Actualization" for a brief 50,000-foot overview showing how his thinking converges with the Voice Code map.

3 Exact quote from C. G. Jung: "Nothing has a stronger influence psychologically on their environment and especially on their children than the unlived life of the parent."

Act II ~ Scene 7

1 The Parable of Ed the musk deer was taken from a story I overheard in college about the behavior of actual Musk Deer. I cannot confirm the original source, but I have long associated this parable with Buddhism and the dangers of letting desire rule our minds.

2 If you are looking for two inspiring real world profiles that illustrate both the indomitable power of Voice and the rocky path those without a map must pave, consider the life stories of Steve Jobs and Albert Einstein as told by biographer Walter Isaacson in *Steve Jobs* (Simon & Schuster, 2015) and *Einstein: His Life and Universe* (Simon & Schuster, 2008). For a broader survey of many different stories of this type, consider the brilliant *The Soul's Code: In Search of Character and Calling* by James Hillman (Grand Central, 1997).

Act II ~ Scene 8

1 "Sacrifice self for future reward" is the mantra for Stage 5 Believers. At this stage many of the undigested Divider shadow energies created in Stage 4 Outlaw become institutionalized

into our personality as part of our Phase I socialization process. Important traits and abilities such as self-discipline and the ability to delay gratification grow from our experiences during this important stage. Problems happen when these inner control structures take over our lives and leave us unwilling to question our beliefs, keeping us stagnated and polarized in Phase I thinking.

Act II ~ Scene 9

1 For a different spin on the separation fallacy undone during Phase II, consider this short (12 minutes) Youtube video called "Shadows of the Past: Teachings from A Course in Miracles" (https://www.youtube.com/watch?v=2sb4FHE21vQ)

2 A strange attractor is a natural systems concept that traces back to Chaos theory. See James Gleik's landmark bestseller *Chaos: Making a New Science* (Cardinal, 1991) for more on this big idea. Through the Voice Code lens, the human mind is essentially a natural system that evolves over time with different "basins of attraction" that govern how we frame the world. The world we experience is formed by how we use our attention to reconcile competing needs rooted in an unchanging 4 variable, 3 level matrix that governs all human perception. More scholarly works detailing this matrix will be released as appropriate and helpful.

3 For a dramatized storytelling of the macro evolution of worldviews from the caveman days (Stage 2 Survivor) through the industrial revolution (Stage 6. Achiever) and beyond, see my free YouTube video "The History of Human Thinking in 6 Minutes, 2 Seconds" at the following URL: https://www.youtube.com/watch?v=3IBRDBuI9bQ (Note: This video was produced prior to the discovery of the Voice Code. As such it does not reference the first (Stage 1) and final three (Stages 10-12) worldview stages that complete the model originally proposed by Graves. But the basic story flow remains accurate and (despite a few inaccuracies) this video has been highly effective at making these ideas accessible and inspiring to mainstream audiences.

4 If you are interested in the intersection between psychology and religion, please read *Varieties of Religious Experience* by William James, the widely acknowledged "father of American psychology" (Createspace, 2009). He tackles this now taboo topic with grace and scholarly wisdom that is rare in modern psychology. From there, good follow up reads would include Aldous Huxley's *The Perennial Philosophy* (Harper, 2009), which shows the essential unity of all mystical traditions and Joseph Campbell in *The Power of Myth* (Anchor, 1991) which colorfully illustrates the universal influence of Jungian archetypes across stories told in all major world religions and spiritual systems.

Act II ~ Scene 10

1 Jung defined inflation as "an overexpansion of the personality through identification with an archetype or, in pathological cases, with a historical or religious figure, which exceeds individual limitations." In both my personal experience and experience helping clients, I've yet to encounter anyone who didn't become inflated at some point along the journey. Each powerful step forward towards Voice alignment tends to be matched by an equal and opposite reaction by the shadow forces within seeking to preserve the status quo. If this

happens to you, don't be alarmed. Understand that this is part of the process and do your best to maintain a humble reverent attitude.

Act II ~ Scene 11

1 See The Allegory of the Cave (P&L, 2010) for a direct telling of this parable. For a deeper and expanded analysis of this story archetype, see Glenn Yeffeths *Taking the Red Pill: Science, Philosophy and Religion in the Matrix* (Smarpop, 2003).

Act II ~ Scene 12

1 See Bruce Lipton's *Biology of Belief* (Hay House, 2008) for host of compelling evidence to support the proposed correlation between frame lock and physical illness.

Act II ~ Scene 13

1 "Die before you die" is an old Zen Saying. In this quote, Eckhart Tolle expands and recontextualizes this wisdom in a way that dovetails perfectly with Voice Code developmental logic: "Death is a stripping away of all that is not you. The secret of life is to "'die before you die' — and find that there is no death." What gets stripped away is Phase I shadow programming. When we reach Stage 12 we release belief in death entirely to know ourselves as immortal as we undo the original choice to be born in Stage 1 (Womb). What's left is who we are and have always been behind the screen of perception. This is our Voice.

Act III ~ Scene 14

1 To quickly wrap your head around the rise in data complexity and how this trend is reshaping our world from the inside out, see the shrewd analysis given by Douglass Rushkoff in *Present Shock* (Current, 2014). For a more "out there" look at where this trend is going from one of the world's most talented and eccentric visionaries, see *The Singularity is Near: When Humans Transcend Biology* by futurist Ray Kurzweil.

2 For an accessible scientific introduction to living systems theory, read *The Web of Life: A New Scientific Understanding of Living Systems* by Fritjof Capra (Anchor, 1997). To see how systems thinking applies to business and society, consider Peter Senge's *The Fifth Discipline: The Art and Practice of the Learning Organization* (Doubleday, 2006) and Donella Meadows' *Thinking in Systems: A Primer* (Chelsea Green, 2008).

3 Verse from T.S. Elliot's "Four Quartets" (Mariner, 1968).

Act III ~ Scene 15

1 This quote comes directly from the intro/overview text of A Course in Miracles (Foundation for Inner Peace, 1992). The quote is given in full below and is intended as a summary of the entire philosophy outlined in the text. I have come to believe that the Voice Code is a practical scientifically grounded articulation of this same paradigm: "Nothing real can be threatened and nothing unreal exists. Herein lies the peace of God."

About the Author

John Marshall Roberts is a behavioral scientist, musician and visionary leadership expert. He's been blowing minds for good causes since his 2008 book *Igniting Inspiration: A Persuasion Manual for Visionaries* first launched him into the public eye. John is founder of Worldview Thinking, a visionary development company with a single focus: to help you awaken and express your true creative potential in your everyday life. In 2012 the Voice Code emerged after two decades of research. Since then, John has been on a mission to make this discovery actionable and accessible through this book and a suite of visionary training solutions.